AMOS & ISAIAH

Prophets
of the Word
of God

AMOS & ISAIAH

Prophets of the Word of God

James M. Ward

ABINGDON PRESS

Nashville   New York

AMOS AND ISAIAH: PROPHETS OF THE WORD OF GOD

Copyright © 1969 by Abingdon Press

Standard Book Number: 687-01271-6

Library of Congress Catalog Card Number: 69-18456

SET UP, PRINTED, AND BOUND BY THE
PARTHENON PRESS, AT NASHVILLE,
TENNESSEE, UNITED STATES OF AMERICA

TO

Elaine,
David,
Mike, and
Tom

Preface

Amos was the first literary prophet of the Old Testament to prophesy to the covenantal community of Israel. Although his home was in Judah, his oracles were addressed primarily to the people of the northern kingdom of Israel. Isaiah was the first canonical literary prophet to address himself principally to the southern, Judean kingdom. They were nearly contemporaries. Thus, together their oracles represent the first great development in the extant, prophetic literary tradition, north and south. However, their affinity was more than temporal; it was also literary and theological. They were much alike in the form of their utterance and the content of their convictions.

The purpose of the present book is to expound the theological and ethical affirmations of these co-pioneers. It has been written in the conviction that the Old Testament prophets' understanding of man's existence in community under God is as lively a possibility for us today as it was for Israel in the eighth century B.C. Many of the forms of our institutional and material environment have changed, but the basic alternatives open to us for understanding and accepting our place in the universe have not. To this extent Amos and Isaiah are our contemporaries.

The place of Amos and Isaiah in the biblical tradition and their theological affinity justify, I believe, treating them together in a single book. Nevertheless, I have chosen to treat each one separately, aiming at as full and synoptic an exposition of the prophetic faith of each as the number and nature of their extant oracles permit. I have not engaged in a concerted and explicit comparison of the two on particular points of their proclamation or the language and literary forms they employed. This is worth doing, and has been done by others. However, it is unnecessary for an adequate understanding of their theology and, therefore, has not been done here.

The translation of the Old Testament text contained here is mine unless otherwise indicated. My dependence upon the standard English versions at many points will be apparent. Brackets used in the translated oracles enclose material that I believe to be secondary, while parentheses indicate emendations of the Hebrew text.

Mrs. Bonnie Jordan typed several drafts of the manuscript with great skill and has won my lasting appreciation.

Much of the writing of this book was done during a research leave in Italy in 1966-67, which was generously supported by the Perkins School of Theology of Southern Methodist University and The American Association of Theological Schools. To them I am indeed grateful. That leave was made possible also by the willingness of my wife, Elaine, to take a year's leave of absence from her professional responsibilities in order to accompany me, and the writing of the book was in no small measure the fruit of her patience and encouragement and those, less articulate but nevertheless real, of our three sons. To the four of them, therefore, I gratefully inscribe this modest book.

James M. Ward

Contents

list of
ABBREVIATIONS

AJSL *American Journal of Semitic Languages and Literatures.*

ANET *Ancient Near Eastern Texts Relating to the Old Testament.* J. B. Pritchard, ed. Second edition. Princeton, 1955.

ASV *The Holy Bible. American Standard Version.* New York, 1901.

BDB *A Hebrew and English Lexicon of the Old Testament.* F. Brown, S. R. Driver, and C. A. Briggs. Oxford, 1907.

BH *Biblia Hebraica.* Rudolf Kittel, ed. Stuttgart, 1937.

BWANT *Beiträge zur Wissenschaft vom Alten und Neuen Testament.*

BZ *Biblische Zeitschrift.*

(B)ZAW *(Beihefte zur) Zeitschrift für die Alttestamentliche Wissenschaft.*

CBQ *Catholic Biblical Quarterly.*

Chicago *The Complete Bible: An American Translation.* J. M. P. Smith and E. J. Goodspeed, eds. Chicago, 1939.

ET *Expository Times.*

Ev.T *Evangelische Theologie.*

FRLANT *Forschungen zur Religion und Literatur des Alten und Neuen Testaments.*

GK *Gesenius' Hebrew Grammar.* E. Kautzsch, ed. A. E. Cowley, trans. Second edition. Oxford, 1910.

HTR *Harvard Theological Review.*

HUCA *Hebrew Union College Annual.*

JBL *Journal of Biblical Literature.*

11

Jerusalem	*The Jerusalem Bible.* Alexander Jones, ed. New York, 1966.
JNES	*Journal of Near Eastern Studies.*
JPS	*The Holy Scriptures According to the Masoretic Text.* The Jewish Publication Society of America. Philadelphia, 1917, 1955.
KBL	*Lexicon in Veteris Testamenti Libros.* L. Köhler and W. Baumgartner. Leiden, 1953.
KJV	*The Holy Bible. Authorized (King James) Version.* 1611.
LXX	*The Septuagint (Greek) Version of the Old Testament.* Joseph Ziegler, ed. *Septuaginta* XIII. *Duodecim prophetae.* Göttingen, 1943. XIV. *Isaias.* 1939.
Moffatt	*A New Translation of the Bible.* James Moffatt. Revised edition. New York, 1935.
MT	*Masoretic (Hebrew) Text.*
Oudt. St.	*Oudtestamentische Studiën.*
RSV	*The Holy Bible. Revised Standard Version.* New York, 1946, 1952.
SBT	*Studies in Biblical Theology.*
(Suppl.) VT	*(Supplements to) Vetus Testamentum.*
ST	*Studia Theologica.*
TLZ	*Theologische Literaturzeitung.*
TR	*Theologische Rundschau.*
TZ	*Theologische Zeitschrift.*
WMANT	*Wissenschaftliche Monographien zum Alten und Neuen Testament.*
ZRG	*Zeitschrift für Religions- und Geistesgeschichte.*
ZTK	*Zeitschrift für Theologie und Kirche.*

COMMENTARIES CITED

The commentaries are cited by the authors' surnames.

Amsler, Samuel. *Amos. Commentaire de l'Ancien Testament* XI a, 159-247. Neuchâtel, 1965.

Cripps, R. S. *A Critical and Exegetical Commentary on the Book of Amos.* Second edition. London, 1955.

Driver, Samuel R. *Joel and Amos. Cambridge Bible.* Cambridge, 1898.

Eichrodt, Walther. *Der Heilige in Israel. Jesaja 1-12. Die Botschaft des Alten Testaments* 17/1. Stuttgart, 1960.

Fohrer, Georg. *Das Buch Jesaja.* Two volumes. Zürich, 1960, 1962.

Fosbroke, H. E. W. "The Book of Amos: Introduction and Exegesis," *The Interpreter's Bible.* VI, 763-853. Nashville, 1956.

Gray, G. B. *A Critical and Exegetical Commentary on the Book of Isaiah. The International Critical Commentary.* New York, 1912.

Harper, William R. *A Critical and Exegetical Commentary on Amos and Hosea. The International Critical Commentary.* New York, 1905.

Kaiser, Otto. *Jesaja 1-12. Das Alte Testament Deutsch* 17. Göttingen, 1960.

Kissane, Edward J. *The Book of Isaiah.* Volume 1. Second edition. Dublin, 1960.

Procksch, Otto. *Jesaia* I. *Kommentar zum Alten Testament.* Leipzig, 1930.

Rinaldi, P. G. *I Propheti Minori I: Introduzione Generale, Amos.* Turin and Rome, 1952.

Robinson, T. H., and F. Horst. *Die zwölf kleinen Propheten. Handbuch zum Alten Testament.* Second edition. Tübingen, 1954.

Scott, R. B. Y. "The Book of Isaiah, Chapters 1-39: Introduction and Exegesis," *The Interpreter's Bible,* V, 151-281. Nashville, 1956.

Sellin, Ernst. *Das Zwölfprophetenbuch. Kommentar zum Alten Testament.* Leipzig, 1922.

Skinner, John. *The Book of the Prophet Isaiah. Cambridge Bible.* Revised edition. Cambridge, 1915.

Weiser, Artur. *Das Buch der zwölf kleinen Propheten I. Das Alte Testament Deutsch* 24/1. Göttingen, 1949.

AMOS

chapter 1

Word of the Prophet—
Word of God

Amos, "who was one of the shepherds of Tekoa" (1:1), a small town on the fringe of the Judean wilderness ten miles south of Jerusalem, during the reign of Jeroboam II, king of Israel, and Uzziah, king of Judah (both, *ca.* 785-745 B.C.), is known only by the small book of oracles that were collected in his name by an anonymous editor at an unknown time. The editorial superscription (1:1) is only slightly amplified by the statement in 7:14 that he trimmed sycamores, in addition to tending flocks, at one time in his life. The date during Jeroboam's reign is also confirmed by the references to Jeroboam in 7:9-11.

This information exhausts the explicit biographical data about Amos provided by the Bible. He is not mentioned in the

17

books of Kings or Chronicles, which provide the main extant record of Israel's history in the eighth century B.C.[1] Therefore, we know next to nothing about the man outwardly. We have only the few prophetic words attributed to him. These, however, have exercised an influence upon Western morality and religion out of all proportion to their bulk. This influence is beyond assessment. Together with the intrinsic worth of his words to the single reader of today, as of any day, it justifies the perennial scholarly effort to explicate his meaning. Although the man is unknown to us, we may be grateful for the slender, but splendid, legacy of his words.

The book of Amos is entirely controlled by the concept—the reality—of the word of God, not merely in substance, in the way that the Bible as a whole might be said to be the Word of God, but also in form. To an unsurpassed degree the words of this prophet come to us in the form of the direct utterance of God. The classical oracular style, which is characterized by brief poetic sayings, dominates the book, and it is punctuated, with a frequency unusual even among the prophets, by the two principal formulas of divine proclamation, "thus says Yahweh," and, "the utterance of Yahweh."[2] The absence of prose sermonic discourse, prolonged biographical narrative, and lyric poetry, in contrast to other prophetic books of the Old Testament, serves to strengthen the impression made by the style of the oracles themselves.

Fully half of the book of Jeremiah is discursive, didactic

[1] Amos is mentioned by name in the Bible only in Amos 1:1; 7:8, 10, 11, 12, 14; and 8:2.

[2] The first occurs in 1:3, 6, 9, 11, 13; 2:1, 4, 6; 3:11, 12; 5:3, 4, 16; and 7:17; and the second in 2:11, 16; 3:10, 13, 15; 4:3, 5, 6, 8, 9, 10, 11; 6:8, 14; 8:3, 9, 11; 9:7, 8, 12, and 13. In addition, "says Yahweh" is found in 1:5, 8, 15; and 2:13; and other variations appear in 3:1 and 6:8. The two primary formulas occur hundreds of times in the Old Testament and with two exceptions (Gen. 22:16 and II Cron. 20:15) they are always used by prophets. In every case but one they are formed with the divine name "Yahweh." Thus it is clear that this type of address was associated exclusively with the prophetic office and with traditional Israelite Yahwism.

prose (sermonic and biographical), and nine tenths of Ezekiel is prose narrative. Isa. 40–55 is a series of fairly lengthy poems which manifest such unity of style and structural design that they may be viewed as a single composition.[3] These are relatively late prophetic works. Their literary forms have undoubtedly been influenced by or, better, called forth by, the cultural and religious situation of the Judean exile (after 598 B.C.). That is to say, they are to a considerable degree extended literary creations meant to be read, and read by men whose religious life was no longer centered in the Palestinian Israelite sanctuaries and whose political life was no longer governed by the Israelite monarchy.

The book of Amos, by contrast, is in many ways the best example in the Bible of a collection of oracles composed initially for oral publication in the capitals of the Israelite kingdoms and their sanctuary cities. Brief, compact, originally discrete utterances have been recorded and subsequently assembled in relatively haphazard fashion. The role of the prophet appears here to have been the oral delivery of messages from Yahweh to the leaders of the Israelite kingdom. The collection of these messages in written form appears to be secondary and may well have have been done by someone other than the prophet himself.

In addition to the two recurring formulas of divine speech, there are several texts in Amos in which the act of Yahweh's speaking is explicitly mentioned.[4]

> Yahweh roars from Zion;
>   his voice thunders from Jerusalem.
> The shepherds' fields wither,
>   and the top of Carmel fades.
>
> (1:2)

[3] See, e.g., J. Muilenburg, *The Interpreter's Bible*, V (Nashville, 1956), *in loc.*
[4] The originality of 9:9 is discussed below, pp. 87-88. Amos 1:2 may be an edi-

> For behold, when Yahweh commands,
>   the large house is struck into pieces,
>   and the small house into bits . . . .
> For behold, I am raising a nation against
>   you . . . .
>   (6:11-14)
>
> For behold, when I command,
>   the House of Israel is shaken among
>   all the nations . . . .
>   (9:9)

Here the word of Yahweh is not merely a message to an Israelite leader delivered by a prophet but the agency of visible happenings in nature and history. It is a physical force of irresistible magnitude. And the same understanding of the word of Yahweh is suggested in other passages in Amos (1:3–2:5; 2:13-16; 6:7; 7:9, 17; and 9:4).

Is this mode of reference nothing more than a manner of speaking about "natural" events? Are these events acts of "Yahweh" only in the sense that they involve powers greater than those of individual men? Or do these oracles betray a belief in a transcendental, personal will which is the hidden cause behind observable happenings in the world? The usual way of reading the Old Testament is to assume that the latter alternative is the right one, that the biblical writers held a simple anthropomorphic conception of God and, correspondingly, a voluntaristic conception of nature and history. The function of the prophet, according to this view, was to announce forthcoming events in human words. Both the prophetic announcement and the actual event comprised the word of Yahweh. God revealed his intention to the prophet before the fact (3:7) and then fulfilled it tangibly in the world. The pro-

---

torial "motto" for the final collection of Amos' oracles since it appears also in Joel 3:16 (Heb. 4:16). See below, p. 99.

20

phetic word corresponded to the actual event because the same God was responsible for both, and he had the power to do what he promised.

There is ample biblical warrant for this interpretation. Perhaps the best exhibit of it is the narrative of I Kings 22. There the prophet Micaiah ben-Imlah describes his vision of the heavenly council of Yahweh, from which the world is governed and from which Micaiah himself carries the advance announcement of the outcome of a forthcoming battle. This is the mythological image of a transcendental world that was held by all the peoples of the ancient, prescientific Near East. One finds it displayed again in graphic form in Isaiah's temple vision (Isa. 6), in the visions of Ezekiel (e.g., Ezek. 1), and in certain of the psalms (e.g., Ps. 82; 89:1-5), to name only a few of the most obvious texts.

Although Amos also expressed an anthropomorphic idea of God, he included in his oracles practically none of the features of the usual mythological picture of heaven and earth. His work presupposes the idea of the prophet as Yahweh's messenger, but the nature and purpose of the message in his teaching are significantly different from those presupposed in the story of Micaiah ben-Imlah. It is the purpose of the present chapter to expound Amos' understanding of how the word of Yahweh affected Israel's life.

Much of this analysis is inferential. Amos' few explicit statements about the nature and function of the word of God have already been quoted, and they provide little help in answering our questions about his understanding. How does the word of God "come" to a prophet? How does it differ from the prophet's own words as these are formulated in his mind and put into audible speech? Does the process of formulation seem involuntary to the man himself, that is, does he imagine he is "receiving" a message from without rather than shaping one himself? If so, does this happen while he is dreaming or in a state of emotional excitement? What is the content of a word of God? May it deal with anything at all, or is its range of subjects limited? Why does God speak? Is it merely to inform, and if so, is the prophet's speech alone the sufficient medium of instruction? Is it to punish, and if so, does it accomplish this unaided, or does it depend upon another agent to actualize the punishment? Is it to inspire the hearer to action, or the cessation of action, in order thereby to bring about the desired outward effect? Does it warn of disaster so the prudent may flee? Does it exhort to repentance in order to avert disaster?

We have only a few oracles from Amos—powerful words which have fascinated, moved, and perplexed a hundred generations. We have practically no words from him about their origin and only a few about his intention in proclaiming them. The data are too meager for us to draw any probable conclusions concerning the psychological concomitants of the formulation and publication of Amos' oracles. The question of their "origin" is almost entirely closed to us in this sense. The question as it is usually put is, "Was Amos an ecstatic?" This question is discussed later in this chapter in connection with the vision reports in Amos 7-8. Although the answer we must give to it is that we do not know, study of the text in the light of the question is not entirely fruitless, for it helps us to clarify significant features of the prophet's published work.

The question of the origin and form of Amos' oracles is not our chief concern in this chapter or in this book. It is rather to discover the prophet's purpose for publishing them and the religious implications of this purpose. We are concerned primarily with the "doctrine of the word" as it is contained in this first great corpus of biblical oracles. We must pursue this study not only because it is an interesting historical question (What did Amos think he was doing?) but because it is an important theological question. What is implied about man and his relation to the world by the conviction that words like these of Amos are the words of *God*? What does it imply about God? These are our ultimate concerns. These questions about the nature of the word of God in Amos are relevant to all his oracles, at least indirectly. However, they may be discussed most usefully in relation to the dialogue of Amos and Amaziah (7:10-17), Amos' vision (7:1-9; 8:1-3), the oracle in 3:3-8, and the exhortations in chapter 5.

AMOS AND AMAZIAH (AMOS 7:10-17)

10 Amaziah the priest of Bethel sent to Jeroboam the king of Israel, saying,
    "Amos conspires against you in the midst of the House of Israel.
    The land is unable to bear all his words.

11 For thus says Amos,
    'Jeroboam shall die by the sword,
    And Israel shall be cast into exile from her land.' "

12 Then Amaziah said to Amos,
    "Go, seer! Flee to the land of Judah.
    Eat bread there, and prophesy there.

13 But prophesy no more in Bethel;
    for this is the royal sanctuary;
    this is the temple of the kingdom." [5]

14 Then Amos answered Amaziah and said,
    "I (was) no prophet, nor son of a prophet,
    But I (was) a shepherd and trimmer of sycamores,

---

[5] The last phrase is literally "house of the kingdom." It has been interpreted as the city itself (Cripps) or the royal residence (ASV, Harper, and Robinson). Similar phrases in Est. 5:1 and II Chron. 2:1 (Heb. 1:18) refer to a palace, but the parallelism in Amos 7:12 and the frequent use of the word "house" for a temple in the OT support this latter interpretation here (cf., e.g., I Kings 6:12 and RSV, Jerusalem, Weiser, and BDB, p. 109*a*).

15 When Yahweh took me from tending the flock,
And Yahweh said to me,
   'Go, prophesy to my people Israel!'
16 "So now, hear the word of Yahweh:
You say,
   'Do not prophesy against Israel;
   speak not a word against the House of Isaac.'
17 Therefore, thus says Yahweh,
   'Your wife shall be a harlot in the city,
   and your sons and daughters shall fall by the sword,
   and your land shall be parceled out by shares.
   You yourself shall die in an unclean land,
   and Israel shall be cast into exile from her land.' "

The conflict reported in this famous narrative concerned the word of the priest and the word of the prophet, or better, the word of the kingdom and the word of God. The narrative is too brief for our liking. It omits innumerable facts we should like to know and forces us to surmise the answers to many questions. The "traditioners," as they are often called today (in order to comprehend the complex process of literary transmission), did not know, or did not wish to preserve, more than they have given us. Or perhaps the report has simply suffered the attrition that inevitably accompanies the oral transmission of historical memories. In any case, we must accept the defects of prophetic tradition along with its qualities. In this instance the defects are the necessary concomitants of the qualities, for the text forces us to consider the heart of the conflict between Amos and Amaziah without allowing us to be distracted by nonessential features of the event.

Amaziah the priest of Bethel, which was the chief sanctuary of the kingdom of Israel, reported to his king that Amos was conspiring against him. We are not told here or elsewhere (he is not mentioned again in the Bible) whether Amaziah was the chief officer of the temple. Was his word alone sufficient to expel Amos from the precinct of the national sanctuary, or did it require the support of the crown? If Amos were a member of the temple staff, as several scholars have recently suggested, the latter alternative would be conceivable. Amaziah's word to Amos may not have been a mere command, but may have been the good counsel of one who did not wish any serious harm to befall the prophet, despite the counselor's need and desire to be rid of him and his conspiratorial preaching.

Again, we are not told whether Amos left Bethel and went to Judah as Amaziah advised (ordered). Interpreters of Amos have generally concluded that he did and, further, that this encounter brought his (brief) ministry to an end and that he responded to his expulsion from Israel by recording his oracles as a permanent testimony to the validity of his words. On the other hand, at least one scholar has concluded that Amos stayed in Israel and was martyred there.[6] The plain truth is that we do not know the result of the conflict or the ultimate destiny of the prophet. We are thrown back upon the words of the two men themselves, as tradition preserved them, Amaziah's charge and Amos' reply.

In the light of the history of prophetic activity in the kingdom of Israel it was reasonable for Amaziah to suspect Amos of conspiracy. In the tenth century the prophet Ahijah had played a major role in the revolution that led to the creation of the north Israelite kingdom under Jeroboam I, abolishing the hegemony of David's Judean dynasty over the northern tribes and depriving the heirs of Solomon's empire of their larger, more prosperous, more populous, and internationally more significant territories (I Kings 11:29–12:24). In the following century the prophet Elisha had instigated the rebellion of Jehu, who annihilated the illustrious

---

[6] R. E. Wolfe, *Meet Amos and Hosea* (New York, 1945), pp. 60-61.

dynasty of Omri and established the royal line in which Jeroboam II stood, who was Amaziah's king (II Kings 9). There might well have been prophets in Israel in the days of Jeroboam who were willing to sanction and abet a rebellion against the ruling house, and prophets in Judah who were champions of the House of David and ready to use their office for the destruction of the (to them) schismatic and heretical kingdom of the ten tribes. Perhaps Amaziah took Amos for such a man.[7] He actually charged Amos with a conspiracy of preaching and nothing more. But the preaching was intolerable to the land; it could not (literally) "contain all his words." These words, as Amaziah summarized them, were a prediction of Jeroboam's violent death and the deportation of the nation from the land of Palestine (Amos 7:11). We do not know whether this was precisely what Amos said on this occasion, but it is a good summary of several of Amos' oracles (2:13-16; 3:9-15; 4:1-3; 5:1-3, 16-17; 6:7; 7:17; 9:2-4).

A prediction of royal catastrophe by an inspired prophet would have alarmed any ancient king, as it would annoy any ruler. The wise monarch might be expected to respond in one of two ways. If the causes of the disaster were within his control, he would take the appropriate action to avert it. If they were not, he would try to accept his destiny in the most constructive way. In the first case he would regard the prophet as his benefactor.[8] In the second he would consider him deluded or prescient, depending on the outcome of his prophecy, and would treat him more as the mediator of a certain kind of knowledge than as a traitor to the crown.[9] However, given the beliefs of ancient men, kings

---

[7] See Robinson and Weiser. Cripps cited Winckler's thesis that Amos *was* such a man!

[8] Note, for example, David's response to Nathan's rebuke and warning (II Sam. 12:13).

[9] This seems to have been the attitude of Zedekiah toward Jeremiah (Jer. 38:14-28).

could not afford to be so dispassionately wise publicly even when they were capable of it privately. For in the eyes of ancient men there was an intrinsic power in a prophet's words that affected the course of events. Orthodox Yahwists in Israel probably did not fear this as a simple magical power since the word which the prophet mediated was for them an expression of the will of God. Yet a prophet was not merely a spokesman of God. He was believed also to be endowed with the authority to intercede with God and thus to influence God's judgments.[10] Furthermore, Yahwistic orthodoxy had certainly not purged all Israelites of superstition, so the popular belief in the self-fulfilling power of the curse must have been a lingering temptation to them.[11]

Therefore, it is not strange that the solemn words of a charismatic prophet should have elicited the grave concern of the protectors of the commonwealth. Amaziah's treatment of Amos betrays the fear that Amos' preaching would provoke the evil events of which he spoke rather than the conviction that these events were already fixed in the purposes of God. It certainly does not imply the suspicion that Amos was a leader of a revolutionary political faction already planning a *coup d'état*. Nevertheless, in a sense Amos' oracles were potentially as dangerous as an armed conspiracy. This was true not only for the reasons that have been stated so far but because of the importance of the Israelite cultus for the normal functioning of the monarchial institutions and the threat that Amos presented to the smooth and effective operation of this cultus. He jeopardized the integrity of the national cult and, therefore, the people's singleness of mind, by challenging the validity of the temple as a means to

[10] See, for example, Jer. 7:16; 14:11; 15:10-13; 17:15-16; 18:20; and Amos 7:2, 5.

[11] On the general question of the magical element in Hebrew prophecy see G. Fohrer, "Prophetie und Magie," *ZAW*, LXXVIII (1966), 25-57,

appropriate the power of God. His assault on Bethel (e.g., 4:4-5; 5:4-5) and on the Israelite system of worship (e.g., 5:21-24; 9:1), coupled with his prediction of Jeroboam's destruction and the nation's exile, was a direct attack upon the foundations of the kingdom.

The temple of the kingdom (7:13) was the nerve center of national life. The well-being of the people depended in various ways upon the services it rendered, and their commitment to the king was affected by the national celebrations conducted there. The importance of the national rites for the integrity of the monarchy is illustrated in the account of the reign of Jeroboam I in I Kings 12:25-29. His kingship was insecure as long as there was no national religious center in Israel and his subjects were tempted to participate in the rituals of the Judean royal sanctuary in Jerusalem. The function of the cult was not merely to satisfy the private religious needs of the people. It was also to reenact the story of God's dealings with the nation and its anointed king; to celebrate royal births, coronations, victories, defeats, and deaths; and thus to maintain God's sanction and support of king and people. The impact of ritual upon the convictions, sentiments, and behavior of a people was incalculably great in ancient times, as it may be in any time. All ancient kings depended upon the sanction and support of the national sanctuaries. None could tolerate lightly the interference of a man who spoke with charismatic power and claimed divine authority for his words. A prophet might undermine the people's confidence in the national rituals and the sanctity of the royal house and thus shake the entire establishment.

Jeroboam II's dynasty had been created nearly a century earlier with the encouragement and intervention of the revered Yahwistic prophets of the ninth century (I Kings 19:15-18; II Kings 9). His heirs would certainly not wish to lose their privileged status in the eyes of loyal Yahwists. This would have been an additional reason for Amaziah's effort to rid the kingdom of Amos.

Amos' attack upon the religious establishment and his condemnation of the leaders of Israel were indeed a national conspiracy. But they were not a political conspiracy in the modern sense of the term. They must be understood in the light of the social institutions of ancient Israel and the convictions and sentiments that nourished them.

Amos' reply to Amaziah's injunction to flee to Judah has occasioned a lively scholarly debate over the question of Amos' relationship to the professional or cultic prophets of his time. Verse 14 is frequently interpreted as the denial of an allegation by Amaziah that Amos prophesied for profit. Any sound analysis of the dialogue in 7:12 ff. must begin with Amaziah's command rather than Amos' reply, although this seemingly obvious rule has not always been followed. The main stress of Amaziah's urging, whether it was command or counsel, fell upon the contrast between the two places, Judah and Bethel. In the one Amos might prophesy; in the other he might not. Amaziah did not describe the measures that would be taken to prevent his prophesying in Bethel, but in sending a message to Jeroboam he obviously expected the king to enforce the prohibition. Clearly Amaziah was gravely concerned over Amos' presence in Bethel. He regarded his preaching so seriously that he invoked the resources of the crown to deal with it. His action implied the greatest respect for the power of Amos' proclamation.

The question why Amaziah told Amos to flee rather than imprison or kill him cannot be answered. He might have lacked the authority or power, or he might have feared a reprisal from Amos' friends or the public. He might have respected Amos' commission as a man of God and feared lest he harm a sacrosanct person. Again, he himself might have

29

been an acquaintance or associate of Amos who was forced by the responsibilities of his office to prevent his preaching in Bethel but who wished him no personal harm.[12] Any of these explanations would be an inference drawn from an inference. But the prior inference certainly seems justified, namely that Amaziah showed the greatest respect for the power of Amos' preaching.[13]

The stress in Amaziah's words falls upon the adverbial modifiers: "Flee *to Judah*. Eat bread *there*, and prophesy *there*. But prophesy no more *in Bethel;* for this is. . . ." His charge to Amos was to leave Israel, and particularly Bethel. And it was to this charge that Amos replied. He answered that Yahweh had given him his orders, at the time he had taken him from shepherding to make him a prophet, and had commanded him to prophesy to Israel. Amaziah had forbidden him to fulfill this commission.[14] Therefore, since Amaziah had set himself against God's command, he would surely fall in the disaster that Amos had been sent to proclaim. This is the main point of Amos' answer to Amaziah: Yahweh

[12] See Würthwein, "Amos-Studien," *ZAW*, LXII (1950), 21, and Reventlow, *Das Amt des Propheten bei Amos*, FRLANT, LXXX (Göttingen, 1962), 14-15. The command might be read as a warning to Amos to flee for his life to Judah.

[13] This respect had nothing to do with Amaziah's personal regard for Amos, about which we know nothing, notwithstanding the dubious inferences sometimes drawn from Amaziah's words (7:12; see the discussion below). Lehming denies that there is any basis for discussing the possibility that Amaziah believed Yahweh actually spoke through Amos ("Erwägungen zu Amos," *ZTK*, LV [1958], 163). Of course we don't know whether he himself believed Yahweh had said what Amos said he had. But Amaziah would not have gone to the trouble to report Amos to Jeroboam, thus invoking the executive power of the royal court, or to expel him from Bethel, if he had not considered Amos a significant threat to the *status quo*. That is to say, he respected the power of Amos' preaching.

[14] The phrase "my people Israel" comprehends both Israel and Judah, but the issue according to 7:10-17 was whether Amos was to prophesy in the kingdom of Israel. The command attributed to God in vs. 15 was therefore clearly meant to obligate Amos to do so. In vss. 10, 11, 16, and 17, "Israel" obviously means the northern kingdom. "House of Isaac" (vs. 16) is unique in the Old Testament (as is "high places of Isaac" in 7:9), but in this context it must refer to northern Israel in some sense.

said, "Go prophesy. . . ." You say, "Do not prophesy. . . ."
Therefore, thus says Yahweh. . . .[15] The first three lines
in verses 14-15 qualify the fourth, thus: "Yahweh said to
me . . . when he took me from the flock, when I was a shepherd and not a prophet." Amos had not been given a general
license to prophesy with the freedom to exercise it however
and wherever he pleased. He had been given a particular
commission to prophesy to Israel, and Amaziah was at-
tempting to countermand it. Amaziah's command did not
entail a minor change in Amos' plans or a mere restriction of
the sphere of his operations. It constituted a denial of Amos'
basic commission as a prophet. This commission had been
not one in a series of assignments given to a man already
a prophet but the sole assignment given to a man who had
not been a prophet at all.

In order to make the point that in principle Amaziah's order
could not be obeyed, Amos described the terms of his commission, and this meant recalling his leaving the flocks to accept the Lord's summons. The biographical recollection has
no other function in the dialogue than this. Amos did not
affirm or deny the title "seer," which Amaziah had used, nor
did he affirm or deny that he was then a prophet (*nabî'*).
Amaziah had not raised this question, and Amos' reply was
not an answer to it. Far less was it a comment on Amos'
possible professionalism or his relation to the offices of the
cult. These are the questions of modern critics, but the text
does not provide answers to them. To obtain answers one must
pile inference upon inference, forcing possible nuances to do

---

[15] In my judgment the emphasis in the dialogue has been treated properly by
Lehming (*op. cit.*, pp. 154-55), despite his interpretation of the verbs in vs.
14 (see pp. 167-68 and the discussion below), by Amsler, and, with certain
qualifications, by Würthwein and Reventlow. However, the conclusions Würthwein
and Reventlow have drawn concerning Amos' professional relationship to
Amaziah are speculative.

service as positive assertions, namely that "seer" was a scornful epithet used to imply the invalidity of Amos' office and that "eat bread there, and prophesy there" implied that Amos was to try to earn his living in Judah by means of his prophesying.[16]

There was perhaps a note of sarcasm in Amaziah's injunction, "Seer, go, flee . . . eat . . . and prophesy." But the burden of it was not to derogate Amos' calling.[17] It was to get him out of Israel. Amos told him why he might not, could not, go. It was not that he was or was not a professional or cultic prophet.

[16] Amaziah's term "seer" (*ḥozeh*, "visionary") has often been interpreted as a scornful epithet. Although none of the literary prophets is called this elsewhere in the Old Testament, other respectable prophets are (e.g., Gad in II Sam. 24:11 and Jehu in II Chron. 19:2). And the corresponding verb, "to see (in a vision)," and noun, "vision," are used in association with the literary prophets in Isa. 1:1; 2:1; Ezek. 12:27; Mic. 1:1; Nah. 1:1; Hab. 2:2-3; and elsewhere. These terms may have been used initially of ecstatic visions, but they developed a wider connotation and finally came to apply to the entire corpus of a prophet's oracles (Isa. 1:1; Obad. 1:1; Mic. 1:1; and Nah. 1:1), including those of Amos himself (Amos 1:1). Although there were corrupt, silly, and pathetic visionaries in Israel (see, e.g., Jer. 23:16 and Ezek. 13:6, 8, 23), the term "seer" itself does not seem to have been derogatory, at least in the pre-exilic period. Zech. 13:2-6 is postexilic. Isa. 30:10 and Mic. 3:6-8 do not disparage the seeing of visions in itself though some scholars have said so (e.g., Rinaldi, commenting on Amos 7:12). In Amos 7:12 "seer" seems to mean simply one who "prophesies," as the parallelism suggests. Cf. II Kings 17:13; Isa. 29:10; and see J. Lindblom, *Prophecy in Ancient Israel* (Oxford, 1962), pp. 90, 147-48; and Lehming, *op. cit.*, p. 163. "Eat bread" nowhere else in the Old Testament means "earn a living" or "pursue a profession" though it is commonly interpreted in this way here (see, e.g., Harper, S. R. Driver, Cripps, and Weiser). It may mean nothing more than "keep alive" or "subsist" or even "live." And it is by no means clearly implied that Amos was to "eat bread" *by means* of his prophesying. See BDB, p. 37*a*; KBL, p. 43*b*; Würthwein, *op. cit.*, pp. 20-21; Reventlow, *op. cit.*, p. 15; and Lehming, *loc. cit.* Ezek. 13:19 condemns certain prophetesses for practicing the black arts "for handfuls of barley and pieces of bread." However, this memorable line is not really parallel to Amos 7:12.

[17] The assumption that Amos chose the term "prophet" (*nabî*) pointedly rather than use Amaziah's term "seer" (*ḥozeh*) has led to opposite conclusions. Smend has argued that Amos was taking no exception to the title "seer" but was repudiating the implication that he was a prophet (*Ev.T*, XXIII [1963], 416-17) while H. N. Richardson has argued that he was repudiating the first title and accepting the second ("A Critical Note on Amos 7:14," *JBL*, LXXXV [1966], 89).

It was that his prophetic responsibility was to prophesy there. And why did Amaziah want him out of Israel? Not because Amos was a professional prophet but because he was "conspiring" against the kingdom so that the land could not tolerate his words.

Since the verbs in the first two clauses of verse 14 are tacit, the reply of Amos may be translated either, "I *was* no prophet nor son of a prophet, but I *was* a shepherd and a trimmer of sycamores, when Yahweh took me," [18] or "I *am* no prophet nor son of a prophet, but I *am* a shepherd and a trimmer of sycamores, and Yahweh took me." [19] The point seems to me to be that Amos was not a prophet at the time when Yahweh gave him the (unforeseen and unbidden) commission to prophesy to Israel. It is not that he was denying being a prophet at the moment of his encounter with Amaziah. Verse 14 is prefatory to verse 15, and its verbs are therefore in the past tense, as are those in the latter. Taken this way, the dialogue makes perfect sense. However, if verse 14 is taken as the present denial of being a prophet, Amos' reply loses cogency. Amaziah has said, "Go, seer! Flee to the land of Judah. Eat bread there, and prophesy there." To this Amos responds, "I am no prophet, nor son of a prophet, but I am a shepherd." What sort of answer is this? It is a *non sequitur* unless we read an allegation of commercialism into Amaziah's command where it is at best a nuance. It is also a denial that Amos is a prophet even though he is now prophesy-

---

[18] Cf. KJV, ASV, JPS, Jerusalem, Robinson, S. R. Driver, Amsler, A. S. Kapelrud (*Central Ideas in Amos* [Oslo, 1961], p. 7), Würthwein (*op. cit.*, pp. 16-17), A. Gunneweg ("Erwägungen zu Amos 7, 14," *ZTK*, LVII [1960], 1-16), R. E. Clements (*Prophecy and Covenant* [SBT No. 43; Naperville, 1965], pp. 36-37), and Reventlow (*op. cit.*, pp. 16-17), among others.

[19] Cf., e.g., RSV, Chicago, Harper, Cripps, Weiser, Lehming (*op. cit.*, pp. 167-68).

ing. This apparent contradiction does not exist if the dialogue is interpreted as we have done.[20]

Whether Amos was a professional or cultic prophet when he prophesied to Israel cannot be decided from the evidence at hand. If the more likely translation of 7:14 is accepted ("I *was* no prophet"), then Amos' reply to Amaziah tells us nothing about the designation of his office subsequent to his call. Although he had not been a prophet (*nabî'*) or a son of a prophet (*ben-nabî'*) before his summons from shepherding, he might well have become one afterward. The implication of his use of the verb "prophesy" to designate his activity is that he was indeed a prophet (*nabî'*), since nothing in the book suggests that the noun carried a narrower or more technical meaning than the verb. The case is perhaps different with "son of a prophet" (*ben-nabî'*) since this term may denote a member of a prophetic guild. It might, however, mean the physical descendant of a prophet[21] or the disciple of a prophetic master.[22] I believe the term in Amos 7:14 is merely a synonym for "prophet" set in parallelism to it.[23]

[20] Several proposals have been made to construe vs. 14 as an assertion that Amos was *indeed* a prophet and a son of a prophet (or, a prophet but *not* a son of a prophet) (G. R. Driver, "Amos vii.14," *ET*, LXVII [1955/56], 91-92, followed by P. R. Ackroyd, "Amos vii. 14," *ET*, LXVIII [1956/57], 94; S. Cohen, "Amos *was* a Navi," *HUCA*, XXXII [1962], 175-78; and H. N. Richardson, *loc. cit.*). However, these are all forced translations, and they magnify greatly one of the chief problems inherent in reading vs. 14 in the present tense, namely that it makes Amos appear to be answering a charge that has not been made.

[21] This is the opinion of A. Guillaume (*Prophecy and Divination Among the Hebrews and Other Semites* [London, 1938], p. 124). The usual term to designate members of a prophetic group is "the sons of the prophets" (*bᵉnê-hannᵉbî'îm*). Cf., e.g., I Kings 20:35; II Kings 2:3; 4:1; 5:22; and 9:1. To refer unambiguously to a person as a member of such a group one would need to say something like "*one* of the sons of the prophets," as is done in I Kings 20:35; II Kings 4:1; and 9:1 (and cf. II Kings 2:7; 5:22).

[22] Elisha referred to Elijah as his "father" (II Kings 2:12). See James G. Williams, "The Prophetic 'Father': A Brief Explanation of the Term 'Sons of the Prophets,'" *JBL*, LXXXV (1966), 344-48. However, King Joash referred to Elisha in the same way (II Kings 13:14).

[23] See Reventlow, *op. cit.*, p. 20.

34

Therefore, we cannot force it to yield an answer to our question about Amos' possible professional associations.[24]

Does Amos' response to Amaziah refer to his initial call to prophecy? It is generally interpreted in this way, and I believe this conclusion is correct. It has been argued that it refers only to the impulse that led him to speak at Bethel on this particular occasion.[25] However, this thesis fails to do justice to the logic of the debate or the plain sense of verse 14b. Neither Amaziah nor Amos was talking merely about a single oracle but about the fundamental issue of Amos' freedom to prophesy in the kingdom of Israel. Another opinion is that 7:14 ff. reports a second call to prophecy, this time as a prophet of judgment, in contrast to a previous call as a prophet of salvation.[26] But this theory makes no sense of the allusion to shepherding and tree-trimming, unless we suppose Amos did these during an interlude between his two prophetic ministries. The theory also requires us to read verse 14 in the present tense ("I *am* no prophet") and interpret it as a denial of some specific form of prophecy (i.e., of salvation), for otherwise it is indeed a denial that he had prophesied at all prior to *this* call. Since there is no positive evidence that Amos did prophesy earlier, there is no reason not to conclude that 7:14-15 describes his call to prophecy, in the usual sense of the term.

Our primary interest in this chapter is to discuss the purpose and authority of Amos' preaching and not to describe the general contents of his oracles concerning Israel. Amaziah's report to Jeroboam (7:10-11) charged Amos with conspiracy.

[24] For a review of the extensive discussion of this issue up to 1947 see H. H. Rowley, "Was Amos a *Nabi?*" *Festschrift für Otto Eissefeldt,* J. Fueck, ed. (Halle, 1947), pp. 191-98. Among the more important recent treatments of the passage are Würthwein, *op. cit.,* pp. 22-24; Lehming, *op. cit.,* pp. 154-57, 161-69; Smend, *Ev.T, op. cit.,* pp. 416-19; and Reventlow, *op. cit.,* pp. 16-24.

[25] See Lehming, *op. cit.,* p. 166. Clements (*op. cit.,* p. 33, n. 4) cites G. A. Danell also in this regard.

[26] See Würthwein, *op. cit.,* pp. 27-28, and the discussion of Amos 7:1-9 and 8:1-3 below.

This to the priest was the apparent purpose of the prophet. It was not the advocacy of a particular political policy, one involving the overthrow of the reigning king, but the demoralizing of the people, the undermining of national unity, and the calling in question of the validity and effectiveness of the royal cultus.

Amos' special denunciation of Amaziah gives us an insight retrospectively into an important function of prophecy, namely to provide the occasion for self-judgment. According to 7:11 and 7:16, Amos had been prophesying the death of Jeroboam and the exile of the northern kingdom. We may fill in the details of his preaching from his other recorded oracles. He had called into question the entire social, political, and cultic establishment. The question of Amaziah's own destiny was inevitably involved in that of the destiny of this establishment, especially since he was an official in Jeroboam's government. But Amaziah was not necessarily doomed because the kingdom of Jeroboam was. His future was open, although the alternatives of action may have been severely limited. But he chose to accept the kingdom's future as his own by rejecting Amos' words. He undoubtedly believed that future to be secure, seeing the threat to the kingdom in Amos' preaching and not in the event which the prophet announced. Therefore, in Amos' judgment he and his family would have to suffer the doom of the nation in all its fullness. Had Amaziah responded differently to Amos' prophecy, he might still have suffered in the debacle or gone into exile, but his destiny would not have been completely closed. There would have been constructive possibilities. However, having repudiated Amos' words and embraced the destiny of the establishment, Amaziah had closed the future for himself and sealed his own fate. Amos' condemnation of Amaziah was not merely an angry act of personal vengeance provoked by the denial of his own privilege. In a sense it was nothing more than the reiteration of what he had prophesied before. The difference was that he now made clear the personal consequences of Amaziah's own decision. The priest had judged himself in the act of judging Amos.

The contest between Amos and Amaziah was one between the authority of the word of God and the authority of the nation. When Amaziah rejected Amos' testimony to the word of God and thus rejected the authority that lay behind it, Amos had no further means by which to appeal to that authority. According to the narrative, he made no effort to prove the validity of his calling or his access to the word of God. He made no appeal to ecstasy, to membership in an accredited prophetic association, or even to Yahwistic orthodoxy. He merely said, in effect, that his prophetic existence was utterly bound up with the particular word he had been preaching. The only test of the authority of his word was the totality of his commitment to it. The authority of the word was intrinsic. For Amos it was compelling; for Amaziah it was not. Therefore, there was nothing more that Amos could do to validate it. He had the wisdom to confront Amaziah with the word alone and not to obscure the confrontation with extraneous, and therefore spurious, considerations. This wisdom is manifested in all the oracles of Amos, as well as those of Hosea, Isaiah, Micah, Jeremiah, Habakkuk, and Ezekiel. This quality of prophecy set these men apart from most of the prophets of the ancient world.

"WHO WILL NOT PROPHESY?" (AMOS 3:3-8)

The question of the nature and authority of the prophetic office is raised most explicitly in Amos in this oracle. Therefore, in addition to discussing the meaning of the oracle itself we will use it as the occasion for pursuing further the general issue of the purpose of Amos' preaching.

37

3 Do two walk together,
    unless they have met?

4 Does a lion roar in the forest,
    when it has no prey?
Does a young lion growl in its den,
    unless it has caught (something)?

5 Does a bird fall into a trap on the ground,
    when the trap is not set for it? [27]
Does a trap spring up from the ground,
    when it has caught nothing at all?

6 If a trumpet is blown in a city,
    are the people not afraid?
If misfortune befalls a city,
    has Yahweh not brought it?

7 [But the Lord Yahweh does nothing unless he has
    revealed his intention to his servants the prophets.]

8 A lion has roared;
    who will not fear?
The Lord Yahweh has spoken;
    who will not prophesy?

Verse 7 is formally not a part of the original oracle so it must be dealt with separately later.[28] The remaining verses (3:3-6, 8) comprise a finely wrought unit, balanced in all its parts.[29]

[27] The last clause is literally, "when there is no *môqesh* for it." The *môqesh* was not the whole trap (RSV) but a part of it, which had to be set (see G. R. Driver, "Reflections on Recent Articles," *JBL*, LXXII [1954], 131-36).

[28] Verse 7 is prose in the midst of poetry, it is an indicative sentence in a series of questions, and it is the only statement in the pericope that does not refer to a causal relation. Once it is removed, the rest is a harmonious unit. Verse 7 has been judged a gloss by Weiser, Fosbroke, Amsler, W. A. Irwin (*AJSL*, IL [1932], 105), I. P. Seierstad (*ZAW*, LII [1934], 35), J. Morgenstern (*Amos Studies* [Cincinnati, 1941], p. 412), Lehming (*op. cit.*, p. 152), Smend (*op. cit.*, p. 412), W. H. Schmidt (*ZAW*, LXXVII [1965], 187), and R. H. Pfeiffer (*Introduction to the Old Testament* [New York, 1948], p. 579). Reventlow believes 3:7 is Amos' own comment and 3:3-6, 8, is merely his adaptation of proverbial sayings (*op. cit.*, pp. 24-28).

[29] Verse 3 is treated independently of the rest by H. Gese ("Kleine Beiträge zum Verständnis des Amosbuches," *VT*, XII [1962], 424-27), W. H. Schmidt

What was the writer's intention in this oracle, and what is its significance for an understanding of Amos' prophetic calling? Two interpretations of the passage have dominated the history of criticism. Each of these has received two alternative emphases. According to the first, the point of the oracle concerns Amos' prophetic vocation. According to the second, it concerns the coming destruction of Israel. In the first case Amos was asserting either the *authenticity* of his commission by Yahweh, perhaps against the charge that he was not an authorized prophet of Yahweh, or the *necessity* of his prophesying, perhaps against an official prohibition. In the second case Amos was asserting either that *Yahweh* was the cause of the coming destruction, against the people's conviction that they would receive only protection from him, or that the destruction *was surely coming*, against the people's blind complacency. Few critics have denied that 3:8 expresses Amos' sense of the urgency of his calling.[30] The debatable issue is whether verse 8 alone conveys the point of the whole unit or whether verse 6 is also an assertion Amos was trying to defend.

The most widely held opinion is that the writer of 3:3-8 sought to show by a series of illustrations from common life that every event has its sufficient cause and that Amos' prophesying was due solely to a prior divine command. In this view the questions in 3-6 are all rhetorical, demanding

---

(*op. cit.*, p. 183), and Harper; and verse 8, by Cripps and Smend (*loc. cit.*), among others. But surely verses 3-6 and 8 are all one piece. The first five lines all begin with the interrogative particle while the last four begin with the letter *'aleph*. The second clause of the first question is formally identical to that of the third, and that of the second to that if the fourth, yielding a balanced alternation. The second half-line is formed the same way in the last five lines. The first six lines begin with a verb, but the last two begin with a noun in order to give it emphasis. The meter is a uniform 3 + 2, except for verse 8, where it is 2 + 2. This shorter line is appropriate to the heightened intensity of the climactic question. The effective repetition of key words is apparent even in translation.

[30] Harper is one of the few.

negative replies. But if verse 6*b* was a simple rhetorical question like the others, it was not a proclamation of something Amos' hearers did not yet know, namely that Yahweh was the source of civic calamities. Rather it was an appeal to what they took for granted. The appeal was then made to win their assent to an analogous proposition, namely that Amos' public proclamation was not a self-generating act but an act with a prior, hidden cause.[31] This cause was Yahweh's command. In order to make this point the prophet drew upon analogies from common experience and cast them in the didactic, rhetorical style of the teachers of wisdom. These were sophisticated men of affairs, and their "empirical" observations about life were probably utilized pedagogically throughout the ancient Near East.[32] The resemblance of Amos 3:3-6 to the wisdom literature has often been noted. It lies especially in the rhetorical and empirical nature of the questions and in the use of an extended series of examples.[33] The sevenfold character of the series is not a mark of dependence upon the canonical wisdom traditions, for groups of seven sayings are uncommon there, although the "house" built by wisdom was seven-pillared (Prov. 9:1).[34] On the other hand, the rhetorical question was probably not one of the basic forms of prophetic address[35] so it seems clear that Amos adopted here the popular, and therefore effective, style

[31] Gese's argument (*loc. cit.*) that "cause" and "effect" are inappropriate here because they separate what in the Hebrew's mind was a "single reality" is unconvincing. Biblical Hebrew has no equivalents for our abstract terms, but this does not necessarily mean the Hebrews' perception of events was different from ours.

[32] See W. McKane, *Prophets and Wise Men* (SBT No. 44; Naperville, 1965).

[33] Rhetorical questions are fairly common in the canonical wisdom literature, e.g., Job 4:7; 6:5-6; 8:3, 10:4; Prov. 6:27-28, 30-31.

[34] There is a list of seven examples in Prov. 30:15-16, but the literary form there is quite different from Amos 3:3-6.

[35] See C. Westermann, *Basic Forms of Prophetic Speech,* Hugh Clayton White, trans. (Philadelphia, 1967).

of the teachers of wisdom.[36] However, 3:3-6 is unique in the Old Testament in its gross configuration and thus exhibits Amos' poetic creativity in adapting various styles to his purpose.

The main point of the oracle 3:3-6, 8 is conveyed by the last verse. The seven analogies (3-6) do not comprise a complete oracle so verse 6 is not to be taken as an independent affirmation which Amos thought it necessary to defend.[37] Nevertheless, there are prophetic overtones in 3-6, not least in the seventh question ("If misfortune befalls a city, has Yahweh not brought it?").[38] In this oracle Amos asserted his own obligation to prophesy, in response to "the lion's roar," and the people's corresponding obligation to fear. Indeed, he himself was not exempt from this second obligation. In a sense his prophesying was the measure of his fear. Furthermore, the urgency of his speaking and the people's fearing was due to the threatening character of what he proclaimed. Apart from a threat of God's judgment the oracle makes little sense.

A considerable debate has been prosecuted over the question of whether 3:7-8 gives evidence of Amos' membership among the professional prophets (nebî'îm) of his day.[39] The evidence is inconclusive. Verse 7 apparently places Amos among the nebî'îm, but this verse appears to be secondary. However, it suggests that the men among whom Amos' oracles were transmitted made no distinction between him and the nebî'îm. Verse 8 has Amos (presumably) prophesying, but he need not have been a professional or cultic prophet to have done so.

[36] For a detailed treatment of the affinities of the book of Amos to the wisdom literature see S. Terrien, "Amos and Wisdom," Israel's Prophetic Heritage, B. Anderson and W. Harrelson, eds. (New York, 1962), pp. 108-15; and cf. W. H. Schmidt, op. cit., pp. 185-86.

[37] This interpretation has been made by Harper, Cripps, Gese (loc. cit.), Smend (loc. cit.), Schmidt (op. cit., pp. 183-88), and Irwin (loc. cit.).

[38] This quality is acknowledged in one way or another by Weiser, Fosbroke, and Amsler.

[39] See Würthwein, op. cit., pp. 17-18; Lehming, op. cit., pp. 151-54; Reventlow, op. cit., pp. 28-29; Smend, loc. cit.; and Seierstad, op. cit., pp. 35-36.

The oracle in Amos 3:3-6, 8 is an appeal to the men of Israel to take the prophet's preaching as seriously as he himself has done. Like the phenomena noted in the series of rhetorical questions (3-6), this preaching had not taken place without a compelling motive. Yahweh had spoken, and his speaking was not empty. It was under his sovereignty that cities fell (6b). He had roared like a lion (8a), and lions did not roar unless they had taken their prey (4). Therefore, who would not fear the prophet's threatening oracle? Might it not be an alarm to a city under assault (6a)?

Amos' argument was not coercive. His analogies were only analogies. They did not constitute a logical proof of his divine authority or the inevitability of what he prophesied. They pointed to the folly of heedlessness to a word of the prophet which might after all be the word of God. Quite simply and without appeal to extraneous tokens of his office, Amos confessed his compulsion to speak in response to what he believed to be God's command. He issued a solemn invitation to his hearers to respond in an equally appropriate way to the awful word of God. He could not prove his word to be God's word. But if it were, woe to him who failed to take heed.

Two of the chief elements of prophetic proclamation in the Old Testament are the demand for a present response and the threat of a future calamity. These are related to each other in various ways in the literary traditions of the Bible. An adequate exposition of prophetic faith requires an acknowledgment of the variations. The writer of the prose comment in Amos 3:7, which we have said intrudes into the poetic oracle in 3:3-8, proposed a dogmatic theory of the relation of prophetic word to historical event that has no counterpart elsewhere in Amos and violates in some respects the understanding of the word that is implied there. It is one of the most oft quoted lines in Amos, and it is theologically important whether it was composed by Amos or by a later editor.

The line reads, "But the Lord Yahweh does nothing unless he has revealed his intention to his servants the prophets." This assertion, if taken literally, would be somewhat naïve and pretentious on the lips of a prophet since according to the Israelite conception of Yahweh's lordship in the world there was an infinite number of the acts of God. It is pretentious also because it limits the sovereign freedom of God.[40] It is one thing to assert that God has chosen on particular occasions to use prophets as heralds of his acts. It is quite another to assert that prophets always have access to the purposes of God before they are carried out. We may note here, however, that this assertion, even if true, would not settle the problem of prophetic authority that we discussed above. For even though God did not act without first giving warning through a prophet, it would not be true therefore that every prophetic warning was an authentic revelation from God.

The general proposition declared in Amos 3:7 belongs among the ideas expressed in the latest stratum of the books of Kings and has an affinity to the theory of prophecy expounded in the prose biographical portions of the book of Jeremiah. The writers of the narrative framework of I and II Kings believed that the destinies of the dynasties of Israel and Judah had been predicted beforehand, often years or centuries beforehand, by prophets of Yahweh. Indeed, according to this source, the chief function of these prophets was to make such predictions. Prediction and fulfillment constitute one of the central motifs in these books. Ahijah prophesied the schism in Solomon's empire (I Kings 11:29-39; fulfilled in 12:15-20). An anonymous prophet forecast Josiah's reform (13:1-2; fulfilled in II Kings 23:15-20).[41] Ahijah predicted

---

[40] Cf. A. Weiser, *Die Prophetie des Amos*, BZAW, LIII (1929), 127-28, and W. H. Schmidt, *op. cit.*, p. 187. This observation is not merely subjective, as Lehming asserts (*op. cit.*, p. 152).

[41] The prediction in I Kings 11:39 seems to point also to Josiah or perhaps to

the death of Abijah and the end of the dynasty of Jeroboam I (I Kings 14:1-16; fulfilled in 14:18 and 15:29). Jehu ben-Hanani predicted the fall of Baasha's house (16:1-4; fulfilled in 16:11-12). Elijah prophesied the death of Ahab and Jezebel and the revolution of Elisha and Jehu (21:17-24; cf. 19:15-18; fulfilled in II Kings 9:1-28, 30-37; 10). Micaiah predicted Ahab's defeat (I Kings 22:17; fulfilled in 22:29-37). Elijah prophesied the death of Ahaziah (II Kings 1:2-4, 16; fulfilled in 1:17). Elisha forecast Moab's defeat by Jehoram and Jehoshaphat (II Kings 3). Elisha repeated Elijah's prediction of the fall of Ahab's dynasty (II Kings 9:7-10). Jeroboam II regained lost Israelite territory in fulfillment of an otherwise unrecorded prophecy of Jonah ben-Amittai (II Kings 14:25). Isaiah made a series of predictions concerning Hezekiah (II Kings 19:6, 20, 32-37; 20:5) and the Judean exile (20:16-18). Anonymous prophets also forecast the exile (21:10-15; fulfilled in 24:2). Huldah predicted the fall of Judah, which was to occur after the death of Josiah (22:16-20).

Throughout this series of narratives the phrase found in Amos 3:7, "my (his) servants the prophets," keeps recurring.[42] Walter Zimmerli has called it a "deuteronomic cliché" because its use is confined virtually to the deuteronomic portions of Kings and Jeremiah.[43] Furthermore, the dogmatic scheme of prediction and fulfillment that provides a structure for the present edition of Kings accords fully with the understanding of the nature of prophecy expressed in Deuteronomy (18:21-22).[44] In this theory the true prophet

___

a postexilic restoration.

[42] I Kings 14:18; 15:29; II Kings 9:7, 36; 10:10; 14:25; 21:10; 24:2; cf. 17:13, 23.

[43] *The Servant of God* (SBT No. 20; London and Naperville, 1957), pp. 22-23. The texts in Jeremiah are 7:25; 25:4; 29:19; 35-15; and 44:4. The phrase occurs only five times elsewhere, always in texts of the sixth century B.C. or later (Ezra 9:11; Ezek. 38:17; Dan. 9:6; and Zech. 1:6).

[44] Cf. also Jer. 28:9.

is the one whose predictions are confirmed by the actual course of events. Naturally this test is useful only retrospectively, but it was not therefore deemed deficient by the deuteronomists, for the interest shown in the prophets by this circle of writers was largely retrospective. By appealing to the record of prediction and fulfillment they were able to support the conviction, which it was their didactic purpose to expound, that the rise and fall of the Hebrew monarchies had transpired in conformity to the covenantal promises of God. They believed God had sworn to bless Israel in the land of Canaan for as long as they obeyed the terms of the Sinaitic covenant, particularly its prohibition of idolatry. Correspondingly, disobedience to the commandments was to have been punished by the destruction of dynasties and the eventual exile of Israel from the land.[45] In the view of the deuteronomists the prophets alone had fully understood these conditions of Israel's life; therefore, their role in her history had been to reiterate the general proposition and to predict the fall of kings in confirmation of it. To be sure, they also had exhorted the kings of Israel to obey the law of God, but their exhortation had been subordinate to their prophecy of disaster.

The deuteronomic writers viewed all the prophets of former times primarily as predictors of the judgmental acts of God. However, as they viewed their own times and sought to interpret the meaning of Israel's past for their contemporaries, they attached greater importance to prophetic exhortation. The lessons of Israel's history seemed clear to them, in covenantal terms, as did the urgent need of obedience to God's law. The reported series of fulfilled predictions made by the prophets of old was meant to prove the present validity of the covenant and the reliability of God's threats and promises. It is within this stream of Old Testament tradition, in which

[45] See Deut. 4:25-28; 6:10-15; 8:1-20; 11:8-17; 28:1-68; and compare II Kings 17:7-23 and most of the deuteronomic passages cited above.

the scheme of prediction and fulfillment defines the prophetic office, that Amos 3:7 finds its natural place.[46]

This rational-ethical interpretation of the prophetic office and the relation of the spoken word to the historical event is the antithesis of the usual ancient belief in the self-fulfilling (magical) power of ritual words, that is, words of blessing and cursing. This belief presupposed an impersonal, mechanical operation of forces that was unrelated to the moral circumstances of the speaker or his object. There may have been some generic link between the earliest Hebrew conception of the prophetic function and the ubiquitous belief in the power of ritual blessing and cursing since remnants of a magical conception of the spoken word may be found in early strata of the Old Testament in association with certain quasi-prophetic figures. For example, the patriarchal blessings described in Genesis were considered self-fulfilling, irrevocable, and ethically unconditional. The well-known story of Isaac's blessing of Jacob and Esau illustrates well these features of the old conception (Gen. 27). However, this notion was fundamentally incompatible with the Israelite belief in a personal God who was the sovereign Lord of creation and the righteous judge of men. Already in the old portrait of Balaam (Num. 22–24), who may be viewed as a forerunner of the prophets, at least as they are depicted in Samuel and Kings, the magical belief in the power of the word has been overcome. Balaam, for all his shamanistic gifts, could not curse effectively what Yahweh had not cursed. It was obvious to the narrator that the function of the inspired person, the man with spiritual "power," was to act as spokesman of the will of God. In this

[46] There are antecedents in the books of Samuel of the theory of prophecy manifested in Kings. See I Sam. 9:15-17; 9:27–10:1; 8:11-18 (cf. Deut. 17:14-20 and I Kings 11); 12:13-18; 16; 28:3-19 (cf. 15:28 with 28:17); and II Sam. 7:8-16. The deuteronomic stereotype of the prophet is not as evident in Samuel as it is in Kings. Elijah and Elisha are the only prophets named in Kings who are not stereotyped. The traditions concerning them were apparently too extensive and well established to be reduced to the usual formula.

story God's will was to bless Israel, so Balaam could do nothing else.

The nationalist sentiment of the writer of the Balaam narrative apparently outweighed any universal ethical ideal he might have held. However, such an ideal became increasingly important among later writers, and by the time of the final edition of the books of Kings and Jeremiah, the old-style nationalism had been displaced fully by covenantal theology. In these books the blessings and curses of God are rationalized completely so that no magical elements remain, and they are made conditional upon obedience to ethical norms. These norms were believed by the writers to have been revealed in the special traditions of the Israelite covenant, but, nevertheless, they were universal in their ultimate scope and intention.

According to the writers of Kings and the prose portions of Jeremiah, the purpose of prophecy was to predict the judgments of God upon his sinful people, in confirmation of his covenantal threats, and to exhort to repentance, as the means of averting further disaster. The predictive and hortatory aspects of prophecy were emphasized, respectively, as the writers' attention moved from time past to time present. The predictive aspect is stressed in Amos 3:7. Nowhere else in Amos is the relation of prophetic word to historical event reduced to such simple, rational terms. It is legitimate to infer from Amos' oracles that his purpose was partly to elicit repentance on the part of his hearers. However, it is never said, nor even implied, that their repentance would avert the calamity he prophesied. Amos 5:6 and 5:15 might be taken to imply such an outcome, but the situation actually implied there is more complex and ambiguous than this, as we have observed in the next section of this chapter.

What Amos himself sought to do and to lead his hearers to do was to acknowledge the justice and sovereignty of God regardless of the practical results of the acknowledgment.

Taken together, his oracles suggest that his central aim was to foster the knowledge of God and secure proper worship and submission to his will in the face of events which would soon occur. It was not to prevent their occurrence. Submission to God's will in the circumstances of his own life was the quality of Amos' response to God (7:10-15), and it seems fair to say that he sought a similar submission in his hearers. If the aim of prophecy may be defined in these terms, then prophetic interpretation of the acts and counsels of God was as important in the wake of social catastrophe as it was in its van. Through the prophet's agency the catastrophe might be more than a mere catastrophe. It might be also the occasion for moral renewal. This was the meaning of the events described in Amos 4:6-12, for example. A prophetic word spoken in the midst of adversity was required to evoke a creative response from the people who experienced it.

Amos 3:7 could perhaps be made to comprehend both the predictive announcement of divine judgments in history and the retrospective interpretation of them if it were translated as in the RSV and taken out of context:

> Surely the Lord God does nothing,
> without revealing his secret
> to his servants the prophets.

However, the line itself is more accurately rendered, "does nothing, unless he has revealed," [47] and the context makes this meaning virtually certain. Therefore the statement accords perfectly with the understanding of prophecy expressed by the writers of I and II Kings.

Our purpose in discussing the place of Amos 3:7 among the literary traditions of the Old Testament has not been merely to argue that it was not an original part of Amos'

---

[47] See GK, par. 163c, Jerusalem, Driver, Harper, Cripps, and Weiser.

oracle. It has been primarily to describe a significant biblical conception of the function of prophecy, to which this verse has the closest affinity and which is partly at odds with the understanding of the prophetic office that is implied elsewhere in the oracles of Amos.[48]

DEVELOPMENTAL INTERPRETATIONS OF AMOS' PREACHING

Amos' preaching of impending catastrophe to the kingdom of Israel was not presented explicitly as a summons to eliminate the causes of destruction in order to prevent its occurrence. The imminent end of the nation was repeatedly announced in his oracles with unqualified certainty (2:13-16; 3:2, 9-15; 4:1-3; 5:1-3, 16-20; 6:7-14; 8:1–9:8a). However, there are several significant passages in the book in which God's judgment is treated as conditional and indeterminate. These have been variously interpreted, and the interpretations have gone hand in hand with differing estimates of Amos' prophetic intention. The passages are 4:6-11 and 7:1-6.

Several developmental interpretations of Amos' preaching have been advocated, largely on the basis of these texts. Robert Gordis defended the view that Amos began his career as a prophet of conditional doom who hoped for national reformation, but became a prophet of unconditional doom as the prospect of repentance grew dim.[49] Martin Buber traced three stages in Amos' preaching. In the first Amos proclaimed a conditional threat to the nation, hoping for the repentance of the whole people. Sobered by the frustration of this hope, he subsequently worked for the reform of a remnant (5:15).

[48] The ideas expressed in Amos 3:7, I and II Kings, and Jeremiah may have been current in Amos' time or even earlier. Our point is not that they are chronologically secondary to the ideas conveyed by the other oracles of Amos but that they are different from these theologically.

[49] "The Composition and Structure of Amos," *HTR*, XXXIII (1940), 239-51.

And ultimately his appeal was narrowed to a single listener (9:11, 13, the first five words of vs. 14, and the last three of 15).[50] Ernst Würthwein argued, mainly on the basis of the above passages, that Amos had originally been a cultic prophet of national salvation but abandoned this role to become a prophet of judgment.[51] These interpretations illustrate the possibilities. The weakness of these and all similar theories is that the present text of Amos manifests a uniform and consistent perspective concerning Israel's future and gives no explicit indication of the kind of change these scholars have assumed to have occurred.

Amos 4:6-11 is a recollection of a series of evils that God had inflicted upon Amos' hearers (apparently citizens or leaders of the kingdom of Israel) during an indeterminate period of time prior to the prophet's speaking. They were a famine (vs. 6), a drought (7-8), a crop blight (9a), devouring locusts (9b), an "Egyptian" plague (10a), a military defeat (10b), and the fall of a city (11). There is no explicit indication given of God's purpose in imposing these misfortunes. They are not explained as punishments for crimes, either moral or ritual. All that is said is that on each of these occasions the victims failed to "return" to Yahweh (4:6, 8, 9, 10, 11).

This catalog of failures has been placed by the editors in juxtaposition to oracles decrying the oppression of the poor (4:1) and the simultaneous maintenance of a luxuriant cultus (4:4-5), and it might be supposed that this contiguity implies a moral explanation of the seven plagues. Surely the people's need to return to God presupposed their having turned away. Nevertheless, the absence of an explanation of the specific causes of the afflictions should probably be considered deliberate on the part of the writer. Nowhere else in the book of

[50] *The Prophetic Faith* (New York, 1949), pp. 103-8. Buber referred to the Hebrew text.
[51] *Op. cit.*, pp. 28-50. See also R. E. Wolfe, *op. cit.*, p. 48.

Amos is a natural disaster cited as a divine punishment for Israel's sinfulness. Elsewhere the punishment is always military conquest, deportation, and attendant evils, that is to say, calamities produced through the agency of men.

The point of 4:6-11 is simply that Israel has been given many occasions for a turning to God and has allowed them all to pass without making the appropriate response. The preceding oracle (4:4-5) mocks the people's delight in sacrificial turning to God. Thus if there is significance in the placement of 4:6-11 beside this other utterance, it is probably to counterpose the denunciation of their failure to turn truly against the acknowledgment of their readiness to turn sacrificially. The antithesis is doubly pointed if 4:6-11 is an imitation of a liturgy from the Israelite temple, as some scholars believe.[52]

Israel had failed to seize the divinely given occasions for her repentance so the opportunities had been exhausted, and it was now too late to return. Therefore God would turn to them in what could only be a terrible and final visitation (4:12a). The prophet may have intentionally left the content of this encounter vague, and therefore more mysterious and dreadful, since the oracle is also vague with respect to the antecedents of the calamities and the content of the desired returning.[53] More likely, in my opinion, he was prophesying an overthrow of the whole kingdom (vs. 12) similar to that which had previously been experienced only by a part (vs. 11). This point will be discussed further in chapter three.

Amos was not announcing one more occasion in an endless

---

[52] See Weiser; Reventlow, *op. cit.*, pp. 75-90; W. Brueggemann, "Amos IV 4-13 and Israel's Covenant Worship," *VT*, XV (1965), 1-15; and below, pp. 125 ff.

[53] The content of a curse, particularly one potentially affecting the speaker, was often left unstated, probably out of fear lest the utterance hasten its fulfillment. See Andrew F. Key, "The Magical Background of Isaiah 6:9-13," *JBL*, LXXXVI (1967), 201. Key mentions Amos 4:6 ff. (p. 204) but not as an illustration of the possible influence of curse formulas upon prophetic style.

series. The event he now proclaimed was of a different order. Moreover, there is not the slightest suggestion that he had previously prophesied the other events himself.[54] These stood in the past, entirely outside the realm of his own encounter with the people. His responsibility was to announce the ultimate visitation of Yahweh to Israel. This turning of God against Israel was determinate and unconditional.

A passage related to this one for purposes of the present discussion is 7:1-9. It is part of a larger narrative about a vision or series of visions (7:1-9; 8:1-3; and possibly 9:1 ff.). The purpose of this report, as it stands, is oracular and not biographical. The writer tells us nothing about the psychological character of the visions themselves. We do not know whether Amos had perceived external objects in nature which he then invested with prophetic significance, as has often been maintained, or whether he had seen these objects only with his mind's eye in a dream or vision.[55] Whatever the original experiences were, they have receded from view. Indeed, the present account is so highly polished, so economical in expression, and so deliberately and articulately structured, that

[54] Amsler rightly rejects the interpretation of the plagues as if they were still to come, on the ground that this makes the refrain meaningless.

[55] The literature on this question is extensive. In addition to the commentaries, see especially I. P. Seierstad, *op. cit.*, pp. 31-35; *Die Offenbarungserlebnisse der Propheten Amos, Jesaja, und Jeremia* (Oslo, 1946); Mowinckel, "Ecstatic Experience and Rational Elaboration in Old Testament Prophecy," *Acta Orientalia,* XIII (1935), 264-91 (particularly pp. 274, 279, 283-84); W. Rudolph, "Gott und Mensch bei Amos," *Gustav Krüger Festschrift,* H. Bornkamm, ed. (Giessen, 1932), pp. 19-31; Lehming, *op. cit.*, pp. 160-61; Würthwein, *op. cit.*, pp. 28-35; and Reventlow, *op. cit.*, pp. 30-56. The following general studies of prophecy may also be mentioned: A. Guillaume, *Prophecy and Divination,* pp. 47-219 (especially the comments on Amos, pp. 149-50); J. Lindblom, *Prophecy in Ancient Israel,* pp. 182-85, 209; H. H. Rowley, "The Nature of Old Testament Prophecy in the Light of Recent Study," *HTR,* XXXVIII (1945), 1-38; H. Knight, *The Hebrew Prophetic Consciousness* (London, 1947); A. R. Johnson, *The Cultic Prophet in Ancient Israel* (Cardiff, 1944, 2nd ed. 1962); A. O. Haldar, *Associations of Cult Prophets Among the Ancient Semites* (Uppsala, 1945); and J. Muilenburg, "The 'Office' of the Prophet in Ancient Israel," *The Bible in Modern Scholarship,* J. P. Hyatt, ed. (Nashville, 1965), pp. 74-97.

one wonders whether there were any prior visionary experiences or whether the whole account is not an imaginative literary creation. In any case, nothing is said, not the least hint is given, about the place of this vision in Amos' career, whether it occurred before he began to prophesy publicly or only afterward, whether it constituted his call to prophecy or marked a later change in the character of his mission, or whether it took place all at once or at various times.[56] Everything in the account serves a single purpose, and it is oracular. It is to proclaim God's decision, "I will never again pass by them. . . . My people Israel is ripe for destruction" (7:8 and 8:2).

THE VISION (AMOS 7:1-9; 8:1-3)

7:1   *The Lord Yahweh showed me this:* behold, he was forming locusts in the first growth from the late sowing—it
2   was the late sowing after the royal mowing. When they had finished devouring the grass of the land, I exclaimed,
      "Lord Yahweh, forgive!
      How will Jacob stand,
      He is so small?"
3   Yahweh changed his mind.
      "It shall not happen," Yahweh declared.

---

[56] The vision is commonly believed to have constituted Amos' call to prophecy, and it is often supposed that the episodes in the narrative betray the seasons of the year in which the series of original experiences took place. The first episode does indeed concern spring mowings, and the fourth summer fruit. However, the third is nonseasonal; and so is the second, apart from the improbable supposition that it was occasioned by the severe heat of a Judean summer. The only positive evidence linking the vision(s) with Amos' call is the proximity of this report to the narartive of 7:10-17, which contains Amos' only reference to his call (vss. 14-15). The common, a priori judgment that all prophets had inaugural visions is hardly supported by the evidence. Samuel's audition was indeed inaugural (I Sam. 3), but only Jeremiah's among the visions (auditions) of the literary prophets is explicitly presented as inaugural (Jer. 1). Neither Isaiah's vision (Isa. 6) nor any of Ezekiel's (e.g., Ezek. 1 f.) is so represented. Any of these may have occurred after the call to prophecy.

4   *The Lord Yahweh showed me this:* behold, the Lord
     Yahweh was summoning to a trial by fire. When it had
     consumed the great ocean and was consuming the dry land,
     I exclaimed,

5   "Lord Yahweh, stop!
          How will Jacob stand,
          He is so small?"

6   Yahweh changed his mind about this.
          "This, too, shall not happen," the Lord Yahweh declared.

7   *He showed me this:* behold, the Lord stood beside a
8   plumbed wall with a plumb-line in his hand. And Yahweh
     asked me,
          "What do you see, Amos?"
     And I answered,
          "A plumb-line."
     Then the Lord said,
          "Behold, I am setting a plumb-line
          In the midst of my people Israel.
          I will never again pass by them.

9   The high places of Isaac will be devastated,
          And the sanctuaries of Israel destroyed,
          When I rise against the House of Jeroboam with the
               sword."

8:1 *The Lord Yahweh showed me this:* behold, there was a
2   basket of ripe fruit. And he asked me,
          "What do you see, Amos?"
     And I answered,
          "A basket of ripe fruit."
     Then Yahweh said to me,
          "My people Israel is ripe for destruction.[57]
          I will never again pass by them.

3   They will wail the temple songs
          In that day, is the Lord Yahweh's utterance.

---

[57] The Hebrew contains a wordplay on *qayiṣ* ("harvested fruit") and *qeṣ*
("end"). The penultimate clause in 8:2 is literally, "The end has come for
my people Israel" (cf. Chicago and RSV). However, the paraphrase adopted
here, which is borrowed from the Jerusalem Bible, obviously commends itself.

So many corpses!
Thrown everywhere!
Silence!"

The first two of the four episodes in the narrative have the same function as the catalog of calamities in 4:6-12. They describe God's previous forbearance as a prelude to his ultimate decision to destroy Israel. Two destructive events, the latter of cosmic proportions, are seen by the prophet as symbols of a terrible threat to "Jacob" (Israel). The prophet twice begs God to be compassionate to the frail people, and each time God accedes to his request. But subsequent symbols of disaster pass before the prophet's eyes, and on these occasions God declares the time for forbearance past and the time for irrevocable judgment at hand.

The vision differs from the oracle in 4:6-12, for it does not explicitly interpret the calamities as occasions for Israel's repentance. In the vision the emphasis is not upon Israel's refusal to turn but upon God's patience and willingness to forgive and upon the final exhaustion of this patience and the necessity of destruction. Moreover, in the present text there is no indication that the evil happenings might be punishments of an apostate people. This, of course, is in keeping with the symbolic role of these events within the visionary drama. They point solely to one end, which is God's final, irrevocable decision. The narrative does not describe actual events in Israel's history or Amos' public career. The events are entirely visionary and symbolical. Only one feature of the vision is meant to correspond directly to Israel's actual situation in the world, and that is the decision of God to destroy.[58]

The events described in 4:6-12 and symbolized in 7:1-6 lay in the past from the viewpoint of the writer. Nowhere in the

---

[58] The view that everything in the narrative transpired within the vision itself has been persuasively argued, e.g., in the works by Seierstad, Würthwein, Rudolph, and Reventlow, cited above.

book is there an indication that Amos' perspective changed during the actual course of his prophetic career. Moreover, the hypothesis of a change is unnecessary in interpreting Amos' oracles and judging the purpose of his ministry. There were indeed conditional aspects of his preaching, to which Buber, for example, has pointed. But I believe Buber and others are wrong to regard these elements as indices of change in the basic orientation of Amos' prophecy.

The vision narrative (7:1-9; 8:1-3) is a superbly integrated whole. It contains a single dialogue between God and Amos which moves dramatically through four episodes marked by scenes of devastating significance. The meaning of the narrative as a whole is unambiguous, and it corresponds fully to what is asserted in Amos' oracles. Chapter 8:1-3 is now separated from the rest by the report of Amos' dialogue with Amaziah (7:10-17). In form and content it belongs with 7:1-9, and the common critical judgment that 7:10-17 was editorially inserted into the midst of the vision narrative because of the catchword similarity of verse 11 to verse 9b is probably correct.[59] Whether or not it is correct, however, there is no question of the formal and material unity of 7:1-9. This is one dialogue leading to one conclusion. Insofar as it reflects an actual vision, and there is no adequate basis for denying that it does, this vision is one. It is conceivable that there were four discrete visions, but if there were, we do not know what meaning might have been attached to them other than the one they have in the narrative before us. This narrative is a single dramatic dialogue whose point is similar to the one in 4:6-12, namely that God's patience with the un-

---

[59] Numerous theories have been propounded concerning the "original" place of 7:10-17 within the book, but all these are highly speculative. See, for example, Weiser, *The Old Testament: Its Formation and Development* (New York, 1961), p. 244; J. D. W. Watts, *Vision and Prophecy in Amos* (Grand Rapids, 1958), p. 49; and Gordis, *loc. cit.*

regenerate kingdom of Israel is exhausted, and its doom is therefore sealed.

Amos 7:1-9 and probably 8:1-3 comprise a single narrative of an impressive vision. Amos is shown a series of calamities developing before his eyes. God repents of the first two (in the vision) when Amos (also in the vision) asks him to forgive "little Jacob." However, the subsequent calamities (which again take place only in the vision) are not turned back. They are symbols of the disaster Amos is commissioned to declare to Israel.

In 4:6-11 Amos apparently described events that had actually occurred in Israel's history, although this conclusion has recently been challenged in the interest of a cultic interpretation of the passage. However, the events in Amos' vision (7:1-9; 8:1-3) are symbolical and need not be correlated with actual happenings in Israel's history. They are episodes in a drama of divine decision, which is symbolized by the vision as a whole. Amos' intercessions (7:2, 5) are probably nothing more than devices to support the movement of this drama. They are made solely upon the stage of the vision and require no correlation to events in Amos' private life or prophetic career. The vision is a parable of Israel's life under God and not a pictorial review of the stages in Amos' ministry.

The announcements contained in 4:6-12 and 7:1-9 (and 8:1-3) are unconditional. There are two other passages in the book of Amos that deal with the possible mitigation of God's judgment, but these do not soften the unconditional quality of the threat to the Israelite kingdom as such. In 5:4-6 Amos admonishes the House of Israel to "seek Yahweh and live" at the same time that he assures them of the coming destruction of the national sanctuaries in Gilgal and Bethel. And in 5:14-15 he again urges them to "seek good and not evil, so that you may live" and so that Yahweh therefore "may be merciful to the remnant of Joseph." What is assumed in both these passages is exactly what is proclaimed elsewhere, namely that the kingdom of Jeroboam was doomed, together with the cultic establishment which supported, and was supported by, it. However, the destruction of the kingdom did not necessarily mean the obliteration of the whole people of Yahweh. The tribal confederacy, based on common faith in Yahweh and common worship of him, antedated the creation of the monarchy and the permanent national sanctuaries. This people of Yahweh, visibly represented by the old tribal communities, might survive the fall of the monarchy. Whether it did depended upon the response of the people to Amos' proclamation and to the events he prophesied. If they "sought Yahweh," that is, reaffirmed their faith in him, and also sought to maintain a just society based upon the Yahwistic covenant, they might endure the destruction of the kingdom and its idolatrous and unjust institutions and remain a truly Yahwistic community, albeit a "remnant" of the old nation.

The word of God, embodied in the oracle of the prophet, was the occasion for self-judgment whether it was spoken in the sanctuary or the street, whether it contained a prediction of ineluctable national catastrophe or an exhortation to personal repentance. The prophet's obligation was to provide this occasion, for it was always an invitation to obedient response. Amaziah's response to Amos' oracles sealed his own destruction, in the prophet's opinion. Thus it was possible for him to turn the prophecy of the nation's fall into a prediction of personal ruin for one man and his family (7:16-17). Alternatively, it was possible for Amos to exhort his hearers to "seek Yahweh and live," even in the face of the imminent fall and exile of the kingdom (5:4-5, 14-15). The lordship of God was operative in every human situation, and men were morally accountable to him even in the most dire circumstances of history. Nothing could happen in the people's life to relieve the prophet of his responsibility to speak the word of God, even though the immediate content of the word was utterly foreboding. It was not his responsibility to trace out all the possible consequences of decision amid the vast complexities of history.

The final punishment of the heedless community was not the fall of the kingdom, which the prophet predicted, but the silence of the prophetic voice itself. The famine of the word of God was the most terrible famine of all (8:11-12). The most evil time was the one in which the prophet himself became prudent and kept silent before the violent hatred of his audience (5:10-13). As long as Israel had an imprudent prophet in its midst, it was not yet swallowed up in darkness.

The creative consequences of prophetic speaking were never completely exhausted even though the prophet might seem to have little to promise. On the other hand, the people's speaking might be futile even though it was full of assurance. To Amos their religious songs were so much noise (5:23), their ritual confessions illusions (8:14), and their complacent boasts the means of their own destruction (9:10, if this verse is from Amos). But in the dark days to come they would finally speak an appropriate word, for it would be a lamentation (5:16). If Amos' characterization of the people's words was correct, then he was their faithful servant in speaking a dark and critical word. This word addressed *to them* was the best intercession the prophet could make for the people with God (cf. 7:2, 5).

TESTING THE PROPHETIC WORD

In his confrontation with Amaziah, Amos appealed to the word of Yahweh against the word of the priest and thus raised the question of the test of the authentic word of God. Two tests are specified in the Old Testament, and a third seems to be assumed. This last is the test of "ecstatic" or visionary experience. Amos himself reports several visions (7:1-9; 8:1-3; 9:1). Although there is no express claim that his "seeing" guaranteed the divine origin and reliability of his oracles, it is possible that the mere public recollection of the experience was intended as an authentication. The recognition that Amos was a seer, however, did not prevent Amaziah from rejecting his prophetic testimony (7:12). In the book of Amos, as in the other prophetic books of the Old Testament, there is no discussion of the psychological forms of prophecy as means of validating the truth of an oracle. The implication of this silence on the part of writers who manifestly struggled with the problem of true and false prophecy is that they did not regard visions and related phenomena as useful criteria of divine authority. One would judge from the allusions to popular consultation of diviners and seers that there were many in Israel who respected these phenomena as necessary marks of "inspiration." [60] However, in the circles out of which the Old Testament came, skepticism toward these marks grew, and they were finally repudiated.[61] The evidence is not sufficient to prove that Amos saw visions even though he did use the conventional visionary form as a vehicle for his proclamation.

The two tests of true prophecy expressed in the Old Testament are that the prophet be a devotee of Yahweh and that his predictions come to pass (Deut. 13:1-5; 18:15-22). Both of these are useful guides though neither is an adequate criterion. The kind of superficial orthodoxy defined in the first case is easily achieved or affected, and in any case, mere orthodoxy may stultify prophetic insight. Amaziah may have been orthodox! Hypocrisy would perhaps disqualify a prophet, if there were accurate tests of hypocrisy, but sincerity alone would not qualify him. Amaziah was surely sincere.

[60] E.g., Deut. 13:1-5; Isa. 8:19; Jer. 23:23-40; Mic. 3:5-8, 11.
[61] See, e.g., Jer. 23:23-40 and Zech. 13:2-6.

The test of historical fulfillment is of course valid for a prophet's analysis of the course of a nation's affairs. Amos himself implicitly invoked this test of his own prophecy in his reply to Amaziah. The entire prophetic canon of the Old Testament is in one respect a testimony to the application of this principle, for it is made up largely of oracles by men who correctly anticipated the fall of Israel and Judah. At the moment of decision, naturally, this test is useless. Amos' prediction must have seemed like eccentric pessimism to his contemporaries. On the other hand, a prophet's moral criticism is not necessarily invalidated by his mistaken estimate of the course of history, although many worthy oracles probably failed to gain admission to the canon merely because their authors were wrong about the fate of the kingdoms of Israel. However, in the conflict between Amos and Amaziah ethical criticism was not explicitly an issue, at least not as the encounter was reported. The issue was solely the prophet's expectation of the destruction of the kingdom and the exile of her rulers.

Amos' judgment about the nation's destiny was confirmed by subsequent events. Yet it is unlikely that his oracles were remembered, inscribed, collected, edited, and transmitted simply in order to ascertain whether his prediction would be fulfilled and to offer the oracles to the remnant of the nation as proof of his astuteness and the people's folly. Although the canonical tradition did not preserve the utterances of prophets who were fundamentally wrong about the future of the Israelite monarchy, it is inconceivable that it preserved the utterances of those who were right about it simply on this account. Who in pre-exilic Israel would have cared, would have gone to all this trouble? The deuteronomic test and the concern it presupposes are too shallow to account for the creation or preservation of the canonical collections of prophetic oracles. It is really a test of the diviner and soothsayer, offered as practical advice to private citizens of Israel in order to prevent their supporting unscrupulous or pagan seers. It serves this purpose admirably, for it is a test that every seer must ultimately fail, regardless of the orthodoxy of his religious convictions. That is to say, it suffices for anyone who will apply it rationally. It did not serve to prevent the superstitious in Israel from continuing to buy the services of diviners.

The canonical prophets were not diviners so the deuteronomic test does not really apply to them.[62] It does, however, point to an analogous consideration that was operative in the process of transmitting their oracles. Similarly, the second deuteronomic test, that is, the requirement of Yahwistic orthodoxy, points to a decisive factor in the recognition and preservation of authentic prophetic teaching even though it is superficial in itself. The prophets' oracles were acknowledged as the word of God because of their continuity with Israelite religious tradition. They were not merely private opinions. They were reformulations of convictions about God and man which had motivated generations of Israelites and had become embodied with varying degrees of effectiveness in their social institutions, patterns of behavior, and forms of worship.

We cannot trace the precise lines of continuity from eighth-century prophecy backward through the centuries to the beginnings of Yahwistic tradition. Of course, literary affinities may be observed between the prophetic books and other portions of the Old Testament. But the virtual silence of the extant sources concerning the development of Israel's literary and liturgical forms makes it necessary to deduce the origin and development of the forms of prophetic utterance and

---

[62] The use of this test was further complicated by the belief that Yahweh might use "lying" oracles to achieve his purpose, as in the story of Ahab and Micaiah (I Kings 22), and by the acknowledgment that even prophets of pagan gods were capable of providing empirical confirmation of their oracles (Deut. 13:1-8).

of their settings in life from indirect evidence. These inferential conclusions are necessarily tentative.

We have already mentioned Amos' use of the literary form of the vision as an indication of his affinity to well-established prophetic traditions.[63] Another mark of this affinity is his use of the conventional formulas of prophetic utterance, "thus says Yahweh" and "utterance of Yahweh." Still another is the apparent imitation of a liturgy of cursing in his oracles on the nations (chaps. 1 and 2), a subject to which we will return later. Finally, we may cite the highly polished character of his poetry and his repeated use of customary forms of prophetic denunciation. One might argue that these forms became customary only after Amos created them and demonstrated their effectiveness, but this possibility seems much less likely than the alternative. It requires the improbable assumption that a whole series of prophets over a period of several centuries depended for a major portion of their oracles upon forms created by a single man (and a shepherd, at that) who is not even mentioned in the Old Testament outside the small collection of his oracles.

The theory that Amos employed forms and language long hallowed by Yahwistic prophets raises the question why Amos' oracles were written down while those of his predecessors were not. This is an important question to which it is not yet possible to give a fully satisfactory answer. However, we actually do not know that Amos' oracles were the first to be written down or even that they were the first written ones to have survived. The canonical books contain many anonymous prophetic oracles. It is possible that some of these are older than those of Amos. Also, there may have been other written oracles that did not survive. However, even if Amos' oracles were the first to be collected in written form, they probably

---

[63] This statement is not meant to preclude the possibility that Amos actually saw visions.

did not differ essentially in style and language from oracles which were published only orally.

The persistence in use throughout subsequent centuries of the oracular forms found in the book of Amos is a testimony to their origin in a well-established tradition. Prophets' words were holy words, and their habits of speech, like all sacred usage, probably evolved slowly under many influences. Amos' words were powerful because they were cast in forms upon which sacred tradition, and perhaps liturgical usage, had conferred authority. They would doubtless not have survived, would not have impressed the men who collected them, if they had not taken these forms. They would hardly have affected Amaziah as they did. The words of this transient herdsman-seer were a threat to the state only because they carried the force of sacred tradition in their shape, in their appeal to recognized modes of revelation, and in the manner of their proclamation. Amos' words were recognizable as words of Yahweh because they were shaped by a well-defined prophetic tradition. Only so could Amos himself, who was a devout Yahwist with an awful sense of the majesty and power of God, have presumed to say of his own proclamation, "Thus says Yahweh."

chapter 2

The Righteousness of God
and
The Righteousness of Man

The prophet Amos spoke out of a long tradition of Israelite faith. His oracles presuppose many fundamental convictions about God and the world, about man and history, that had been formed and reformed in the minds of his ancestors during a period of at least five hundred years. The heritage may be traced with relative clarity back through Elijah in the ninth century B.C. and the historical writers of the tenth century to those who shaped the religious convictions and ethical norms of the Israelite confederacy in the period from Moses to Samuel (thirteenth to eleventh centuries). The line becomes obscure as we approach the time of Moses, but it probably reaches back before him for another five hundred years to Jacob and Abraham. The literary sources of the Bible are too recent to provide access to the convictions of these remote fathers of the faith; yet all the sources affirm that Israel's faith was a gift of God, transmitted from the fathers in unbroken succession for a thousand years.

Amos' hearers were heirs of this tradition as much as he. Because of their knowledge of it and implicit obligation to it, he did not need to articulate all the convictions upon which his oracles were based. Indeed, it probably never occurred to him to do so. Outwardly his preaching was simple and uniform. It was the proclamation of impending disaster to Israel and her neighbors as the judgment of God upon unrighteous nations. Everything he said served this purpose. Therefore, he was silent about many things that interest the modern reader. An exposition of Amos' theology is largely an exposition of his idea of God's righteousness and of the righteousness demanded by God from men.

Amos' oracles are negative and critical. Their explicit subject is the unrighteousness of men. However, one implicit purpose of his speaking was to call men to obedience to God, and the nature of this obedience may be inferred from what is denounced. The accusation which recurs again and again in the oracles of Amos is that the privileged oppress and exploit the powerless and indulge themselves proudly in the fruits of their exploitation (2:7-8; 3:10, 15; 4:1, 4-5; 5:7, 10-12; 6:1-7, 8, 13; 8:4-5). The means are extortion, dishonesty, and corruption of judicial processes, and the ends are luxury and arrogance. The strong become stronger and richer, of course, and their victims more destitute.

There are twenty accusations among the oracles, and fifteen of them involve this compound evil. The innocent poor are "sold" by the powerful (2:6). Concretely this meant either that they were denied their legal rights by judges who had been bribed[1] or that they were forced into debt-slavery on the least pretext.[2] Enslavement of the poor is the charge in 8:6, along with crooked business practices directed to the same end (8:4-5). In 5:7 and 5:10 it is perversion of justice in the courts ("the gate"). This offense is also mentioned in 2:8, in one of its concrete forms, namely withholding pledged garments in defiance of the law (cf. Deut. 24:12-13). Unspecified acts of oppression and extortion are referred to in a number of oracles (2:7a; 3:10; and 4:1). The resulting luxury enjoyed by the powerful in confident self-indulgence is decried repeatedly (3:15; 4:1; 5:11-12; and 6:1-8, 11-14). It is also implied that the luxuriant sacrificial cult was maintained out of the same resources (4:1-5).

In the five remaining accusations the prophet charged the Israelites with abuse of Nazirites and prophets (2:12),[3] unrepentance (4:6-12), idolatry (5:26-27), superstition (8:13-14), and the sexual exploitation of certain women (2:7b). Thus he attacked purely ritual offenses only rarely. It was social injustice and immorality with which he was primarily concerned. However, he was not unconcerned with the profanation of the Yahwistic cultus, as we shall try to show in chapter three.

Amos' critique of Israelite life was not confined to the overt act of oppression or self-indulgence, important as this was. It involved equally the disposition of the will. This constitutional quality of Israel's unrighteousness is described in the litany of impenitence (4:6-12). It is also referred to sarcastically in 4:4-5 and in the reproaches in chapter 6. The prophet's distress over the intractability of the proud and

---

[1] See, e.g., Cripps.

[2] See Fosbroke, and Robert Bach, "Gottesrecht und weltliches Recht in der Verkündigung des Propheten Amos," *Festschrift für Gunther Dehn*, W. Schneemelcher, ed. (Neukirchen, 1957), pp. 28-29.

[3] Unless 2:10-12 is a secondary addition to the Israel oracle in 2:6-16, as Weiser, Schmidt (*ZAW*, LXXVII [1965], 168 ff.), and others maintain.

selfish becomes clearer as his invectives exert their cumulative impression upon the reader.

In every case but one the evils cataloged in the oracles on the foreign nations are acts of cruelty against neighboring peoples. Some of them are simultaneously violations of international treaty or kinship. The Arameans of Damascus had slaughtered their southern neighbors in Gilead with iron-spiked threshing sledges (1:3, if the accusation is literal and not figurative). This could only have been done to captives or noncombatants and was therefore not one of the routine evils of combat. This atrocity had been matched by the Ammonites, Gilead's neighbors on the other side (1:13). Such gratuitous butchery was not uncommon in the Old Testament world (cf. Hos. 13:16). The moral perversion exhibited here was the greater because the acts were committed against peoples who had in part a common history and culture with their assailants.

The crime of the Philistines of Gaza and the Phoenicians of Tyre was wholesale slave-trading (1:6, 9). For Tyre, it entailed the violation of a treaty (1:9*b*) so their guilt was magnified, even though the external consequences of their actions were the same as those of Gaza's. This selling of individual persons as slaves, even in large numbers, is to be distinguished from the deportation and resettlement of whole communities that was done by Tiglath-pileser III and subsequent Assyrian kings. Not that one was a greater evil than the other; they were simply different.

In the Edom oracle we encounter again that emphasis upon the *will* to do evil which we found in the oracles against Israel. All military conflicts were evil, but Edom's passion for the sword was pitiless and insatiable, even against "brother" peoples (1:11). Moab's offense against Edom, namely profaning a king's corpse, seems trivial by comparison with Edom's crime although the intention was fully malicious (2:1).

In content and tone the oracle against Judah (2:4-5) is markedly different from the other oracles on the nations. While the oracles against the non-Yahwistic nations (1:3–2:3) and the one against Israel (2:6-16) all contain concrete charges of social wrong, this one contains only a general charge of disobedience to the precepts of Yahwism. This difference is one of the bases for assigning the oracle to a secondary stratum of the collected oracles.[4]

The oracles against the foreign nations were meant to be heard by Israel. The prophetic intention in publishing them was similar to that in publishing the other oracles of Amos. This is not to say that the prophecies contained in them were not expected to be fulfilled. Amos surely believed that these events would take place. The execution of God's judgment throughout the world would not be forestalled by men's ignorance of his intention. Nevertheless, although the purpose of the oracles themselves was defined by their meaning for Israel, it is interesting that the prophet charged the foreign nations with violations of common standards of human decency and not of special norms defined by Israel's religious tradition. Indeed this was also true of most of Amos' accusations against Israel. Only a few of these presupposed specifically Israelite norms. Those that did so were the misappropriation of pledged garments (2:8) and possibly the sexual exploitation of the same woman by father and son (2:7).[5] On the other hand, the persecution of Nazirites and prophets (2:12), like the Moabites' crime against Edom (2:1), was a violation of basic human rights and not merely the violation of special religious tradition.[6]

---

[4] See below, p. 99.

[5] Assuming that the law of consanguinity (Lev. 20:11) was extended in oral tradition to cover sexual intercourse with servants and concubines. See below, p. 136.

[6] R. Bach argues that Amos' oracles show a dependency upon the apodictic legal traditions of Israel but not upon the casuistic ones (op. cit., pp. 23-34). He

Amos exhorted his hearers to "hate evil, and love good, and establish justice in the gate" (5:15), to "seek good and not evil, that you may live" (5:14), and to "let justice roll down like water, and righteousness like a perennial stream" (5:24). These are the principal positive ethical injunctions contained in Amos' oracles. In order to give concrete meaning to them we must infer from his denunciations what behavior he expected from members of the Yahwistic community. This may be described as an active zeal to protect the rights and welfare of one's fellow citizens, and a subordination of self-interest to the interest of the community.

The foundation of righteousness was the acknowledgment

---

concludes that the two streams of tradition may not have been fused in Amos' time as they were by the time of the final compilation of the Covenant Code (Exod. 21–23) and the Code of Deuteronomy (Deut. 12–26). However, there are several weaknesses in his analysis. First, he assumes as valid the theory of Alt that there were two quite distinct legal traditions in Israel, the casuistic, which was similar in form to other bodies of case law in the ancient Near East and was based upon the secular "law of the gate" of the towns of Palestine, and the apodictic, which was unique in the ancient world and was derived from the religious covenant of Israel with Yahweh. However, the validity of this theory has never been demonstrated, and it has recently been challenged (see E. Gerstenberger, "Covenant and Commandment," *JBL*, LXXXIV [1965], 38-51; *Wesen und Herkunft des "apodiktischen Rechts"* [Neukirchen, 1965]). It is also questionable whether the formal differences in the two types were a simple result of different institutional origins. The differences in form may be due merely to differences in content. The apodictic "laws" consist largely of general norms of attitude and behavior, the very ones that would have found their way naturally to the center of the Yahwistic covenantal traditions, regardless of their origin. Alt's theory oversimplifies the history of Israel's legal traditions. It is probably incorrect to speak of "the two sources" of Israelite law. At least four *institutions* made contributions to it: the corporation of town judges (the court "in the gate"), the priesthood, the royal state, and the Israelite tribal confederacy (i.e., the covenantal community). Furthermore, the two "forms" of law are little more than conditional and unconditional formulations of injunctions (or prohibitions), respectively. This difference does not justify isolating them as distinct literary traditions. Indeed, it is often insufficient to justify separating them at all. Bach refers to one law as apodictic in substance and casuistic in form (*op. cit.*, p. 26, n. 27, referring to Exod. 22:24)! Amos dealt mostly with unconditional moral principles so we would expect the Pentateuchal parallels to his oracles to be among the unconditional laws. That they are there hardly justifies Bach's conclusions concerning the history of the legal traditions.

of Yahweh's lordship. Therefore, to "seek good that you may live" meant to "seek Yahweh and live" (5:6, cf. 5:4). Moreover, to "love good" meant, concretely, to "establish justice in the gate" (5:15). One could not worship Yahweh truly without an active commitment to the welfare of others. The failure of the Israelite cultus and its patrons to foster justice was Amos' chief charge against the religious establishment. By catering to the pride and self-satisfaction of the privileged it undermined justice and showed itself morally corrupt.

Amos' purpose was as much to proclaim the righteousness of Jahweh as to reproach the unrighteousness of Israel. He did this in various ways but chiefly by announcing the coming judgment of Yahweh. As the consequence of Israel's failure to "seek Yahweh and live," this event was largely destructive, but it might force Israel to acknowledge in the midst of her despair what she had neglected in her complacency.

Amos' vocation was to proclaim the judgments of God in history so it is not surprising to find that he said relatively little about the acts—or presence—of God in nature. However, the priority given in his oracles to history over nature as the scene of God's activity was not due merely to his special calling. To a considerable extent it was a reflection of the basic quality of Yahwistic faith. It was characteristic of the religious leaders of Israel to be preoccupied with history rather than nature, with man in society rather than man in solitude, with the just will rather than the ecstatic feeling.

It was once popular among biblical critics to attribute this characteristic of Israel's religion to its historical development. Thus the stages in Israel's religious growth were traced from tribalism through nationalism to universalism, and the Old Testament writings were arranged chronologically in accordance with this scheme. There is an element of truth in this theory. Thus, for example, there is more interest in the cosmos shown in the poems of Second Isaiah, from the sixth century B.C., than in the oracles of the eighth-century prophets. However, the difference was not due to inferior knowledge or capacity on the part of the earlier writers. It was due primarily to a difference in their historical situation. The cosmological religions of the ancient world were older than Israel, and she had intimate contact with them from the beginning of her history. Cosmological considerations were important in Israelite worship at least from the beginning of the monarchy, as is shown by the royal psalms. However, from first to last, history had priority over nature as the focus of Israel's religious concern. This priority was not merely chronological; it was theological. And it is as evident in the poems of Second Isaiah as in the oracles of Amos.

Amos' intention was to predict the destruction of the Israelite kingdom and to interpret the event as an act of God. It was an act of Yahweh, the one who spoke from Jerusalem (1:2) and who had been known from the time of the exodus from Egypt as the God of Israel (3:1, cf. 2:9-10; 5:25). However, he was not merely the genius of Israel, a personification of her national ambition and energy. He was for Amos the same one who guided the destinies of other nations.

9:7   "Are you not like the Ethiopians to me, House of Israel?"
    The oracle of Yahweh.
    "Did I not bring Israel up from the land of Egypt,
    And the Philistines from Caphtor,
    And the Arameans from Kir?
  8 Behold, the Lord Yahweh is watching the sinful kingdom,
    And I will destroy it from the surface of the ground,
    Even though the House of Jacob I will not utterly destroy."
    The oracle of Yahweh.

Yahweh was not the genius of the Israelite kingdom, and he could therefore set a limit to its ambition and punish the excess of its self-interest. He could, and did, do this also for the other nations of the world (1:3–2:5). He could do it anywhere only because he could do it everywhere.

Yahweh was not merely the guide and judge of nations. He was also the lord of nature (1:2; 4:4-13; 5:1-8; 7:1, 4; 8:9; 9:1-6). Indeed, he was the one only because he was the other. Amos, like the other prophets of Israel, was the messenger of Yahweh's judgments in history, but his message presupposes that the only God worth taking seriously is the creator of the world.

Amos did not begin with a rational theory about the rise and fall of nations and then select concrete examples to prove the thesis. He began with concrete events, which he believed to be under the control of God, and he sought to call men to obedience to God in the light of these events. He believed that the justice of God was partly visible in the destinies of nations. This is the premise of his entire proclamation. But he did not pretend to explain every event in history in terms of a theory of retribution. The destruction of the Amorites, for example (2:9-10), is not explained, as it is in Gen. 15:15-16, as a just punishment for their iniquity. It is perhaps implied that God destroyed them to make way for Israel. However, considering the prophet's explicit denunciation of acts of aggression (1:3–2:3), it is better to take his statement simply as an acknowledgment of a historical fact—an act of God whose justification is not evident to men.

As we might expect in a book of prophecies of the coming judgment of God, there is little said in Amos' oracles about God's revelation to man. The exodus is once referred to as the medium of Israel's knowledge of Yahweh, a knowledge unique among the peoples of the earth (3:1). Once, the design of nature is referred to as something revealed by God to men (4:13*a*).[7] Israel knew Yahweh, but not truly. This is the burden of Amos' prophecy.

Amos' assertion that the prophets were God's gift to Israel, comparable in importance to the deliverance from Egypt and the gift of the land (2:9-11), must be interpreted in relation to the conception of the prophetic office implicit in his own oracles. He was a prophet of the destruction of the Israelite kingdom and was regarded as a menace by the priest Amaziah (7:1-17). If he was typical of the prophets, what sort of gift were they? We must remember that Amos never suggested his ministry might be a means of averting the destruction by effecting a social reform.

A prophet of God's justice was a means of knowledge and, therefore, of reconciliation and obedience, even in the face of unavoidable disaster. He himself would not know what concrete result his preaching might produce. It was not a part of his responsibility to predict that. Of course, his sense of vocation was not fully rational. Amos felt compelled to speak even though he believed disaster was at hand. This compulsion, coupled with the conviction that prophecy was a mark of Israel's unique relationship to Yahweh, can only mean that Amos believed his speaking was indispensable to the continuation of this relationship. Without prophecy there could be no people of Yahweh. Therefore, silencing the prophets was Israel's most self-destructive act (2:12). It sealed the fate of the contemporary kingdom of Israel (2:13-16) just as it sealed the fate of Amaziah (7:16-17).

Another oracle that should be mentioned in this context is 5:7, 10-13.

> 7 Those who turn justice to wormwood
> degrade righteousness to the ground. . . .

[7] "His design" is often interpreted as man's design, but the parallelism suggests that the design is Yahweh's ("his design"/"his name").

10 They hate the arbiter of justice in the gate,
   and despise the one who declares truly.

11 Therefore, since you exploit the poor,
   and take a percentage of his grain,
   Your hewn stone houses
     you will not inhabit,
   And from your lovely vineyards
     you will never drink the wine.

12 For I know the multitude of your iniquities,
   and the magnitude of your sins,
   Punishing the innocent,
     accepting bribes,
       and denying justice to the poor.[8]

13 Therefore, the prudent will keep silent in that time,
   for it will be an evil time.

The oracle alternates between accusation (vss. 7, 10-11a, and 12) and threat (vss. 11b and 13), forming a self-contained unit once the stray verse 7 has been restored to its place at the beginning.[9] It is closely akin to other oracles in this section of the book. Indeed, it is possible that it originally began, "Woe to those who turn justice to wormwood. They degrade righteousness to the ground." The textual difference is minor, and the change might have been made after the

---

[8] Literally, "they turn aside the poor in the gate."

[9] See below, p. 119. Amos 5:10-13 is complete without vs. 7; but vs. 7 does not seem to belong in 5:1-6, 8, and it goes well with 5:10 ff. The editor of 5:1-17 created a well-structured poem. It is perfectly balanced chiastically. (a) It begins and ends with a lamentation over Israel's fall (vss. 1-3 and 16-17). The first is the prophet's present lament, before the event; the second is the people's future lament, after the event. (b) "Seek me (Yahweh) and live" (4-6) is matched by "Seek good and not evil that you may live" (14-15). (c) The motif of the remnant occurs in vss. 3 and 15. (d) The reference to the judge who now speaks truly (10) is complemented by that to the prudent man who will then keep silent (13). (e) "Justice" appears in the second and the second-to-last sections (7 and 15). (This fact favors the retention of vs. 7 in its canonical place, incidentally.) This list includes only the most obvious symmetries.

verse was displaced from its original position. It would then have been another in the series of "woes" which have been collected here (cf. 5:18; 6:1, 4).[10]

According to Amos 2:12 and 7:1-17 the voice of prophetic criticism had been stifled in northern Israel. In the oracle before us now Amos depicted the subversion of juridical processes in the kingdom. The civil judges, he said, were in collusion with the upper class to use the courts for self-aggrandizement. Naturally, the victims were those who could not afford "justice." An uncorrupted judge (or witness, perhaps) was as unpopular with the leading citizens as an outspoken prophet (5:10). The leadership of the community despised the unbought, fearless word.

Amos prophesied a time when the people would be forced to forego the advantages they derived from the subversion of justice (5:11). In the present time, whose evil was moral corruption, the spokesman of justice was denied free voice. In the coming time, whose evil would be military conquest, advocacy of the truth would be doubly imprudent, for it would be both dangerous and futile—a fitting end for those who disdained the truth in the present age.[11]

This curtailment of speech, present and future, was for Amos the ultimate evil. In two other oracles he described additional forms of it that would appear in the impending age of ruin. The first of these (6:10) is obscure in some details though the crucial point is clear, namely that in the midst of the terrible evils which are coming it will be too dangerous to mention the name of Yahweh. The reason seems to be that Yahweh himself will be the destroyer, so that his

[10] Jerusalem, Weiser, Fosbroke, and Amsler, among others, treat 5:7, 10 ff., as one of the woe oracles.

[11] The tense of vs. 13 is more likely future (Chicago, RSV), like that of the parallel vs. 11, than present (Jerusalem). Some critics have gone to great lengths to find a place for vs. 13 outside the oracle 5:10 ff., but it is neither a gloss (e.g., Cripps and Weiser) nor an independent fragment (Robinson, Amsler).

presence must not be invoked. "Hush! Don't mention Yahweh's name!" (6:10) will be the desperate exclamation of the last survivors, attending the corpses all around.

Finally, in 8:11-12 the prophet depicted the Israelite refugees stumbling pathetically about in the world in search of the vivifying word of Yahweh, which they had formerly despised. To Amos, who lived by the word, this "famine of the word" was the worst of God's punishments. The word of prophecy was the word of judgment in the midst of the people who had been created by God's word. In disobedience they had lost the knowledge of God's purpose. Therefore the prophet's judgmental word was potentially a means of renewal of this knowledge. Final rejection of the prophet cut them off from the source of their being. Banishing the word from their midst, they could only perish as the people of God.

This feature of Amos' prophecy of the righteousness of God is less obvious than others to which we now turn. Some of these are well-known features of Hebrew prophecy generally and do not require extended comment. Others deserve special attention because they are distinctive of Amos' oracles. We are concerned particularly to define the instruments, the content, and the objects of God's justice as they are treated in the book.

We may begin by observing that a physical calamity is never prophesied as a punishment for moral evil. This point is important because other biblical writers, and many whose faith is based upon the Bible, have interpreted physical evils as divine punishments for sin and physical "blessings" as corresponding rewards for virtue. There is no trace of this belief in Amos or in the contemporary book of Hosea. Amos 4:6-11 describes a series of natural calamities caused by God, but they are presented in the oracle as occasions for repentance and not as punishments for sin. The locust-plague (7:1-2) and the cosmic fire (7:4-5) in Amos' vision are symbolical events which happen only in the vision. They do not correspond to actual physical punishments suffered by Israel from the hand of God. The remaining events described in the vision (7:7-8; 8:1-2) are also symbolic. In all four episodes of the vision the acts of God symbolize the imminent fall of the Israelite nation. Even the earthquake in 8:7-10 is figurative, like the darkening of the noonday sun in the same passage.

The actual punishments prophesied by Amos were political, military, and economic. In the oracles against the foreign nations the punishments nicely match the crimes. They teach the general moral lesson that "they who live by the sword shall die by the sword." This adage does not cover all the details of these oracles, but it serves as a valid summation. The agents of punishment are not mentioned in these oracles. The oracles against Israel lack this fine matching of the punishment to the crime.[12] Whereas the offenses of the foreign nations were international and were to be requited internationally, the offenses of Israel were domestic but were also to be requited internationally. Amos' logic is questionable at this point. The incongruity can be overcome dogmatically by asserting that God is the lord of all life and may punish sin anyway he chooses. However, this solution hardly eliminates the empirical question whether God does punish in the way Amos alleged. Even though the sins Amos

---

[12] The introductions to the oracles on the nations (1:3–2:16) read, "for the three transgressions, and for the four," although only one transgression is recounted in each accusation in 1:3, 6, 11, 13; and 2:1; and two (at most) in 1:9 and 2:4. In the Israel oracle there are six (2:6, 7a, 7b, 8a, 8b, and 12). However, the introductions are rhetorical (a simple repetition of the same introduction in all eight oracles) and not to be taken literally. The novel theory of B. K. Soper ("For Three Transgressions and for Four: A New Interpretation of Amos 1, 3, etc.," ET, LXI [1959/60], 86-87), that Amos in oral delivery of the oracles mentioned "the three," then gave a gesture of dismissal to indicate that God in his long-suffering had passed these by, and concluded by saying, "But because of the fourth, I will not turn away the punishment thereof," is implausible. In any case the stylized character of the introduction remains clear.

described were perpetrated and the disaster he predicted came to pass, it would not be clear that the one was the cause of the other. Could Amos have been right in principle and wrong in application? Or morally right and empirically wrong?

Lest we magnify the problem unnecessarily, we need to be aware of the exact terms of the proclamation. We have already enumerated the moral evils for which Amos held Israel guilty. What, now, were the punishments he expected Israel to suffer for these crimes? We may simply list them all in order: (a) 2:13-16, military defeat; (b) 3:9-11, military invasion and conquest; (c) 3:14-15, ruin of altars and homes of the rich; (d) 4:2-3, disgraceful expulsion of the proud women from the city of Samaria; (e) 5:2-3, general collapse of the nation and decimation of the male population (possibly only the fighting men); (f) 5:5, exile of the people of Gilgal and ruin of Bethel; (g) 5:11, prevention of extortioners from living in their stone houses and drinking their choice wines; (h) 5:16-17, general bereavement; (i) 5:18-20, "darkness" in the day of Yahweh; (j) 5:27, exile (if this verse is genuine); (k) 6:7, exile of the rulers of Samaria and Jerusalem ("Zion," vs. 1); (l) 6:8-11, widespread death; (m) 7:9, destruction of the cultic high places and sanctuaries of "Isaac"; (n) 7:17, exile of Amaziah, death of his children, and prostitution of his wife; (o) 8:3, lamentation over the many dead; (p) 8:7-10, cosmic upheaval (figurative) with great lamentation; (q) 8:11-13, famine of the word; (r) 9:1-4, destruction of the sanctuary and slaying of all the worshipers. This is the entire list of Amos' threats against Israel. Each of these evils may be accounted for as the result of foreign conquest of the Israelite kingdom.

Before forming general conclusions about these threats and the accusations to which they are joined, we need to establish more precisely the identity of those who are threatened. This exercise is one of the less exciting aspects of interpretation, but failure to perform it can lead to erroneous estimates of prophetic preaching.

To judge by the superscription to the book (1:1) and the introductory announcement (1:2) Amos' oracles were concerned with the north Israelite kingdom and were spoken from the standpoint of Jerusalemite Yahwism. One might suppose therefore that Amos endorsed the national religion of Judah. There is an element of Judean nationalism in the concluding oracle of the book (9:11), but this is probably editorial, as the superscription is, of course. Surely the oracles of Amos are more than a Judean condemnation of the rival Israelite kingdom.

The first oracle against Israel (2:6-16) threatens military defeat as a punishment for the crimes of the ruling class against the powerless. The oracle stands at the end of a series, each part of which is aimed at a monarchial state. The punishments threatened in these oracles are to fall upon political capitals, palaces (or fortresses), kings, and princes (1:4-5, 7-8, 10, 12, 14-15; 2:2-3, 5). Neither the indictments nor the threats are directed against all the people of these kingdoms. The reproach in 2:6-8, 12, is against the powerful in Israel, not the general population. Therefore the conclusion seems inescapable that the threat in 2:13-16 is also against the leaders of Israel alone.[13] Under the monarchy the Israelite army was not a popular militia but a corps of professional soldiers; therefore, those who fell in battle were servants of the state first of all and representatives of the people only secondarily.

The brief oracle 3:1-2 concerns all Israelites of both kingdoms. It states the general proposition that God will punish

---

[13] They were "sons of Israel" (2:11), of course. The use of this phrase does not mean that *all* the sons of Israel were under indictment. The same comment applies to 3:12, where the phrase occurs again.

them, above all others, for their sins. It is not a prophecy of particular judgment but a statement about the nature of Israel's special relation to Yahweh. It was intended to correct the popular misunderstanding that Israel had a special claim upon God, or enjoyed certain immunities, in virtue of her covenant with him.

The threat in 3:9-12 is against Samaria, the capital of the northern kingdom, while that in 3:14 is against its national sanctuary in Bethel, and that in 3:15 is against its wealthy (ruling) class. In the opening lines of the oracle 3:13-15 Yahweh orders the prophet to testify against "the House of Jacob," and he goes on to say, "In the day that I punish Israel for her transgressions." The allusion is apparently to a day of general punishment for Israelites, or indeed of universal judgment. It signifies that all are subject to the justice of God. However, this particular threat was meant for certain persons and institutions in Israel.

It is the prominent women of Samaria who are addressed in 4:1-3. In the following oracle, however, the threat is universal ("sons of Israel," vs. 5; "Israel," vs. 12). It is also vague (vs. 12). The warning to Israel to prepare to meet their God seems to presuppose the same idea of a day of universal reckoning alluded to in 3:13-14. Here Amos appears to be especially dependent upon the stylized language of traditional prophecy. This was meant doubtlessly as a serious threat. However, it lacks the concreteness of the other oracles. It rebukes the devotees of the sacrificial cult (4:4-5), who are content with a purely ritual atonement and disdain the opportunity for repentance (4:6-11). This group might have included most Israelites. Nevertheless, the oracle is above all a condemnation of the national cultus itself.

The oracles in chapter 5 are addressed to the northern kingdom. This is the meaning of the phrase "House of Israel" in Amos, as it is in Hosea and Isaiah.[14] The term appears in Amos 5:1, 3, 4, 25; 6:1, 14; and 7:10. The places threatened in 5:4-5 are again the national sanctuaries of the north, Bethel and Gilgal. The "remnant of Joseph" means the survivors of destruction in the north Israelite territories of Ephraim and Manasseh (the two Joseph tribes). And the territory to be harassed, according to 6:14, i.e., "from the pass of Hamath to the Wadi Arabah," belonged to the northern kingdom in the time of Amos (cf. II Kings 14:25).

If the reference to Beersheba in 5:5 is original, it concerns northern pilgrims to the ancient sanctuary there. Since the parallel line (5b) omits any mention of Beersheba, the reference in 5a may well be secondary. In any case, Beersheba is not mentioned with Gilgal and Bethel as a place marked for destruction. It was in Judah and therefore outside the scope of the prophet's threat. What he was interested in was the devotion falsely given by his listeners (whoever they were) to the prevailing rituals in the popular sanctuaries. When he mocked the superstitious swearing by Beersheba (8:14), he was not referring in particular to residents of the place.

The woe oracles in chapters 5 and 6 (including 5:7, 10-13) apply in principle to anyone guilty of the behavior described in them. However, the threats in these oracles show that Amos actually had in mind the prosperous and powerful in the northern kingdom. The only exception is 6:1, where he mentions "those who are at ease in Zion." This reference to the rich rulers of Judah is the only one to Judeans in the book of Amos outside the Judah oracle in 2:4-5. As in the latter case, we may assume that the *audience* here is in the northern kingdom. The indictment includes the irresponsible rich of both kingdoms, but it expresses a particular concern

---

[14] See Ward, *Hosea: A Theological Commentary* (New York, 1966), pp. 7, 239-42, and below, pp. 172-73.

for those who "do not care about the ruin of Joseph" (6:6),
that is, do not care about the northern Israelite people.

Most of Amos' oracles have a universal relevance, at least
for all the "sons of Israel," but they were addressed first of
all to the leaders of the kingdom of Israel and dealt with
the destiny of that kingdom. Amos reported that he had been
commissioned by God to "Go, prophesy to my people Israel"
(7:15). However, for reasons that are not disclosed in the
book, Amos chose to fulfill this commission in the political
and religious capital of the northern kingdom and to direct
his words chiefly to those who controlled its national institutions.[15] These remarks are not meant to imply that Amos'
prophecy of imminent judgment was limited to this kingdom
and its rulers. In addition to the allusions to a universal day
of judgment that we have already cited (1:3 ff. and 3:14),
there is the oracle about the day of Yahweh in 5:18-20:

> 18 Woe to those who long for the day of Yahweh!
>   Why would you have the day of Yahweh?
>   It is darkness, not light!
> 19 As if a man fled from a lion
>   And ran into a bear;
>   Then entered a house to rest against the wall,
>   And was bitten by a snake.
> 20 The day of Yahweh,
>   Is it not darkness, and not light?
>   And unrelieved gloom?

The allusion to a popular hope for the day of Yahweh is
too indefinite to satisfy our curiosity about its specific content
although many theories have been proposed.[16] However,

[15] In the vision accompanying the statement about the commission (7:1-9),
"Jacob" (7:2, 5) and "my people Israel" (7:8; 8:2) apply to all Israel, but the
actual threat (7:9) is against the northern kingdom and its cultic establishment.

[16] Gressmann traced the expectation of the day of Yahweh back to an

there is a note of universality here that goes beyond the specific threats in the other oracles and reflects, probably, Amos' belief in the limitless sovereignty of Yahweh.

The origin of Amos' belief in the universality of Yahweh's rule has been the subject of considerable scholarly interest. This is natural since the book of Amos is the oldest prophetic book. Several theories have been proposed to account for his belief. In the days when the book was considered the earliest part of the Bible, Amos was credited with being the first monotheist, and many critics thought it necessary to account for his belief on the basis of his personal experience of the presence of Yahweh.[17] It was supposed that because this experience was overwhelming, Amos concluded that Yahweh must be a universal God. The argument is illogical, but the theory had a surprising popularity for many years. Today Amos' conception of the unity and universality of Yahweh is considered to have been largely dependent upon Israelite tradition. His distinctive teaching is generally seen to be the proclamation of Yahweh's destruction of the Israelite kingdom.

Although Amos was indeed the heir of an ancient tradition, a belief in Yahweh's universal rule is not articulated in the older sources of the Old Testament in quite the way it is in Amos' oracles, in particular, the conviction that Yahweh cared for (and judged) the other peoples of the world as much as he did Israel. Was Amos simply giving expression

---

alleged preprophetic, cosmic eschatology shared by Israel with Babylonia and other nations (*Der Ursprung der isr.—jüd. Eschatologie*, FRLANT, VI [Göttingen, 1905]). Mowinckel considered it the projection of a cultic experience of the presence of God (*Psalmenstudien*, II [Kristiania, 1922], 214 ff.). Cerny, rejecting both these notions, believed the hope to be the fusion of several Israelite ideas about Yahweh's coming, for example, the day of battle, the day of the exodus, and the day of pestilence (*The Day of Yahweh and Some Relevant Problems* [Prague, 1948]).

[17] See, e.g., Weiser, *Die Prophetie des Amos*, BZAW, LIII (1929), 291-324.

to something implicit in the faith of his fathers, or was he influenced in part by ideas encountered elsewhere? Several scholars have argued that the cosmic universalism of Amos is ultimately derived from Canaanite religion, especially the cult of the god El, although it was probably already embodied in the cult tradition of Israel in Amos' time.[18]

It is probable that Yahwism was influenced by the natural theology of the Canaanite cults. However, it is impossible to discover the precise source and nature of the influence or the time when it was exerted. All the literary sources of the Old Testament presuppose the universal sovereignty of God, and most of them give open expression to the belief, in one way or another. How then can we test the hypothesis? How can we be sure that universalism was not a feature of Yahwism from the very beginning of Israel's history? In any case, we cannot trace any direct influence of non-Yahwistic beliefs upon the oracles of Amos.

Was there any hope in Amos' expectation of the future, or was he solely a prophet of doom? Was there any love in Amos' conception of God, or did he think of him entirely in terms of unrelenting justice? His oracles have often been judged to be hopeless and loveless. Is this judgment fair?

The God of Amos was no cruel and uncompassionate judge, but the vigilant champion of the oppressed. He punished violence, oppression, and deceit because he was the protector of the lives and dignity of men. Amos defined, albeit in negative terms, the conditions under which a people might enjoy "life." "Seek Yahweh and live" (5:6). Reject Yahweh and die. Seeking Yahweh meant striving for justice. The neglect of justice was apostasy and, in Amos' view, always had fatal consequences. This was the quality of existence under God. To affirm this was not to deny the love of God. Amos

---

[18] E.g., Kapelrud, *Central Ideas in Amos*, pp. 33-47, and Reventlow, *Das Amt des Propheten bei Amos*, pp. 72-75.

did not say so explicitly, but the force of his teaching is to affirm that this is the way the love of God works.

> Seek good and not evil,
> So that you may live,
> And so Yahweh, God of hosts,
> May be with you,
> Just as you have claimed.
> Hate evil and love good,
> And establish justice in the gate.
> Then perhaps Yahweh, God of hosts,
> May be merciful to the remnant of Joseph.
>
> (5:14-15)

Amos affirmed the patience of God and his readiness to forgive (4:6-11; 7:1-6). But he was persuaded that there was a limit to God's patience with injustice, pride, and self-indulgence. To reestablish the possibility of righteous life required the end of such patience.

According to Amos there was no hope for the north Israelite kingdom as he knew it. He believed it would be conquered by an alien power and its leaders exiled. This could only take place with great suffering for the people of Israel. Amos' expectation proved to be correct. He also believed the fall of the kingdom, including its cultic, economic, and legal institutions, was a just punishment for the injustice that had been allowed to develop in the nation's life. He blamed the powerful minority for this, chiefly. His analysis and prediction involved imprecision in the assignment of guilt and the calculation of causal relationships. It was not his purpose, though, to explain the dynamics of human behavior and the processes of national history. His oracles testified to the righteousness of God. This was no strict, retributive justice, impersonally constituted and mechanically executed. It was personal and free. Nor was it wholly within the rational grasp of men. It was partly hidden in the mystery of God.

Amos did not attribute to God the full range of human feelings that Hosea did, for example. Yet it is clear that he conceived of God as a person. His word, spoken by the prophets and embodied in the traditions handed down from the fathers, was the source of man's life and the guide of his obedience. The famine of the word of God was the final curse of the faithless community (8:11-12). Obedience to the word, attendance upon the dialogue between God and his people, was the chief blessing of existence.

The conclusion of the book of Amos (9:8b-15) contains several promises which have long been judged as postexilic additions to the original oracles. The threat that sinners in Israel will be sifted out and destroyed (9:8b-10) implies the corresponding promise that the righteous will be preserved. Other promises are the renewal of the Davidic empire among the peoples of Palestine (9:11-12) and the restoration of the civil and economic fortunes of the uprooted people of Israel (9:13-15). The old critical arguments for a postexilic (i.e., post–587 B.C.) date for these verses are still powerful in spite of recent efforts to reclaim them as part of the original collection.

The new factor that has been introduced into the defense of these verses is a form-critical one. It is supposed that the prophetic oracles were products of the cult and that oracles of doom and oracles of hope were used side by side in the liturgies of Israel, without there having to be any internal connections between them. Therefore, when we find negative and positive oracles side by side in the Old Testament without logical continuity, we should not necessarily attribute them to different authors or periods. Their coherence derives from the continuity of the liturgy, with its several moods, and not from the verbal consistency of the oracles themselves.[19]

---

[19] See, e.g., Reventlow, *op. cit.*, pp. 90-110 (he defends the originality of

I find the argument incredible in the case of Amos 9:8b-15. The ethical gulf lying between these lines and the oracles of Amos cannot be bridged by a theory of ritual origins, whatever may be said for the theory with respect to the origin of the basic oracular forms. There is not a single word in these lines about the righteousness that God demands of men. They are wholly devoid of moral earnestness, and they never once allude to the ethical conditions under which life may be received from God. In this respect they are totally different from the oracle of promise which concludes the contemporary book of Hosea (Hos. 14:1-9). They promise Israel joy and power and say nothing whatever about repentance or responsibility. Therefore, it is not so important whether the historical allusions in them demand an exilic date or permit a pre-exilic one. They are simply incompatible prophetically with the oracles of Amos.[20] To appeal to the rhythm of an alleged liturgical setting, that is, one that moves naturally from judgment to promise, is to compound the difficulty; for Amos' condemnation of Israel's liturgies, if it meant anything at all, was a rejection of the belief in unconditional blessings as these were allegedly assured and appropriated in the contemporary cult.

The implied promise of salvation for the righteous in 9:9-10 is perhaps not wholly incompatible with the theology of Amos, although it is more akin to later Jewish orthodoxy, where the distinction between the righteous (pious) and the sinful is more sharply drawn (e.g., Ps. 1). Of all the lines in this section, 9:9a, which I have quoted in chapter one as a word of Amos, is alone free from the objections I have

---

9:13-15 only), and E. Florival, "Le jour du jugement (Amos 9, 7-15)," *Bible e Vie Chretienne*, VIII (1954/55), 61-75.

[20] Amos 9:8b-15 might have been written before the fall of Judah in 587 B.C. if the "fall" of David's booth (9:11) means the breakup of the Judean empire in 922 B.C.

raised. It might well have been the remembered fragment around which the rest of this promise was constructed.

Amos affirmed, even in the midst of Israel's national debacle, that there were genuine possibilities of obedience to God for those with the will to obey. Therefore, for them there was the promise of "life." This was the grace which the "remnant of Joseph" might expect (5:15). The same sort of promise is made in Amos 5. The oracles there are saturated with moral urgency and revulsion toward the amoral Israelite cult. The hope they offer is a "perhaps." It preserves the prophet's usual stress upon the conditional nature of blessedness. The promises in 9:8b-15 lack any such emphasis.

I cannot imagine what prophetic purpose these final lines of the book would have served during the time of Amos' ministry. All indications point to a date before 745 B.C. for this. We might suppose that he lived after the fall of Israel in 722 B.C., or during the last tragic years of the kingdom, and added an appendix to his oracles in order to give hope to a despairing remnant. But even then we must reckon with the completely non-ethical character of the appendix. In short, we are forced to declare them secondary theologically, regardless of their origin. Again we may contrast the situation of Hosea. His oracles of judgment reflect the political chaos of the last decade of the Israelite kingdom (732-722 B.C.) so it is much more likely than in the case of Amos that he was called upon to minister to his people's despair. Furthermore, the ethical perspective of the oracles of hope in the book of Hosea is consonant with that of the oracles of judgment.[21] Thus a comparison of the two books is devastating to the theory of the originality of Amos 9:8b-15.[22]

[21] The promises are contained in Hos. 2, 3, 11, and 14. There are a few secondary elements in them, such as the reference to David in 3:5. See the discussion of Hos. 14 in Ward, *op. cit.*, pp. 228-37.

[22] The historical and literary objections to the originality of these verses are presented in all the standard introductions. A. Bentzen, *Introduction to the Old*

Amos' hope was restricted in its social content by the nature of his prophetic mission in eighth-century Israel. Nevertheless, it was real. It was a hope for the fulfillment of God's righteousness in the world. This righteousness was an eternal barrier to the fulfillment of the unrighteous purposes of men, but it was the foundation and guarantee of every righteous act. Not, of course, a guarantee of extraneous reward, but a guarantee of the ultimate triumph of justice and the eternal worth of every just human relation.

Amos did not speak of the love of God. His extant oracles are few and brief, and they leave most things about God unsaid. We must look elsewhere for the biblical sources of the doctrine of God's love. We may say, however, in affirmation of Amos' prophetic insight, that any doctrine that fails to account for the realities Amos affirmed is a sentimental illusion. Amos was no heartless prophet. His sympathy lay with "little Jacob" (7:2, 5). But Jacob (Israel) was dying of injustice. Amos' prophetic responsibility was the master of his personal inclination. He would surely have been happier tending sheep, but fidelity to God left him no choice. In a way his submission to the word of God was the model of

---

Testament, II (Fifth ed.; Copenhagen, 1949, 1959), 141-42, contains an especially cogent evaluation of the arguments. The effort to secure these verses as part of the primary collection on the ground that Amos as a Judean shared the messianic claim and hope centered on the Davidic dynasty (thus E. Hammershaimb, *Amos* [Copenhagen, 1946], *in loc.*) is desperate. There is not a shred of evidence in the indisputable oracles of Amos to support it. Engnell's theory, cited by Bentzen, that 9:8b-15 and the doxologies constituted an old messianic poem incorporated in the book by the "congregation" which later used Amos' oracles is unconvincing. Amos 9:8b-15 is totally unrelated to the doxologies in content, and none of the signs of postexilic origin manifested in 9:8b-15 appears in the doxologies. Amos 9:8b-15 clearly presupposes the exile of Israel, and probably that of Judah. A prophecy of return could have been made before the exile itself occurred, but what religious or moral purpose might such a prophecy have served? In the midst of the death throes of the kingdom of Israel it might have offered reassurance to those in despair and thus have invited a new moral commitment. This was one of the functions of Hosea's words of hope. But by all the evidence Amos prophesied during the heyday of Israel. The assurances in 9:8b-15 would have been utterly gratuitous in that time, either in Israel or in Judah.

the obedience he asked of the leaders of Israel. He prophesied the end of the kingdom of Israel and the end of the social oppression and illusory religion within it, but he did so in the name of the righteous God, who waited, Amos believed, at every moment of shattering judgment to be gracious to the remnant who turned in obedience.

Amos' oracles contained the only sure basis of hope, namely faith in the unwavering righteousness of God. They did not offer the remnant of Joseph specific hopes defined in terms of their familiar political, economic, and cultic environment. In this sense the remnant was forced, in T. S. Eliot's words, to "wait without hope," lest their hope be "hope for the wrong thing." Amos' criticism of conventional expressions of faith was therefore radical, even more radical than that of his contemporaries, Hosea and Isaiah. But Amos' faith was far from hopeless. Indeed, it was one of the truly hopeful factors in the religious consciousness of Israel in his time.

chapter 3

The Book of Amos
and
Israelite Worship

One of the preoccupying interests of contemporary Old Testament scholars is the influence of ancient Israelite ritual upon the forms of Old Testament literature. Nearly every page of the text has been scrutinized for signs of a cultic setting and a corresponding liturgical influence upon the shape of the documents. The psalms were naturally the first part of the canon to be subjected to this analysis. The Pentateuch was next and then, somewhat tardily, the books of the latter prophets. In spite of the limited and disputed results that have been achieved up to the present time in the case of the prophets, the investigation is important for the history of Israelite worship and literature and also for biblical exegesis and theology. It also has implications for the modern liturgical use of the Bible. The study of the cultic dimensions of the prophetic *office* has accompanied that of the liturgical influence on prophetic *literature*. In fact, interest in cultic prophecy, and particularly the question whether the literary prophets of the Old Testament were cult functionaries, has taken precedence over the study of the ritual background of the literature. Yet the latter is at least as relevant for exegesis and theology. One of our purposes in the present chapter is to examine those sections of the book of Amos that seem to bear the marks of ritual influence and to inquire into the consequences of such influence for the interpretation of Amos' prophecy.

Study of the liturgical context of the prophetic literature, especially the pre-exilic books, is complicated by several factors, in addition to the general dearth of liturgical rubrics in the canon. One of these is the editing of the collections of prophetic oracles for subsequent use by the Jewish religious community. As a result of this adaptation some of their litugical features are secondary, although it is often impossible to discover whether or not they are. Another factor is the existence within the books of the prophets of oracles condemning Israel's rituals. This polemic against the cultus has immunized many scholars against the idea that the prophets' oracles might themselves have been influenced positively by Israel's worship. The second purpose of the present chapter is to ponder the implications of Amos' anti-cultic polemic in relation to the evidence for his own indebtedness to ritual forms.

LITURGICAL FORMS IN THE BOOK

Three segments of the book of Amos give particular evidence of having been influenced formally by earlier Israelite ritual practice, or adapted for use in later worship. These are

1:2–2:16; 4:6-12; and the passages marked by the doxologies in 4:13; 5:8; and 9:5-6.

ORACLES ON THE NATIONS (AMOS 1:2–2:16)

1:2 Yahweh roars from Zion;
    his voice thunders from Jerusalem.
The shepherds' fields wither,
    and the top of Carmel fades.

I. Damascus   *Type A*

3 *Thus says Yahweh:*   Introductory
  "For the three transgressions of Damascus   Formulas
    —and for the four,
    I will not turn it back.

  "Because they threshed Gilead   Accusation
    with iron sledges,   (one Hebrew line)

4 "I will cast fire upon Hazael's house,   Announcement
    and it shall consume Ben-Hadad's fortresses. (three lines)
5 And I will break the bar of Damascus,
    and cut off the inhabitants from the Aven Valley,
And him who holds the scepter from Beth-Eden.
And Syria's people shall be exiled to Kir,"
Says Yahweh.   Concluding Formula

II. Philistia   *Type A*

6 *Thus says Yahweh:*
  "For the three transgressions of Gaza
    —and for the four,
    I will not turn it back.

  "Because they carried a whole people away captive,
    to deliver them to Edom,

7 "I will cast fire upon Gaza's wall,
    and it shall consume her fortresses.

8 And I will cut off the inhabitants from Ashdod,
     and him who holds the scepter from Ashkelon.
  And I will turn my hand against Ekron,
     and Philistia's remnant shall perish,"
Says the Lord Yahweh.

III. Tyre   *Type B*

9 *Thus says Yahweh:*   Introductory
  "For the three transgressions of Tyre   Formulas
     —and for the four,
     I will not turn it back.

  "Because they delivered captive   Accusation
     a whole people to Edom,   (two lines)
  And did not remember
     the covenant of brothers,

10 "I will cast fire upon Tyre's wall,   Announcement
     and it shall consume her fortresses." (one line)

IV. Edom   *Type B*

11 *Thus says Yahweh:*
  "For the three transgressions of Edom
     —and for the four,
     I will not turn it back.

  "Because he pursued his brother with the sword,
     and lost all compassion,
  And his anger raged perpetually,
     and he harbored his wrath forever,

12 "I will cast fire upon Teman,
     and it shall consume Bozrah's fortresses."

V. Ammon   *Type A*

13 *Thus says Yahweh:*
  "For the three transgressions of the Ammonites
     —and for the four,
     I will not turn it back.

"Because they ripped up Gilead's pregnant women,
   in order to enlarge their own border,

14 "I will kindle a fire against Rabbah's wall,
   and it shall consume her fortresses,
With shouting on the day of battle,
   and a tempest on the day of the whirlwind.
15 And their king shall go into exile,
   he and his princes together,"
Says Yahweh.

VI. Moab   Type A

2:1 *Thus says Yahweh:*
"For the three transgressions of Moab
   —and for the four,
   I will not turn it back.

"Because he burned to lime
   the bones of the king of Edom,

2 "I will cast fire upon Moab,
   and it shall consume Kerioth's fortresses.
And Moab shall die in an uproar,
   amid shouting and blasts of a trumpet.
3 And I will cut off the ruler in her midst,
   and slay all her princes with him,"
Says Yahweh.

VII. Judah   Type B

4 *Thus says Yahweh:*
"For the three transgressions of Judah
   —and for the four,
   I will not turn it back.

"Because they have rejected Yahweh's teaching,
   and have ignored his precepts,
While their lies have led them astray,
   into the way their fathers walked,

5   "I will cast fire upon Judah,
    and it shall consume Jerusalem's fortresses."

VIII. Israel   *Expanded Type B*

6   *Thus says Yahweh:*   Introductory
    "For the three transgressions of Israel   Formulas
      —and for the four,
    I will not turn it back.

    "Because they sell the innocent for silver,   Accusation
      and the needy for a pair of shoes,   (six lines)
7   They who trample [1] the heads of the weak,
      and push the humble (from) the way.
    And a man and his father go to the maiden,
      to profane my holy name.
8   And they stretch out upon pledged garments
      beside every altar.
    And drink wine taken in fines
      in the house of their God.
12   And (they) force the Nazirites to drink wine,
      and command the prophets, saying, 'Don't prophesy!' [2]

9   "Yet it was I who destroyed   Recollection
      the Amorite before them,   (six lines)
        who was as tall as the cedars.
    Though he was as strong as the oaks,
      I destroyed his fruit above
      and his roots below.

---

[1] "Into the dust of the earth" overloads the poetic line and therefore appears to be a secondary expansion. Cf. Weiser.

[2] Vs. 12 is an accusation and therefore belongs formally with 6*a*-8 rather than with the historical recollection (9-11) or the announcement of punishment (13-16). I suppose the person of the line was altered from third (like vss. 6*a*-8) to second (like vss. 10-13) when it was moved from its original place (after vs. 9) to its present one. It is conceivable that the verse was inspired by 7:10-17, but the supposition is an inadequate ground for deleting it as a gloss (Amsler). Schmidt's deletion of 2:10-12 as a deuteronomic addition is also subjective (*ZAW*, LXXVII [1965], 178-83).

10 And it was I who brought you up
    from the land of Egypt,
    And made you walk in the wilderness
      for forty years,
        in order to inherit the Amorite's land.
11 And I raised up some of your sons as prophets,
    and your stalwart youths as Nazirites.
    Isn't this so, O Israelites?"
    The oracle of Yahweh.   Concluding Formula

13 "Behold, I am about to make you totter   Announcement
    in your place,   (four lines)
    as a wagon totters that is full of sheaves.
14 Refuge will vanish from the swift;
    the strong will not exert his strength,
      nor the warrior save himself.
15 The archer will not stand,
    nor the fleet runner save himself,
      nor the horseman save his life.
16 But the stout-hearted warrior
    will run away naked in that day."
    The oracle of Yahweh.   Concluding Formula

This is certainly the best known of all the biblical oracles against the foreign nations.[3] The eightfold introduction is arresting and memorable. The prophet's moral indignation is evident and is easy for us to share. And the oracle embodies a universal ethic transcending sectarian dogma and national self-interest. The poem is finely constructed. The marginal headings that I have inserted alongside the translation indicate the perfectly patterned alternation between two similar forms, which are here designated type A and type B. These

[3] Isa. 13–23; Jer. 45–51; Ezek. 25–32; etc.

are placed together in pairs. The climactic Israel oracle breaks the mold somewhat because of its greater length and formal freedom. However, in the relative size of its accusation (which formally includes the historical recollection) and its announcement, it conforms to type B rather than type A. This gross structure is elegant. It is more impressive, in my opinion, than it would be if all its components were identical in form.[4]

The introductory verse (1:2), the splendid cry of Yahweh's herald, is repeated in part in Joel 3:16, which in the canonized Bible comes only seven verses before Amos 1:2. Since both larger poems (Joel 3:15-21 and Amos 1:3–2:16) are broadly liturgical in form and neither is apparently dependent upon the other, there is no way of knowing which, if either, of them was the original setting of this herald's announcement. Both may be quotations from a common liturgical tradition.

When modern interpreters of the prophets have tried to imagine the social setting in which this oracle was delivered,

[4] Because the Tyre, Edom, and Judah oracles do not conform precisely to the shape of the others, they have sometimes been regarded as secondary expansions of Amos' original composition (e.g., by Weiser). It should be clear, however, from the above display of the components that these three parts belong to the pattern of the whole as much as the other four. Other objections have been raised against the three, namely that they are less concrete than the others in their accusations, that they are imitative of the other four, and in the case of the Judah oracle, that it exhibits the language of the deuteronomists, whose chief literary monuments come from the seventh and sixth centuries B.C. However, the Edom and Tyre oracles are not more vague than those against Damascus and Philistia. And the similarity in the accusation of Tyre to that of Philistia may be due to historical facts rather than to editoral imitation. The Judah oracle is admittedly vague and "deuteronomic" and therefore has the poorest claim to originality. If the Israel oracle was meant originally to include all Israel, i.e., the kingdoms of Judah and Israel, as many scholars believe, then the Judah oracle may have been composed after the fall of the kingdom of Israel (722 B.C.) in order to apply Amos' strictures unambiguously to the surviving kingdom of Judah. Nowhere else is Judah mentioned in an oracle of Amos. This suggests, though it does not prove, that he made no sharp distinction between the two kingdoms but regarded them as segments of one people.

they have frequently turned to that most important religious festival in ancient Israel, the autumn Feast of Tabernacles. They have imagined Amos going from the little pastoral village of Tekoa to Bethel, the cultic center of the kingdom of Israel, and standing up in the midst of the throng to prophesy the wrath of God against the enemies of justice. They see him capturing the people's attention and arousing their assent with the oracles directed at the foreign nations, who were at least rivals if not enemies of Israel, and then suddenly, to the crowd's surprise, proclaiming God's wrath against them, too. Caught off guard, they were asked to apply the same logic to themselves that they applied so easily to their enemies. Thus, according to this imaginative reconstruction, began Amos' public career, which ended, probably a short time later, with his expulsion from Israel by Amaziah (7:10-17).

This hypothesis is reasonable. However, it would be valuable to know whether such a proclamation by a prophet was unprecedented in Israel or whether Amos had drawn upon literary conventions in composing his oracle or ritual conventions in announcing it. In seeking an answer to this question we must remember, of course, that we have the *text* of the oracle before us but have only imagined a possible *setting* for its publication. In order to achieve truly objective results in our inquiry we would need to find texts whose form and content were similar to this one and for whose social setting there was explicit ancient testimony. Such a discovery would not prove that Amos 1:3–2:16 was used in the same way as the comparative texts, but it would greatly increase the probability of our historical reconstruction. There are useful comparative materials in the Bible, as we shall see, but the best parallels found so far come from outside Israel. Aage Bentzen has compared Amos' eightfold oracle with Egyptian execration texts from the second millennium B.C., and this comparison has provided the focus of current discussion of the oracle's setting.[5]

The Egyptian texts are curses upon neighboring peoples that were pronounced ritually to the accompaniment of the magical smashing of clay effigies.[6] The priest uttered the curses in a geographical sequence, naming the neighbors lying around the home land at the points of the compass. Finally he cursed also the evildoers among the Egyptians themselves, who were construed as enemies of the gods. This sequence resembles the pattern in Amos 1:3–2:16. Damascus lay to the northeast of Israel, Philistia to the southwest, Tyre to the northwest, Edom-Ammon-Moab to the southeast. Judah-Israel of course comprised the center of Amos' oracular map.[7] The formal similarity is remarkable. Since the Egyptian texts were used in recurring rituals, we wonder whether this was true also of Amos' oracle or its prototype. Bentzen believed that it was. He accepted Sigmund Mowinckel's theory that an annual judgment of Yahweh upon his enemies was celebrated in the Feast of Tabernacles,[8] and he supposed Amos 1:3–2:16 to have been modeled upon traditional texts used for this occasion. He believed the "curses" were accompanied by appropriate rites of purgation on behalf of the Israelite people, which later evolved into the Jewish Day of Atonement. His thesis has been well received by other scholars.[9] Reventlow

---

[5] "The Ritual Background of Amos i.2–ii.16," *Oudt. St.*, VIII (Leiden, 1950), 85-99.

[6] Cf. Jer. 19.

[7] The similarity of Amos 1:3–2:16 to the Egyptian cursing ritual with respect to the geographical pattern employed has been used as an argument for the originality of the Tyre, Edom, and Judah oracles (see, e.g., Kapelrud, *Central Ideas in Amos*, pp. 23-27, and Reventlow, *Das Amt des Propheten bei Amos*, pp. 61-62). The pattern in Amos does indeed require the Tyre oracle, i.e., in the northwest corner. However, it would remain intact without the other two, for Moab and Ammon would still occupy the southeast corner without Edom, and Israel the center without Judah.

[8] See *Psalmenstudien*, II, and *The Psalms in Israel's Worship* (Nashville, 1962).

[9] See, e.g., Clements, *Prophecy and Covenant*, p. 43, and Amsler.

goes even further than Bentzen and declares 1:3–2:16 to be an actual ritual text, which was recited by Amos in fulfillment of his office as a cultic prophet.[10]

Another striking parallel to the Israelite prophets' denunciations of foreign nations has been discovered recently among the royal archives of Mari from the eighteenth century B.C. In one of the documents a diviner is reported to have predicted the loss of Babylonian territories to Mari, apparently (although this is not stated in the oracle) as a punishment of Babylon for breaking a treaty with Mari.[11] The basis for such a denunciation was generally provided in the international treaties of the ancient Near East, which contained curses that were invoked prospectively against a defaulting party to the treaty.[12] Many of these curses resemble the threats proclaimed by the Israelite prophets. Among them the following appear in Amos: (a) the transgressor will be killed and have no descendants (Amos 7:17; 9:4, 10); (b) his corpse will be exposed without burial (8:3); (c) his dwelling will be destroyed (4:11; 6:11); (d) his wife will be given to the enemy (5:2; 7:11); (e) light will be turned to darkness and joy to sadness (5:18; 6:4-7; 8:9, 10); (f) the women will become prostitutes (7:17); (g) the warriors will become "women" (cf. Amos 2:14-16); (h) natural calamities will occur (4:6-9); (i) the transgressor's sceptre will be removed and his weapons broken (1:5, 8; 2:3). In general the relevant Old Testament passages are distributed evenly among the oracles against Israel and those against the foreign nations.[13] This is what one would expect

[10] Op. cit., pp. 62-65.

[11] See A. Malamat, "Prophetic Revelations in New Documents from Mari and the Bible," Suppl. VT, XV (Volume du Congrés, Geneva, 1965; Leiden, 1966), 214 ff.

[12] See D. R. Hillers, Treaty-Curses and the Old Testament Prophets (Rome, 1964), and F. C. Fensham, "Common Trends in Curses of the Near Eastern Treaties and kudurru-Inscriptions Compared with Maledictions of Amos and Isaiah," ZAW, LXXV (1963), 155-75.

[13] Hillers, op. cit., p. 78.

since the prophets' oracles were not primarily against the enemies of Israel but against the enemies of God.

As a result of his research, Delbert Hillers concludes that the new comparative data confirm the long-held conviction that the prophets used traditional material in their doom oracles, and in particular that their curses were closely related to the traditions lying behind Deut. 28 and Lev. 26. He wisely refrains from trying to surmise the mode or extent of *literary* borrowing by the prophets from any of the older traditions but concludes, plausibly, that they used international treaty curses as the basis for some of their oracles.[14] Not all Old Testament oracles against foreign nations specify the grounds of the announced disaster, but those of Amos 1–2 do. Interestingly, a breach of treaty is explicitly cited in the Tyre oracle in the phrase "the covenant of brothers" (1:9),[15] and the other accusations in the series may have had similar references, especially 1:11, where Edom is accused of injuring "his brother." [16]

It is one thing to recognize affinities between Amos' oracles and other Near Eastern texts in language, idea, and form; it is quite another to assert that Amos 1–2 or its prototype was traditionally recited in a liturgy of cursing at a sanctuary in the fashion of the Egyptian execration texts. No such liturgy is mentioned in the ritual prescriptions of the Pentateuchal codes of law. Nevertheless, this silence does not preclude the possibility that one existed in the usage of the preexilic Israelite sanctuaries. We may assume that some of the liturgical practices of the Israelite monarchies died with them

[14] *Ibid.*, pp. 79, 85.

[15] John Priest, in "The Covenant of Brothers," (*JBL*, LXXXIV [1965], 400 ff.), cites the use of the term "brother" in Hittite and Hellenic treaties to designate the relation between the treaty partners.

[16] This allusion is usually interpreted to mean Israel (or Judah) in the light of the Jacob(Israel)-Esau(Edom) tradition recalled in Gen. 25 ff. Priest, e.g., reads it this way (*ibid.*, p. 406). However, the term may have the same meaning in Amos 1:11 that it does in 1:9.

in 722 B.C. and 587 B.C. and were not mentioned in the post-exilic editions of the codes for the reason that they could no longer be performed by the Jewish community. A public liturgy embodying curses upon surrounding peoples would have appeared treasonable to the imperial authorities who ruled Palestine after the exile. The influence of such pre-exilic liturgical practices upon the later literature would therefore have been indirect.

The tribal blessing (Gen. 49; Deut. 33; and Judg. 5) is in some respects a prototype of the serial oracular utterance; therefore, prophetic usage may have been influenced by this ancient and memorable literary form.[17] These "blessings" contain some curses (e.g., Gen. 49:5-7; Judg. 5:23) so the development of a whole series of curses out of this form is conceivable. The poem of tribal blessing was a "cultic" composition in a sense, for every blessing or curse was charged with sacral power. Deathbed blessings were especially significant in ancient Israel, as the story of Esau and Jacob illustrates (Gen. 27). The concentrated benediction of a patriarch near the end of his life was respected as a dynamic factor in the welfare of his survivors, quite apart from its function as a legal testament.[18]

There are other features of early Israelite ritual (using the term again in the broad sense), as it is reflected in the Pentateuchal narratives, that perhaps influenced the shape and function of later prophetic utterances. The legend of the ten plagues which preceded the exodus from Egypt appears to be an expanded version of a ritual celebration of this event (Exod. 7:14–12:42).[19] As it now stands, the narrative repre-

[17] Lindblom considers Amos 1:3–2:6 an adaptation of the old "tribal poem," enlarged to include other nations than Israel (*Prophecy in Ancient Israel*, pp. 239-40).

[18] This conclusion is suggested by comparison with similar practices in Mesopotamia in the Patriarchal Age, particularly those documented by the Mari texts. See E. Speiser, *Genesis* (New York, 1964), pp. 212-13.

[19] In calling this narrative a legend I do not mean to deny the historicity of

sents the fusion of several originally discrete versions of the story, and it contains much later didactic material relating to the celebration of the Passover (12:1-34). Once allowances have been made for these editorial operations, we may discern a highly stylized report of an artificial series of events. It resembles a ritual drama far more than a simple historical recollection. The tenfoldness of the series is especially significant in this regard. Moses' declarations to the king of Egypt are in the form of prophetic oracles. This legend, therefore, points to a plausible liturgical setting for the development of oracles against foreign nations. In this case, of course, there is only one nation, but the model could easily have been adapted to other ritual purposes.[20]

Two practices associated with the ancient holy war in Israel provided precedents for the utterance of oracles against foreign nations. These were the devotion of the enemy to the ḥerem (ban) and the consultation of diviners. The ḥerem involved a promise to Yahweh that all spoils of battle would be sacrificed to him in exchange for his aid against the enemy. In effect this was the most terrible sort of curse upon the enemy, although formally it was a vow and not a curse.[21] The consultation of diviners prior to battle was common before and after the establishment of the Israelite monarchy. In the earliest times sacred lots were employed. These were probably associated with the holy ark, the battle-paladium of Yahweh that led the tribes to war (Num. 10:33-36). The lots were in the custody of the Levites, champions of militant

---

the exodus itself or the actual, temporal association of some of the plagues with this event. However, the manner in which the dialogue and the ten marvelous plagues are described is surely legendary.

[20] See J. Pedersen, "Passahfest und Passahlegende," *ZAW*, LII (1934), 161-75, and *Israel*, III-IV (London and Copenhagen, 1940), 726-37; G. von Rad, *Das formgeschichtliche Problem des Hexateuch*, BWANT, LXXVIII (1938) (English trans. in *The Problem of the Hexateuch and Other Essays* [New York, 1966], pp. 1-78).

[21] Examples of the use of the ban are reported in Num. 21:1-3; Josh. 7:17-19; and I Sam. 15:1-23.

Yahwism (Exod. 32:25-29; Num. 3:31; 27:21). They ministered before the Lord in the tent of meeting, where God's oracles were received (Exod. 25:21-22; 29:42; 33:7-11; Num. 8:15). The lots were used also during Saul's reign (I Sam. 14:36-46) but not thereafter. In their place prophets were consulted about the outcome of a projected battle and about divine instructions for its conduct (I Sam. 28:6, 15-19; I Kings 20:13-14; 22:5-28). All of this oracular activity was cultic. It concerned holy wars and consecrated ministers of Yahweh, who performed carefully prescribed rites of divination, from which came formal prophetic announcements. It is not difficult to imagine the development of a liturgy of judgment upon the nations from these well-attested practices.

Perhaps the most interesting biblical account of early prophetic activity is the story of Balaam. Balaam's oracles concerned the destinies of the Moabites, Edomites, Amalekites, Kenites, and Philistines (Num. 24:17-24) in addition to Israel (23:7-10, 18-24; 24:3-9, 15-19). The grouping of oracular utterances against several foreign nations anticipates formally the serial oracle in Amos 1–2. It is a transformation of the old tribal poem because the peoples to which it refers are non-Israelite. In this respect it resembles the old Noachic curse on Canaan (Gen. 9:25-27). Thus it may be said to lie midway between the ancient tribal blessing and the later prophetic oracle. Balaam's oracles are described explicitly as ritual acts. He erected seven altars for a sevenfold sacrifice as part of the oracular process (Num. 23:1-7, 14-15, 29-30). The oracles put in Balaam's mouth are the creations of an anonymous poet (or poets) of unknown date and provenance, and the narrative in which they are set is only partly historical. Nevertheless, the traditioners have done their best to give it historical verisimilitude, and we may use it as evidence of prophetic practices during the period of the Israelite monarchy, at the latest. The cultic setting of Balaam's oracles is therefore highly significant for our present inquiry.[22]

The list of foreign nations in Amos 1–2 (Aram, Philistia, Phoenicia, Edom, Ammon, Moab) does not recur in other prophetic or ritual contexts in the Old Testament although there are similar lists. One of these occurs seventeen times with minor variations. It is the list of pre-Israelite peoples who were displaced by Israel in her settlement in Palestine. Its most common form is "Canaanites, Hittites, Amorites, Perizzites, Hivites, and Jebusites."[23] It appears regularly in covenantal contexts.[24] Several of these are explicitly liturgical, namely the covenant-renewal ceremony in Josh. 24 and the prescription for the annual pilgrimage festivals in Exod. 23:14-23. The number of nations listed is usually six or seven. Amos 1–2 lists six foreign nations plus Judah and Israel.

The book of Psalms provides evidence of the ritual use of oracles against the nations in Judah under the monarchy. Ps. 2 is probably a coronation psalm for a Davidic king. It contains an oracular decree of the king's dominion over the nations (vss. 7-11). Ps. 89 refers to the oracle of Nathan, which contained a promise of Davidic rule over the nations "from the sea to the rivers," that is, from the Mediterranean (or the Red Sea) to the Tigris and Euphrates (89:25; cf. II Sam. 7:5-6). This territory comprised just those lands enumerated in Amos 1–2. It was the territory of the Davidic empire at its greatest extent. Perhaps the liturgy behind Amos 1–2, if there was one, was part of the royal cultus in Jerusalem. Its purpose would have been to reassure the king and the people of God's promise to David and to reinforce the

[22] Some of the oracular activities of the prophets of Mari were also associated with sacrifice. See Malamat, op. cit., p. 215.

[23] Exod. 3:8, 17; 23:23; 33:2; Deut. 20:17; Josh. 9:1; 11:3; 12:8; Judg. 3:5; cf. Gen. 15:20; Exod. 13:5; Deut. 7:1; Josh. 3:10; 24:11; I Kings 9:20; II Chron. 8:7; Ezra 9:1; Neh. 9:8.

[24] Gen. 15:20; Exod. 3:8, 17; 13:5; 23:23; 33:2; Deut. 7:1; 20:17; Josh. 24:11; Neh. 9:8.

judgment of God upon the "subject" nations. The grounds of judgment are different in Amos 1–2 from those reflected in the royal psalms (cf. Pss. 18, 20, 21, and 144), but the difference may be accounted for in terms of Amos' distinctive ethical concern. The oracles found in other royal psalms (Pss. 110 and 132), although they are not against foreign nations, give further indication of the prophetic element in the Israelite royal cult.

Elsewhere among the psalms there are references to God's judgments against the nations, but no oracles of judgment are quoted directly (Pss. 96:10-13 and 98:2-9). Similar psalms celebrate God's triumph over cosmic powers of disorder and his support of Israel as his vicegerent in the world (Pss. 47, 93, 95, and 97). Mowinckel grouped all these psalms together and deduced from them an annual liturgy for the Feast of Tabernacles, in which, among many other things, there was a dramatized act of judgment against the foreign nations, who were conceived as terrestrial embodiments of the cosmic opponents of God's order.[25] Würthwein and Reventlow regard Mowinckel's case for the ritual setting of the oracles against the nations as demonstrative and deem it unnecessary to defend it in their own discussion of related issues.[26] Actually, Mowinckel's theory is still unproved and widely contested. However, whether or not it is correct in all respects, it is probably correct to the extent that the motifs contained in the extant royal and enthronement psalms were prominent in the royal liturgies of pre-exilic Israel, at least in the southern kingdom. The forms of these liturgies are partly irrecoverable, but the surviving cultic songs provide ample evidence of the religious convictions fostered by the monarchial cult.

[25] *Psalmenstudien*, II. Mowinckel's pioneer study of the oracular element in the Psalter is also important for the present discussion (*Psalmenstudien*, III. *Kultprophetie und prophetische Psalmen* [Kristiania, 1923]).
[26] Würthwein, ZTK, XLIX (1952), 12; Reventlow, *op. cit.*, p. 63.

There are other psalms relevant to our discussion also; however, since these are not explicitly royal psalms, the probability of their having been pre-exilic in origin is not so high as in the case of those previously mentioned. Psalm 82 is the closest parallel to a prophetic oracle against the nations among all the extant Hebrew psalms. Here we have not merely a warning to the nations to respect Yahweh's chosen king (Ps. 2), nor merely an announcement of God's approaching world judgment (Pss. 96 and 98), nor yet a summons to remote powers to behold Israel's trial before God (Ps. 50), but an actual sentence of judgment against the world's rulers, delivered in oracular form. The trial is depicted mythologically. God takes his place in the heavenly assembly and sentences the erstwhile immortal governors of the peoples to mortal existence as a penalty for unjust rule.[27] The psalmist responds to the vision of judgment with the plea to God to execute his decree among the nations of the earth (82:8), which are the empirical embodiments of the mythically imagined heavenly powers. The motive of God's decision in this cosmic trial is similar to that of his promised judgments upon the foreign nations in Amos 1–2. In the former it is the punishment for failure to champion the afflicted against the powerful within a nation while in the latter it is the just punishment for one nation's cruelty toward another. The ethical situation in the Israel oracle (Amos 2:6-16) is the same as in Ps. 82.

In the other psalms to which I have referred the dominant ethical interest is to maintain Israel's God-given privileges among the nations of the world, and these are defined largely chauvinistically. Among the royal psalms, Ps. 72 alone describes the moral responsibilities of the Davidic king and praises him as the upholder of justice amidst otherwise unjust

[27] The belief that Yahweh used these lesser divine beings as his lieutenants in governing the nations is expressed in Deut. 32:7-9 (LXX, cf. RSV). Compare also I Kings 22:19-22 and Job 1–2.

nations (72:8-14). However, there is no note of prophetic self-criticism even here. The ethical perspective exhibited in Amos 1:3–2:3 is genuinely transnational and is thoroughly consonant with the rest of the book of Amos. They are far more than nationalistic imprecations against rival nations such as we may imagine a cultic prophet of salvation (*Heilsnabi*) to have uttered as part of the effort to secure the state in a precarious world.[28]

Ps. 60 and 108 contain the recollection of a divine oracle exalting Ephraim and Judah as the helmet and scepter of God and scorning Moab, Edom, and Philistia (60:6-8; 108:7-9). Although the connotation of *b°qodhshô* in 60:6 (Heb. 60:8) and 108:7 (Heb. 108:8) is not absolutely clear, the line seems to refer to an oracle delivered "in his sanctuary." [29] It is noteworthy that seven names of peoples or tribes are enumerated in this oracle (assuming that Shechem, in the first line, is of a different order). Why is there no new oracle to lift the psalmist's hope? At the end he seems reassured of God's help against Israel's foes (60:12; 108:13). Has a cultic prophet intervened to answer his question ("Hast thou not rejected us, O God?" 60:10; 108:11) with a denial?

Scrutiny of the historical allusions in Amos 1–2 provides evidence neither for nor against authorship by Amos. Of the six international crimes referred to in the accusations all but one are of indeterminate date. The charge against Syria (1:3) may refer to Hazael's conquest of Israelite territory in Gilead at the end of the ninth or beginning of the eighth century

---

[28] Contrast the view of Würthwein in "Amos Studien," *ZAW*, LXII (1950), 35-40. It is criticized by Weiser, Amsler, Kapelrud (*op. cit.*, pp. 23 ff.), Lehming (*ZTK*, LV [1958], 157-60), and many others. Weiser's view that the oracles against the foreign nations in Amos 1:3–2:6 were meant solely as a rhetorical prologue to the Israel oracle has also been rejected on all sides.

[29] See BDB, p. 871*b* (2.d.); KBL, p. 828*b*; RSV; Jerusalem; H. Gunkel, *Die Psalmen* (Göttingen, 1926), *in loc.*, and H.-J. Kraus, *Psalmen* (Neukirchen, 1960), *in loc.* Contrast Kissane ("by his holiness"), *The Book of Psalms* (Dublin, 1953), *in loc.*

B.C. (II Kings 13:3-7, 22-25; cf. 8:9-13), as many scholars believe.[30] However, this judgment is uncertain. The conflict between Syria and Israel over possession of Gilead lasted a long time, and the particular instance alluded to in Amos 1:3 might have occurred at any time during the tenure of "the House of Hazael" in the kingdom of Damascus, that is, down to the time of the Assyrian conquest (732 B.C.). Thus it may have happened a generation before Amos or during his own lifetime. Ammon's crime was similar to Syria's (1:13), but unless it was the same event, its date is indeterminate in the light of the extant sources. The remaining four events are of completely uncertain date. The omission of Gath from the list of Philistine cities in 1:7-8 has been interpreted by some scholars as an indication that the oracle was composed *after* the city's destruction by Sargon II in 711 B.C.,[31] but the inclusion of Ashdod in this list has led others to date it *before* Sargon's destruction of that city, in the same year.[32] The historical allusions, therefore, are not precisely datable so they do not help us to date the composition of Amos 1:3–2:5 except within wide limits, namely from the ninth century B.C. to a time after the career of Amos.[33]

Our survey of the literary affinities of Amos 1–2 has produced no actual liturgies from the pre-exilic Israelite cult incorporating oracles against the nations, but it has, I believe, shown there were numerous antecedents to this kind of oracle in a variety of ritual settings in early Israel. The evidence is sufficient to justify the conclusion that Amos adapted literary forms of a broadly cultic nature that were widely used in Israel and the ancient Near East generally. However, it does not justify Reventlow's conclusion that Amos 1–2 is itself a

[30] E.g., Amsler and N. K. Gottwald (*All the Kingdoms of the Earth* [New York, 1964], p. 104).

[31] E.g., Fosbroke.

[32] E.g., Amsler.

[33] The historical background of Amos 1:3–2:5 is discussed thoroughly in Gottwald, *op. cit.*, pp. 103-10.

traditional prophetic liturgy which Amos simply made use of in his capacity as an official cultic prophet.[34] Amos 1–2 has strong affinities to other ancient texts, but it is in many ways a unique literary creation. Comparison with other texts makes evident the independent poetic imagination and rhetorical skill of its author. It is rightly esteemed as one of the master oracles of the Old Testament.

THE DOXOLOGIES (AMOS 4:13; 5:8; 9:5-6)

The hymnic character of these fragments has always been recognized by interpreters of the Bible, but during the last four decades particular attention has been given to their possible ritual background. In the course of this discussion nearly every conceivable explanation of their origin and function has been proposed. At one time the dominant critical opinion was that they were secondary embellishments of the oracles of Amos, made in adapting them for reading in temple or synagogue. A prominent rival to this theory, which has gained adherents in recent years, is that Amos himself quoted a hymn from the repertory of the Jerusalem temple, in order perhaps to add solemnity to his oracles. It is impossible at the present time to answer the question of the authorship of these lines, and it must therefore be put aside in favor of the question of their function in the text as it is. Only after this question has been answered is there any hope of answering the other satisfactorily.

The fragments are much alike in content and form. Together they constitute a hymnic celebration of Yahweh's power to create and control the structures of the world and to disrupt them at will. The first fragment (4:13) exalts him as the cosmic creator. The second (5:8) develops this theme further but introduces an ominous tone in the second line.

[34] *Op. cit.,* pp. 64-66, 73.

The third (9:5-6) converts this tone into a major theme, in the first two lines, recapitulates the creation motif, in the third, and, in the fourth, repeats the second line of the second fragment.

4:13   For behold, he who forms mountains,
   and creates the wind,
    and reveals his purpose to man;
  Who makes dawn and[35] darkness,
   and walks upon the heights of the world;
    Yahweh, God of hosts, is his name.

5:8   Maker of the Pleiades and Orion,
   who changes deep darkness to morning,
    and darkens day into night;
  Who summons the waters of the sea,
   and spills them upon the surface of the earth;
    Yahweh is his name.

9:5   The Lord, Yahweh of hosts,
   who touches the earth and it melts,
    and all its inhabitants mourn;
  And the whole of it rises like the Nile,
   then sinks like the Nile of Egypt;
9:6   Who builds his high chambers in the heavens,
   and founds his vault upon the earth;
  Who summons the waters of the sea,
   and spills them upon the surface of the earth;
    Yahweh is his name.

There can be no doubt about the unity of these three pieces. Placed side by side in this manner, they form a nearly complete and well-rounded hymn. Indeed, they exhibit a closer interweaving of themes, a more strategic repetition of words,

---

[35] Following the Greek. The Hebrew reads, "He makes the dawn darkness"; cf. 5:8a.

and a more symmetrical arrangement of lines and cadences than do many of the hymns of the Psalter. In 1917 Hans Schmidt declared these pieces to be hymns to Yahweh. In 1925 Karl Budde lifted them out of their canonical places, rearranged them, and declared them to be a single hymn of thanksgiving to Yahweh as Creator, the components of which had been strewn by an editor across the book of Amos. In 1929 Friedrich Horst modified Budde's treatment somewhat, particularly by restoring the lines to their canonical order, and furnished an imaginative explanation of the role of the fragments in the book.[36] Since that time the Budde-Horst separation of the fragments from their context has dominated critical interpretation of them. The separation itself was not altogether new. But whereas many previous critics had merely deleted these passages as late interpolations made presumably "to relieve the gloom of the prophetic picture" by a pious editor,[37] the direction now taken was to study the three as parts of a single hymn, and to inquire into the possible significance of the interpolations for the later worshiping community. Horst's article was especially constructive in this respect, and it has had a wide and continuing influence.

First of all, Horst observed (correctly, I believe) that "the hymn" is not a thanksgiving for creation (Budde) but an acclamation of the cosmic power of God, which is exhibited both in creating the world and in shaking its foundations.[38] Further, he proposed a new thesis to account for the addition of the hymn segments to the collected oracles of Amos. The life situation of the present composition, he said, was the liturgy of postexilic Judaism, where the doxologies functioned as a part of the ritual of atonement. By reciting the prophet's

[36] H. Schmidt, Der Prophet Amos (Tübingen, 1917), p. 23; K. Budde, "Zu Text und Auslengung des Buches Amos," JBL, XLIII (1924), 105-6; F. Horst, "Die Doxologien im Amosbuch," ZAW, XLVII (1929), 45-54. The first two works are cited by Horst (p. 46).

[37] See Harper on all three passages, with references to like-minded interpreters.

[38] Op. cit., pp. 46-47.

oracles of denunciation, which had been addressed initially to a former generation, the worshipers implicitly engaged in a confession of sin. This confession was followed by an acclamation of the majesty and power of God. The conjunction of confession and acclamation was in effect an acknowledgment of God's justice in destroying the Israelite kingdom and was made in the hope that no further expiation of sin, in the form of divine punishment, would be necessary. Horst saw other examples of the practice in Josh. 7:16 ff.; II Chron. 30:8; Job 4–5; Ps. 118:17-21; and Jer. 13:15 f., and discovered extrabiblical parallels in a number of Greek inscriptions.[39]

Some of these biblical parallels cited by Horst are apt, particularly Josh. 7:16 ff. and II Chron. 30:8. However, Ps. 118 is a confession of *innocence* in which God is praised for his *love,* so it is quite different from Amos 4, 5, and 9. Nor is any one of the remaining parallels especially close. There are several other psalms, however, that exhibit a pattern similar to the one suggested by Horst and that lend a certain plausibility to his thesis. The book of Psalms is the best testing ground available for any theory pertaining to the worship and piety of Judaism in the postexilic period. In the case of Horst's theory it is the penitential psalms that provide the comparative data. There are a few of these psalms that do indeed exhibit the elements named by Horst. One of these is Ps. 106, whose formal affinity to Amos 4 we have already described. It contains a confession of sin, a charge of guilt against the fathers (vs. 6), a recollection of the historical calamities which resulted from the father's sin (the bulk of the psalm), and an interjection of praise to God (vss. 1-2). It goes beyond Horst's pattern by adding a plea for deliverance from present oppression and exile (vss. 3-5, 47).[40] Ps. 106 is a communal

---

[39] *Ibid.,* pp. 50-53 (the citation of I Chron. 30:8 is obviously a misprint for II Chron. 30:8).

[40] Vs. 48 is not a part of this psalm but is the doxology which closes the

prayer, as was the hypothetical one proposed by Horst. Ps. 51 is perhaps the closest parallel in the Psalter to the atonement ritual proposed by Horst. The worshiper confesses his guilt and acknowledges his suffering as well deserved and thus exalts God's justice. He begs for the gift of a clean heart, as the necessary condition of blessedness. He does not praise God in the manner of the doxologies in Amos but asks for deliverance in order to praise. The psalmist's logic is explicit at every point in this psalm while in Horst's hypothetical liturgy some of the logic is only implicit. Moreover, Ps. 51 is not a communal psalm. Most of the prayers for atonement preserved in the book of Psalms do not fall into the pattern described by Horst. Nevertheless, since there are significant points of contact between this pattern and the extant psalms, we may consider Horst's explanation a possible one. After all, the canonical psalms do not provide a complete picture of Jewish worship after the exile but are only suggestive of some of the main forms.

Horst's treatment of the doxologies in Amos was important mainly because it was an effort to discover a liturgical life-setting for the text in its present form. Other scholars writing since 1929 have taken a similar approach.[41] It seems to me that this method is more likely to be correct than the older one of inquiring into the possible motives of individual editors.[42] Among those who interpret these portions of Amos in the context of the history of worship, not all date them in the postexilic period. Some believe the doxologies were added to the oracles at an earlier time either by the traditionalists who collected and transmitted Amos' oracles or by Amos himself.[43] The older argument that the language and theology

---

fourth of the five "books" of the Psalter. Cf. Pss. 41:13; 72:18-19; 89:52; and 150 (entire).

[41] E.g., Weiser, and Lindblom (*op. cit.*, p. 117).

[42] E.g., Cripps and Fosbroke.

[43] See Kapelrud, *op. cit.*, pp. 38-39, with additional references.

of these pieces are clearly postexilic is no longer valid in the light of the Ugaritic texts and other cognate materials from the biblical world. Therefore, there is no compelling reason to prohibit their inclusion among the "authentic" portions of the book of Amos, particularly if the conception of God that they reflect is consonant with the oracles of Amos.[44]

My only objection to this line of reasoning is that it is negative. According to the argument, the doxologies are to be retained because there is insufficient evidence to prove them secondary ("late," "inauthentic"). However, a stronger case than this can be made for these lines. The doxologies are not as haphazardly placed as is normally supposed, and it is possible to view them as forming integral parts of the poems in which they stand. This is not necessarily to say that these poems were originally proclaimed oracularly by Amos in their present form, although this possibility may not be ruled out. It is rather to say that the placement of the doxologies in the poems manifests a conscious design, and that, as far as the *book* of Amos is concerned, this design may be assumed to be original.

The three doxologies occur in similar contexts, and the poems of which they are part form a logical sequence, to which the doxologies themselves contribute. These poems are 4:4-13; 5:1-6, 8; and 9:1-6. Amos 4:4-13 begins with an ironic disparagement of the cults of Bethel and Gilgal (4-5). It continues with a catalog of providential chastisements (6-11). Thus the self-imposed cultic occasions are here contrasted with the divinely imposed historic occasions for renewal. The people's relish for a ritual turning to God is contrasted with their refusal to grasp nonritual opportunities for repentance. They are warned, therefore, to prepare for the most solemn possible encounter with God (12). The meaning of the transitional clause "therefore, thus I will do to

[44] For example, Kapelrud deals with them on just this basis (*loc. cit.*).

you, O Israel" (12*a*) is uncertain. Some commentators believe the original lines explaining the "thus" are now missing. Others believe the oracle was left intentionally vague at this point in order to create a sense of awesome mystery. A few believe the line refers to the evils previously enumerated. This last interpretation deserves more serious consideration than it has received generally.[45] The final catastrophe in the catalog (6-11) is the overthrow of "*some* of you" in the manner of the ancient destruction of Sodom and Gomorrah. The sense of the oracle is perfectly clear when verse 12 is taken as a threat of the same sort of ruin "to you, O Israel," that is, to the whole nation. A more complete destruction is inconceivable. Such a threat is therefore no mere repetition of what has been described before. I prefer this interpretation to the more popular ones. In any case, the pericope closes with a solemn affirmation of the power of God, whom Israel must now prepare to meet (vs. 13). The last line of all, "Yahweh, God of hosts, is his name," is a ringing climax, which draws together the sixfold repetition of Yahweh's name in the preceding lines (4:5, 6, 8, 9, 10, and 11). The God whom Israel is now to meet is not the one imagined in their cult, whom they so love to seek (vss. 4-5), but the creator of the world, who may also be its destroyer.

In Amos 5:1-6, 8, the oracle begins with a lamentation over the fall of Israel (1-2). Here, as in 4:6-11, the poet has imitated a standard form of ritual utterance. The vast dimensions of the nation's loss are declared in the oracular line which concludes the first section (3). The middle section of this pericope returns to the topic of the cultus at Bethel and Gilgal,[46] linking the poem directly to 4:4-13. Now, however, the *nation's* coming destruction is declared, together with that of the chief sanctuaries. Therefore, those few who do

---

[45] See, e.g., Harper's summary dismissal of this suggestion.
[46] Beersheba is also mentioned, but the line may be a gloss.

not wish to perish with the establishment are urged to seek Yahweh and repudiate the futile cultus. The practical content of this seeking is not specified in this oracle, or in 4:4-13, and must be inferred from other parts of the book. Verse 7 is not part of the oracle (5:1-6, 8). It belongs with 5:10 ff.[47] The present poem concludes in the manner of 4:4-13 with an acclamation of the transcendent power of Yahweh (5:8). As we have previously observed, this portion of "the hymn" reiterates the creation motif of the first part (4:13) but adds an ominous word in the final line, where the habitable earth is shown flooded by the divinely controlled ocean. Of course, we do not know whether 4:13, 5:8, and 9:5-6 were originally components of a single hymn. If they were, the sequence of themes exhibited by them in the book of Amos might be derivative. But they may never have existed in another form than their present one. Amos 5:9 appears to me to be an editorial expansion and not part of the primary oracle (5:1-6, 8) despite the fact that its inclusion would strengthen my case for the development of themes in these three poems. This verse ("who makes destruction flash forth against the strong,/so that destruction comes upon the fortress," RSV) comes after the closing formula ("Yahweh is his name"), and it repeats the word "destruction" without achieving any poetic effect. Therefore, it were better left out of consideration in the present discussion.

Amos 9:1-6 is constructed more simply than the other two oracles, having only two parts instead of three. The first part (9:1-4) is a visionary scene in a sanctuary. Thus the setting of the oracle is similar to that of the other two although Bethel and Gilgal are not specified here. The Lord is envisioned standing above the altar and ordering the destruction of the temple (1). This then is the climactic poem in the series. In 4:4-5 the cult is satirized. In 5:4-6 the wise

[47] Cf. Weiser, Amsler, and Kapelrud (op. cit., p. 39), among others.

are warned to avoid the sanctuaries lest they fall with them. In 9:1-4 the ruin itself is envisioned, and every worshiper remaining in the temple is killed, or pursued to his hiding place, ferreted out, and slain. The God who does this is the one whose mighty works in nature are acknowledged in the concluding doxology (9:5-6). In this part of the poem the ominous undertone heard in 5:8 becomes the dominant theme, and we hear the sound of the shaking of the earth's foundations. The hymn acclaims the universal sovereignty and terrifying power of God, who can pursue those who are to perish to the ends of the earth. Once again, as in the previous poems, no moral justification is made of God's destroying act. Thus the only explicitly ethical comment in the series of poems is the observation in 4:6-11 that the people have refused to "return" to Yahweh. Yet even this is unexplained.

To recapitulate, each of the three oracles is against the cult of Israel. Bethel and Gilgal are mentioned in the first two, and the third depicts the demolition of "the temple," that is, the whole ritual edifice, whose center was the royal sanctuary of Bethel. The interplay of the themes of creation and destruction, which rises in a crescendo through the doxologies, is matched by the interplay of threat and exhortation, which appears in the oracular segments of the poems. What begins in disparagement of the cult (4:4-5) changes to dire warning against patricipation in it (5:4-6) and ends in a vision of its annihilation (9:1-4). In the denouement everyone perishes (9:2-4) who has disregarded the prophet's counsel (5:4-6) and persisted in seeking satisfaction in the fleshpots of the temple (4:4-5). If this analysis is correct and the three passages we have been discussing comprise a single series of oracles, why has the third one been separated from the other two and placed at the end of the book? Naturally, one cannot answer this question absolutely. Nevertheless, it is not unlikely that the editors were induced

120

by the visionary character of the opening lines of the third poem (9:1 ff.) to place it with the other visions in the book (chaps. 7 and 8). In spite of this dislocation and the oft mentioned syntactical discontinuities that exist in these pericopes, that is, between the oracles proper and the doxologies, I am convinced by the affinities among them that the three constitute a series, governed by a conscious rationale. We may call them Three Oracles on the Meeting with Yahweh.

Amos 4:4-13

I

4   "Come to Bethel and transgress,
      to Gilgal and heap up transgression.
    And bring your sacrifices in the morning,
      your tithes on the third day.
5   Burn leavened bread in thanksgiving,
      and call out free will offerings, proclaim them!
    Because this is what you love to do, O House of Israel."
      The oracle of the Lord Yahweh.

II

6   "And yet I gave you cleanness of teeth in all your cities,
      and a famine of bread in all your villages.
    But you did not return to me." The oracle of Yahweh.
7   "And then I withheld the rain from you
      just three months before the harvest.
    I made it rain on one city,
      and not rain on another city.
    One field was watered,
      but the unwatered field dried up.
8   And two or three cities trekked to one city
      to drink water, but were not supplied.
    But you did not return to me." The oracle of Yahweh.
9   "I smote you with blight and mildew,
      and blasted your gardens and vineyards.
    Locusts devoured your fig trees and olive.
    But you did not return to me." The oracle of Yahweh.

121

10 "I sent upon you a plague like that of Egypt;
    and I slew your young men with the sword,
        with your splendid [48] horses;
    And I raised to your nostrils the stench of your camp.
    But you did not return to me." The oracle of Yahweh.

11 "I overthrew some of you
    as God overthrew Sodom and Gomorrah;
    And you were like a brand snatched from the burning.
    But you did not return to me." The oracle of Yahweh.

12 "Therefore, I will do the same to you, O Israel.
    Since this is what I will do to you,
    Prepare to meet your God, O Israel!"

III

13 For behold, he who forms mountains,
    and creates the wind,
        and reveals his purpose to man;
    Who makes dawn and darkness,
        and walks upon the heights of the world;
        Yahweh, God of hosts, is his name.

Amos 5:1-6, 8

I

1 Hear this word that I take up for you
    in lamentation, O House of Israel:

2 "Fallen, never to rise,
    is the virgin of Israel.
    Forsaken on her land;
    none to help her up."

3 *For thus says the Lord Yahweh:*
    "The city that went forth a thousand
    will have a hundred left;

---

[48] Reading *ṣᵉbî* for *šᵉbî*, with Budde, Sellin, Amsler, and others. This clause spoils the regular chiasmus (cf. 4:6, 9, and 11) so it may be a gloss. Vss. 7-8 do not conform at all to the pattern of the rest. Lines two to four seem to have been expanded from an original **half-line.**

That went forth a hundred
will have left but ten,
for the House of Israel."

4 *For thus says Yahweh* to the House of Israel:
"Seek me and live!

5 But don't seek Bethel,
and don't go to Gilgal;[49]
For Gilgal is destined for deportation,
and Bethel will become a thing of nought.

6 Seek *Yahweh* and live!
lest he flash like fire (on) the House of Joseph,
and consume, with none to quench for Bethel."

II

8 Maker of the Pleiades and Orion,
who changes deep darkness to morning,
and darkens day into night;
Who summons the waters of the sea,
and spills them upon the surface of the earth;
Yahweh is his name.

Amos 9:1-6

I

1 I saw the Lord standing above the altar,
and he said:
"Strike the capitals,
and let the lintels fall!
Smash them on the heads of all,
and I will slay the survivors with the sword.
None who flees will get away;
no fugitive will escape.

2 If they dig down to Sheol,
my hand will pull them out.
If they scale to the heavens,
I will pull them down from there.

---

[49] "And don't go over to Beersheba" appears to be a Judean gloss opposing the rival sanctuary of Beersheba on behalf of the Jerusalem temple.

3 And if they hide on the top of Carmel,
    there I will search and seize them.
    If they conceal themselves from my sight in the depths
      of the sea,
    there the sea-monster will bite them at my command.
4 And if they go into captivity before their foes,
    I will order the sword to slay them there.
    I have fixed my gaze upon them,
    for evil and not for good."

II

5 *The Lord, Yahweh of hosts,*
    who touches the earth and it melts,
    and all its inhabitants mourn;
    And the whole of it rises like the Nile,
    then sinks like the Nile of Egypt;
6 Who builds his high chambers in the heavens,
    and founds his vault upon the earth;
    Who summons the waters of the sea,
    and spills them upon the surface of the earth;
    Yahweh is his name.

It is evident from the study of the literary affinities of Amos 1:2–2:16 and the oracles translated above that Amos was familiar with the forms of liturgical utterance employed in Israelite worship. It is equally evident that he adapted these forms to his own purposes with considerable originality. We have not surveyed the Old Testament parallels to the doxologies because they are legion. Yet the same originality is displayed in these as in the other portions of the book. They employ the vocabulary which was defined by cultic and popular tradition, but they are unhackneyed and remarkably suited to their oracular context. When we judge the quality of early Israelite worship, we must not forget that the liturgical traditions were an important resource for the oracles of Amos. He was deeply indebted to them even though he was severely critical of contemporary ritual practice. That Amos used these traditions does not necessarily mean he was a cultic prophet. The recollection contained in 7:14-15 makes this conclusion highly improbable. It is much more likely that he was a regular worshiper in the temple of Jerusalem who was compelled by his devotion to the word of God to become a prophet to the north Israelite kingdom.

A LITANY OF IMPENITENCE (AMOS 4:4-13)

Several recent theories of the cultic origin of this poem occasion our commenting further on this one of the Three Oracles on the Meeting with Yahweh. The older critical view that Amos was referring in 4:6-12 to a series of historical events known to his audience was partly abandoned by Weiser (in his commentary) when he said that the prophet had imitated a cultic recitation of God's acts of salvation but had reversed it (i.e., made it into a series of unredemptive acts) to suit his oracular purpose. H. Reventlow has recently proposed a more ambitious thesis. He argues that Amos 4:6-12 is a straightforward adaptation of a liturgy of cursing which was part of the covenant-renewal festival.[50] This hypothesis has been accepted by W. Brueggemann, who has gone on to argue that the whole of Amos 4:4-13 is patterned after such a ritual.[51] According to Reventlow, a stereotyped series of curses which were to fall upon Israel for breach of her covenant with Yahweh was recited in the covenant-renewal ceremony.[52] The original ritual setting is reflected,

---

[50] *Op. cit.*, pp. 75-90. Reventlow's thesis is a modification of Hugo Gressmann's interpertation in *Der Ursprung der israelitisch—jüdischen Eschatologie, FRLANT,* VI, 169 ff.

[51] *VT,* XV (1965), 1-15.

[52] For general treatments of the festival and its historical development see, among others, A. Weiser, *The Psalms* (Philadelphia, 1962), pp. 35-52; A. R.

he believes, in Lev. 26, which contains several curses like those in Amos 4:6-11, particularly the triple curse of hunger, sword, and pestilence (Lev. 26:25-26, cf. Amos 4:6, 10). This triad became fixed liturgically and was simply taken over intact into prophetic preaching (e.g., Jer. 14:12; 21:7; Ezek. 6:11; 12:16). In his view, Amos converted the old curse formulas from future threats to past realizations in order to proclaim the people's incorrigibility and to introduce a new and unprecedented threat, namely the direct appearance of God as destroyer (4:12).

Reventlow is correct about the remarkable affinity between the contents of Amos 4:6 ff. and the curses and blessings of Lev. 26; however, he has understated its extent. He has looked chiefly for verbatim agreements, but there are others also. First, the entire group of blessings in Lev. 26:3-13 is parallel antithetically to the curses in Amos. There, there is *"rain at the right time"* (Lev. 26:4, Jerusalem); here there is "(withholding of) rain *just three months before the harvest"* (Amos 4:7). There, the thriving of fruit trees and vines (26:4-5); here, the wasting of garden and vineyard, fig tree, and olive (4:9). There, abundance of bread throughout the land (26:5); here, shortage of bread everywhere (4:6). There, peace without fear, security from the sword of the enemy, military prowess, and the fruitfulness of the people (26:6-9); here, destruction of cities, pestilence, and the slaying of the young with the sword (4:10-11). Secondly, both Amos 4:6-11 and the two lists in Lev. 26 (the blessings, 26:4-13, and the curses 26:14-43) are divided into groups marked by formalized repetitions. Note especially the recurring statement in Leviticus, "If, in spite of this you do not listen" (26:18, 23, 27), which is directly comparable to the refrain in Amos, "And yet you did not return to me"

Johnson, *Sacral Kingship in Ancient Israel* (Cardiff, 1955); and H.-J. Kraus, *Worship in Israel* (Oxford, 1966), pp. 60, 108, 141-45.

(4:6, 8, 10, 11). All three lists are cast in the form of divine address, something that is by no means characteristic of all curse formulas in the Old Testament. The more primitive style is to use passive participles (e.g., "blessed," and "cursed," as in Deut. 27:15-26; 28:3-6, 16-19). Nor do all the old lists of curses have the subgroupings seen in Amos 4 and Lev. 26 (contrast Deut. 28). Thirdly, the climax of Lev. 26, like that of Amos 4, is the assurance of God's *turning toward* his people. In Lev. 26:9-12 it is to bless; in Amos 4:12 it is to punish. Perhaps the most significant parallel between the two texts is that in both, the calamities brought by God are interpreted in part as means of educational discipline.[53] Since Lev. 26:41-46 shows clearly that the text in its present form is postexilic, that is, at least two hundred years later than Amos' oracles, it cannot be used to demonstrate a pre-Amosean ritual pattern. Rather, it would appear to illustrate the adaptation for use in the congregations of later Judaism of a hortatory style developed by the pre-exilic prophets. Formalized curses were used in various ritual situations in the ancient Near East, including Israel. The prophets adapted some of these to their oracular purpose. And their oracles in turn influenced Jewish preaching in a later age.

There are other interesting parallels to Amos 4:6-13 in the Old Testament. Several of these are more extensive even than those mentioned so far. They are to be found in I Kings 8 and Pss. 78, 81, and 106. In Solomon's prayer for the dedication of the Jerusalem temple (I Kings 8), which is part of the didactic framework of the books of Kings, there is a list of afflictions which were to have come upon the Israelite kingdom because of its godlessness. The list sounds familiar to us after studying Amos 4—(a) defeat by an

---

[53] This feature of Lev. 26 is brought out clearly in the Jerusalem Bible: "And if, in spite of this, you do not listen to me, I will discipline you again." (26:18, 23, 27).

enemy; (b) drought; (c) famine, pestilence, blight and mildew, locust and caterpillar, siege, plague and sickness (I Kings 8:33-40). In this recital the list is divided into three groups, in comparison to four in Lev. 26:3-13 and 26:16 ff. and five in Amos 4:6-11. Each part of the prayer contains a petition for forgiveness of the people on condition of their repentance. The list of calamities here is virtually identical to the one in Amos except for the lengthy section on the exile in I Kings 8. The calamities are grouped for rhetorical effect. The motif of repentance dominates both pericopes (positively in one, negatively in the other). This comparison suggests that the authors of Kings imitated the prophetic style exemplified by Amos 4. Whether this style was developed in the liturgies of the pre-exilic cult is a question that cannot be answered merely by comparing these two texts.

Pss. 78 and 106 rehearse the history of Israel from the time of the fathers, through the period of the judges, up to (Ps. 78) the Davidic epoch. The history is interpreted as a series of divine leadings and Israelite transgressions. In the midst of Israel's faithlessness, ingratitude, and hypocrisy, God chastened them with one affliction after another. These had no enduring effect. Ps. 78 closes by celebrating God's rejection of the north Israelite kingdom and his choice of Judah and David as bearers of the sacred heritage. Other psalms also rehearse the salient events in Israel's history (e.g., Pss. 44 and 105). But what is distinctive about Pss. 78 and 106 is their interpretation of this history as a series of providential disciplines. These were at once punishments for previous iniquity and occasions for repentance, although the occasions were seldom seized. The parallel to Amos 4:6-11 is clear. However, the relation is one of content more than form; and even in content there are sharp differences. The calamities in Amos 4:6-11 are not explained as punishments for prior transgressions although they presuppose a general state of religious or moral apostasy (i.e., the need to "return"). Moreover, the two psalms describe hardships inflicted upon Israel primarily during the period before their settlement in Palestine; whereas Amos 4 is addressed to farmers and townsmen.

The events recalled in these psalms are recognizable episodes of Israel's history as it is described in the narrative portions of the Old Testament. Those related in Amos 4 are not recognizable as singular happenings but are typical calamities that might have befallen a Palestinian people at any time. Reventlow is correct, therefore, to call the recitation abstract and cultic. However, by being typical, a declaration of this sort is not thereby cut off from the actuality of history. On the contrary, it is precisely by being typical that a ritual utterance may call to mind the actual experiences of various hearers. If it describes events that are altogether singular, it is irrelevant to the remembered experience of most persons. Thus it is their very generality that makes them perennially relevant. Amos' recital of typical calamities is comparable to the use of stereotyped expressions in the psalms. The terms of his catalog were probably customary and were perhaps familiar to his audience from national rituals. However, they would not therefore have been "merely cultic" actualities.[54] A curse or blessing may be merely cultic until such time as it is fulfilled. But how could the realized events which Amos recalled have been merely cultic? Was the coming disaster (Amos 4:12) also a purely cultic event? This objection has equal force whether the tense of the oracle is past or present, for a grammatical present in this case ("I give you . . . yet you do not return") is effectively a past tense.

Lastly, we may compare Amos 4:6-13 to Ps. 81. The psalm begins with a multiple injunction to praise God with voices

---

[54] Reventlow, *op. cit.*, p. 89.

and musical instruments, and to "blow the trumpet at the new moon,/at the full moon, on our feast day" (81:3, RSV). The allusion seems to be to the Feast of Tabernacles, which began at the full moon following the New Year, which in turn was marked by the new moon of the seventh month, when a trumpet was blown (Lev. 23:23-24, 34-36; cf. Num. 29:1 ff.). This sequence follows the postexilic liturgical calendar rather than the older form, which had no celebration of the New Year separately from the Feast of Tabernacles (Exod. 34:22-23; Deut. 16:1-16). It is possible that Ps. 81 preserves some of the stuff of the older ritual of the Feast of Tabernacles, but it is postexilic in its present form.[55] The psalm continues with an oracle, apparently delivered in the sanctuary (81:5b-16). The prophetic voice recalls the people's exodus from Egypt (6-7a), their testing at Meribah (7b), and their disobedience to Yahweh (8, 11, 13). It contains a divine self-asseveration identifying "Yahweh your God" (10). This feature resembles the doxological poem on the name and power of Yahweh in Amos 4:13, although it comes in the middle of the psalm and not at the end. The reiteration of Israel's refusal to listen, which is explicit in verse 11 and implicit in verses 8 and 13, also recalls the litany in Amos 4:6-13 with its fivefold refrain. In Amos 4 there are several "tests" of the people. In the psalm only one is described (vs. 7b), although another is alluded to (vss. 12 ff.). Ps. 81:14-15 offers Israel, now in exile, the promise of a reversal of fortunes with respect to their conquerors as the reward for fidelity to God's "ways." This is not the ethic of Amos 4.[56] Nevertheless, the formal parallels between the two texts are interesting. They show again that there

[55] See, Gunkel, *op. cit.*, pp. 358 ff., Kraus, *Psalmen*, II, 563-64, and Weiser, *op. cit.*, p. 553.

[56] It is, however, the ethic of Amos 9:12, a verse whose origin is uncertain. See the discussion above, pp. 87-88.

was a certain consistency in the pattern of prophetic and liturgical utterance developed in ancient Israel.

The opening part of Ps. 81 is a postexilic poetic rubric for the liturgy of the Feast of Tabernacles. The lines immediately preceding Amos 4:6-13 treat the ritual practices of Israel in the eighth century. Since the latter passage (4:4-5) mocks these practices, it differs radically from Ps. 81:1-5 in content. Yet the themes of the two are similar so we may say that the affinities between Amos 4 and Ps. 81 extend throughout the entire passage Amos 4:4-13. Furthermore, the reference to Bethel and Gilgal in Amos 4:4 may link the passage to Ps. 81. Bethel was the seat of the national sanctuary of the northern kingdom and therefore the principal site for celebrating the three annual pilgrimage festivals, of which tabernacles was the most important. Gilgal was also an important sacred site, which had strong associations with the ark of Yahweh and the Israelite tribal confederacy (Josh. 4:1-9; 19-20; 5:9-10; 9:6, 15; I Sam. 11:15; 13:14-15). It continued in prominence throughout the age of the monarchy (Hos. 4:15; 9:15; 12:11; Mic. 6:5) and was very likely another place for celebrating the annual feasts, especially for the tribe of Benjamin. The mockery in Amos 4:4-5 is probably not restricted to the pilgrimage festivals, but the excesses it derides would have been especially evident at these feasts. The verbs "go" and "bring" in verse 4 imply that the oracle was addressed to pilgrims to Bethel and Gilgal rather than to local adherents of the cult in these places. It has yet to be established that the rituals of cursing, to which Amos 4:6-12 is parallel, were peculiar to the autumn festival. However, the affinities of this text to Ps. 81, which contains most of the formal elements of Amos 4:4-13, suggest the possibility that such litanies were employed at the major national festivals. One further point of possible association between Amos

4:4-13 and the pilgrimage festivals is the phrase *lishlosheth yamîm* (4:4), which may be translated "on the third day." [57] The phrase is found in Exod. 19:15 in the Sinai pericope. The ritual of the third day was a feature of the traditions surrounding the Sinai covenant. It is alluded to again in Hos. 6:1-3, which depicts a pilgrimage ritual, and in other texts influenced by the pilgrimage traditions (Exod. 3:18; 5:3; 8:27; Josh. 9:16-17; II Sam. 20:4; Ezra 10:8-9).[58]

The relation of Amos 4 to Ps. 81 is not mentioned in Brueggemann's study of the background of Amos 4.[59] His thesis is that there is an organic unity in Amos 4:4-13 derived from the liturgical pattern upon which the passage was based. However, he has not shown that *the pattern* in 4:4-13 is exhibited in other Old Testament texts. Yet such parallels would do more to prove the hypothesis than the demonstration of fragmentary affinities. And it is just such a parallel that Ps. 81 appears to provide. This comparative survey has covered numerous points of contact between Amos 4:6-11 (and to a lesser extent 4:4, 5, 13) and certain texts that may be called liturgical in a broad sense. In its present form Amos 4 is older than most of the other materials studied here; therefore, they may not be claimed to illustrate the ritual tradition upon which Amos drew. Instead they illustrate the way in which the Israelite religious community employed this kind of litany of divine judgment in its liturgical life at various times.

AMOS' CRITIQUE OF THE ISRAELITE CULT

The purpose of the ensuing discussion is to evaluate the significance of Amos' polemic against Israel's cult for the

---

[57] Cf. e.g., Jerusalem, Driver, Weiser, and Amsler.
[58] See Ward, *Hosea*, pp. 118-20.
[59] *Loc. cit.*

interpretation of his collected oracles in the light of the evidence for his own indebtedness to ritual forms. The moral consequences of private acts of worship are infinitely various, and they are largely hidden to the observer's eye. Some of the ramifications of personal piety remain unknown even to the worshiper himself; therefore, the critic of an individual's religion presumes to have more knowledge than he has, especially when he judges the piety of others. The critic of public ritual is on safer ground. The motivation and intention of communal worship are relatively perceptible to the eye of a discerning observer. In particular, he may judge any discrepancy between precept and performance. The classical prophets were critics primarily of public worship. As such they are not liable directly to the later biblical censure of those who judge (e.g., Matt. 7:1-5).[60] Still, the prophets' denunciation of Israel's worship may leave the thoughtful reader uncomfortable and even a bit skeptical of their reliability as observers, for their critique is immoderate and relentless.

Our evaluation of the oracles against the cult is complicated by our relative ignorance of the verbal content of Israelite rituals in the pre-exilic period. We know too little of what was professed in them to judge their moral value or the fairness of the prophets' attack. In recent years the cult has been credited with the formation and transmission of many of the Old Testament writings, or the traditions lying behind them, and as a result the hypothetical rituals constructed by historians of worship have become increasingly rich in verbal content. They differ markedly in this respect from what is explicitly prescribed in the ritual laws of the Pentateuch. A reader perusing the biblical regulations for daily, monthly,

[60] Note the difference between the warning against judging others as individual persons in Matt. 7:1-5 and the actual judgment of communal customs in Matt. 6:7-9.

and annual rites, uninstructed by form criticism, would imagine them to have been almost devoid of moral precept or of a spoken liturgy of any kind. This inference would surely be incorrect, for the results of form criticism are not purely subjective. Nevertheless, form criticism does not provide answers to all the questions resulting from the silence of the biblical prescriptions for worship. Do the extant writings, insofar as they reflect liturgical practice, contain only the best that the Israelite cultus produced, or do they reflect the typical liturgies of the national sanctuaries? Do they provide evidence of worship in Israel as well as Judah? In the provincial temples as well as the central ones? For which periods are they useful sources? To what extent do they mirror the piety of the general population as well as that of special groups of "traditioners"? The task of interpretation is further complicated by our relative ignorance of the prophets' involvement in the cult. How thoroughly did they know and understand the worship they decried? Were their oracles in some sense products of the cult, and may they therefore be taken as the self-criticism of the religious establishment? An adequate evaluation of Israel's worship depends upon the answers to these questions, none of which can be supplied fully. The evidence at our disposal permits great latitude in interpretation. It is especially ambiguous in the case of Amos and the eighth-century cultus.

Several types of reference to cultic acts must be considered in judging Amos' attitude toward contemporary worship. There are some that imply respect by the prophet himself for a ritual law or custom. Another group consists of predictions of the ruin of Israelite sanctuaries without any moral criticism. A third group contains explicit denunciations of the rites conducted at the sanctuaries. However, it is not always clear even in these last cases why the prophet considered the rituals evil.

In the first group of texts Amos criticizes acts involving the breach of ritual laws or customs. Therefore, one may ask whether his criticism implies a positive acceptance of the laws which have been violated. In his oracle against the Moabites he condemns their desecration of the corpse of an Edomite king (2:1). The main burden of this charge is moral, for the act violated the rights and sensibilities of the Edomites. Amos' condemnation does not necessarily imply approval of the burial law broken by this act. However, it seems likely that in this, as in the other oracles against the foreign nations (1:3-15), the prophet regarded the act itself, not merely its secondary consequences, as evil. Amos 2:12 is a similar text. It reproaches Israelites for forcing Nazirites to break their vow of abstinence from drinking wine. One need not be a Nazirite to condemn the persecution of Nazirites. However, in the accompanying line (2:11) the Nazirite vocation is represented as a gift of God along with the vocation of the prophet. A third text of this sort is 8:5. Here the prophet deplores the impatience over sabbath restrictions of those who are eager to do business every day of the week. By itself this comment seems to imply approval of the sabbath regulation. However, the oracle goes on to condemn the profiteering of these people so it is not clear whether Amos is denouncing their attitude toward the sabbath or merely their greed and dishonesty.

The last text in this group is at once the most important and the most difficult to assess. It is 2:7b-8.

> A man and his father go to the maiden,
> to profane my holy name.
> And they stretch out upon pledged garments
> beside every altar,
> And drink wine taken in fines
> in the house of their God.

Were these acts violations of cultic sanctity, and did the

prophet himself respect this sanctity? The crimes in this accusation are usually interpreted by commentators as moral and not cultic, as violations of personal rights guaranteed by covenantal law. The first law prohibited sexual intercourse by father and son with the same woman.[61] The second allowed a man who had pawned his only coat to use it during the night.[62] The third was presumably a limitation on the size of fines if indeed the allusion is to a breach of law and not to the callousness or greed of the judges.[63] The second and third crimes were perpetrated in the sanctuary, according to Amos, but this setting is usually regarded as incidental to the act itself. The accused may have been cultic officials. The first crime may have involved sacred prostitution, though this interpretation no longer represents the consensus of scholars as it once did.[64] I do not wish to challenge the thesis that Amos was concerned here with violations of human rights. However, I believe there is a larger cultic factor in the indictment than is generally acknowledged.

The ritual interpretation of 2:7b has been rejected recently by several scholars on the ground that "the maiden" cannot be shown to mean a sacred prostitute.[65] However, the real issue is the meaning of the phrase "to profane my holy name." This usually means in the Old Testament to profane Yahweh's sanctuary, the place where his name has been "made to dwell" (Lev. 18:21; 19:12; 20:3; 21:6; 22:2; Jer. 34:16; Ezek.

---

[61] Cf. Lev. 20:11 and Exod. 21:7-11. The first prohibits intercourse with one's father's wife, and the second defines the marital rights of girls sold as slaves. Neither is exactly parallel to Amos 2:7b so the latter seems to represent the extension of a moral principle contained in one of the ancient laws.

[62] Cf. Exod. 22:26-27 and Deut. 24:12-13.

[63] We might compare Lev. 10:8-9 (and parallels), which prohibits the drinking of intoxicants by priests.

[64] See, e.g., Amsler.

[65] See M. A. Beek, "The Religious Background of Amos II. 6-8," Oudt. St., V (1948), 132-41, and Robert Bach, "Gottesrecht und weltliches Recht in der Verkündigung des Propheten Amos," Festschrift für Gunther Dehn, pp. 30-31 (with additional references).

20:39; and Mal. 1:12).[66] It may be used to cover both ritual and moral profanation (Lev. 22:32 and Ezek. 36:20-23) but always includes the former. In the present passage the phrase is parallel poetically to "beside every altar" and "in the house of their God." Thus the general meaning of the phrase and its context here make it highly probable that Amos was referring to a desecration of the sanctuary of Yahweh.[67] The inference commonly drawn from the reference to "the house of *their* God" is that Amos repudiated this sanctuary. It was not the house of *his* God. Probably not. But it was supposed to be; and what occurred there might therefore be described as a profanation of Yahweh's name. Therefore it seems virtually certain to me that Amos regarded these three acts as simultaneously abuses against persons and profanations of the cult. That he should denounce the behavior as a profanation of Yahweh's name implies a profound respect for the original intention of the cult, namely to sanctify the name of Yahweh, even though it involves a total repudiation of the contemporary establishment.

There are three announcements of the impending doom of the Israelite cultus in the book of Amos that contain no explicit explanation of the cause of the punishment. They are 3:13-15; 5:4-6; and 9:1 ff. These clearly imply condemnation of the cult but do not help us to understand the concrete basis of it. However, two of Amos' oracles are more explicit. In 4:4-5 he mocks the Israelites' delight in abundant sacrifices and thus contrasts the fullness of their ritual turnings to Yahweh with their failure to turn to him truly (4:6-

[66] On the identification of the name with the sanctuary, see Exod. 20:24; Deut. 12:5, 11; Josh. 9:9; Ps. 83:17; and Isa. 60:9.

[67] M. Dahood interprets 2:8a as a reference to garments pledged to a prostitute, comparing the text to a second-century graffito in the necropolis of Marissa and to several biblical passages (Gen. 38:15-19; Prov. 23:27-28; and 27:13). See, "To Pawn One's Cloak," *Biblica*, XLII (1961), 359-66.

11). In the context of the book as a whole this failure must be interpreted as social injustice and moral indifference. Amos' clearest denunciation of the Israelite cult is 5:21-27.

> 21 I hate, I despise your (pilgrimage) feasts,
>   and take no satisfaction in your assemblies.
> 22 Though you send up burnt offerings to me,
>   and grain offerings, I do not accept them,
>   and pay no heed to gifts of fattened beasts.
> 23 Take your noisy songs away from me;
>   I will not listen to your music.
> 24 But let justice flow down like water,
>   and righteousness like a perennial stream.
> 25 Did you bring me flesh and grain offerings
>   during forty years in the wilderness, O House of Israel?
> 26 You will carry away Sakkuth your king-god,
>   and Kaiwan your star-image,
>   these gods you have made for yourselves,
> 27 When I lead you into exile beyond Damascus,
>   declares Yahweh, whose name is God of hosts.

This oracle is unambiguous. God desires Israel's righteousness but not her ritual offerings. Still we may ask whether the oracle expresses a rejection of the cult in principle. Amos' oracles were addressed primarily to the privileged and powerful in Israel, who exploited the lower classes and lavished their substance on their temples, their palaces (3:15), and themselves (6:4-6). *Their* worship was therefore a profanation. Would it have been if it had been accompanied by the quest for social justice? Verse 25 suggests that Amos considered sacrifices to Yahweh to be superfluous, whether or not the allusion to the wilderness era in this verse is historically accurate. Verses 26-27 are difficult to interpret, and their connection to the rest of the passage is uncertain.[68]

[68] See H. Junker, "Amos und die 'opferlose Mosezeit.' Ein Beitrag zur Erklärung von Am 5, 25-26," *Theologie und Glaube,* XXVII (1935), 686-95;

The reference to cultic images is unique in the book.[69] Idolatry in the narrow sense was not one of the main features of Amos' indictment of the contemporary cult. Verse 26 might be an allusion to an ancient idolatry, like that of the golden calf (Exod. 32), or it might be a prediction of the future loss of valued images. "Sakkuth" and "Kaiwan" may be explanatory glosses, or the whole verse may be a gloss. So may verse 27. Verse 25 is the least uncertain part of 5:25-27. Most scholars agree that it comes from Amos and is a rhetorical question demanding a negative answer. As such it is a rejection in principle of Israel's sacrificial system though it does not constitute a rejection in principle of all forms of public worship. Because of the textual uncertainty of the passage no further conclusions are warranted.

Worship at the Palestinian sanctuaries during the period of the Israelite monarchy was an amalgam of customs derived from ancient tribal religion, the cults of local Canaanite deities, and the covenantal traditions of the Israelite confederacy. The basic system of daily and monthly sacrifices, which were supported out of temple revenues and royal subsidies, and of occasional private sacrifices (vows, thanksgivings, etc.), was not distinctively Yahwistic. It had probably been practiced in Palestine immemorially. Everything cultic that Amos repudiated is attributable to this sacrificial system. On the other hand, Amos' oracles are partly dependent, in form, language, and theological conception, on traditions that appear to have been celebrated in Israel's worship. All these are attributable to ancient tribal usage (blessings and curses, oracles against foreign nations, etc.) as it was transmitted and modified by the covenant community.

E. Würthwein, "Amos 5:21-27," *TLZ*, LXXII (1947), 143-52; and W. H. Schmidt, *ZAW*, LXXVII (1965), 188-91.

[69] Jerusalem interprets the "lies" in Amos 2:4 as "false gods," but this is exegesis, not translation.

The doxological fragments probably reflect the influence of Canaanite natural theology as it was transformed by the Israelite belief in the sole sovereignty of Yahweh. This influence might have been exerted at any time after the formation of the confederacy. However, the chief impetus to the use of hymns of this sort in Israel's worship was probably given by the establishment of the temple in Jerusalem by David and Solomon. We are not sure when, where, how, and by whom the covenantal traditions were celebrated in public worship. Perhaps it was at one or more of the annual pilgrimage festivals, at one or more of the places (like Gilgal) which were centrally located and hallowed by historical association or ancient usage. Perhaps the means was a dramatic reenactment of covenant-making. This is probably the aspect of Israel's worship to which Amos was most indebted and which he affirmed most fully.

Historically the most important implication of Amos' dependence upon traditional liturgical forms is that the system of public worship in ancient Israel contained within itself, if not official cultic prophets who were like Amos, then at least the resources and occasions that gave rise to proclamations like his. It was not only the people of Israel that had the courage and insight to be self-critical through the medium of her own prophetic voices, but it was also her ritual establishment. It would be unfair to credit the establishment—which, after all, was composed of individuals—with the individual literary and ethical achievement of Amos. But it would be equally unfair to discredit it by overlooking its creative influence upon the great canonical prophets, of whose very oracles the religious establishment subsequently made continuous use, transmitting them through the centuries with their judgmental words intact.

ISAIAH

chapter 4

Isaiah's Commission as Servant of the Word

Isaiah's first prophetic word was:

> "Woe is me! I am lost!
> For I am a man of unclean lips,
> And I dwell among a people of unclean lips,
> For my eyes have seen the King, Yahweh of hosts!"
> (6:5)

Chronologically this was not the first word spoken to his Judean audience. That word was characterized by the commission, "Go, and say to this people . . ." (6:9), and it may be represented by one of the oracles preserved in the canonical collection. However, his cry of woe (6:5) expressed his self-understanding as a prophet and was therefore the foundation of his peraching. It was theologically his first word.

As spokesmen for God all prophets were by definition servants of the word. However, in Isaiah's thought the importance of the prophetic word was not defined merely by the special vocation of the prophet, at least as this vocation was conventionally conceived. For Isaiah, all service of God was service of the word, not only for the prophet but for the entire Israelite community. This conviction undergirded his critique of contemporary Israelite worship and dictated his prophecy concerning the future of worship among the people of God. It was also implicit in his ethical judgments. A defense of these assertions cannot be compressed into a single paragraph but will engage our attention again and again as we try to interpret Isaiah's oracles.

Chapter 6 is the report of a commission to prophesy. It has been almost universally regarded as a report of Isaiah's inaugural vision. Among the few scholars who have demurred from this judgment A. C. Welch has argued skillfully that the experience related here was a turning point in the middle of Isaiah's prophetic career. Beforehand he had prophesied the unrelieved destruction of Judah as God's punishment of Israel's moral and religious apostasy, but afterward he was ruled by the conviction that God's final purpose for Judah, as for himself, was to forgive and renew. Therefore he altered his message in the second half of his career and preached about the remnant and the messianic king.[1] In Welch's opinion, the oracles in Isaiah 1–5 come largely from the period prior to this experience of forgiveness and recommission, and chapter 6 has been placed deliberately where it is now, rather than at the beginning of the book, by one who knew the significance of the event it described.

[1] *Kings and Prophets of Israel* (London, 1952), pp. 210 ff.

Welch's interpretation of Isaiah's preaching is one of the better general treatments published in the twentieth century. One of its virtues is the emphasis it places upon the relation of the prophet's own experience of forgiveness (6:1-7) to the message he declared (6:9-13 and various oracles). However, Welch's theory of the chronology of Isaiah's recorded oracles is conjectural. The content of the oracles in chapters 1–5 is too similar to that of other oracles in the book to be separated from the rest either chronologically or theologically. Nor is there any evidence in chapters 1–5 themselves that they originated before the year of King Uzziah's death, when the experience of chapter 6 occurred (6:1). On the other hand, nothing in chapter 6 dictates the conclusion that the vision was inaugural, so we should beware lest too much weight be placed exegetically upon the common inference that it was. Among the biblical accounts of prophetic visions the one with the closest affinity to Isa. 6 is I Kings 22:19-23. But the vision of Micaiah that it records was obviously not inaugural. Micaiah was already a well-known prophet when he saw the vision (22:8).

The process of recording, transmitting, and supplementing Isaiah's oracles is not described in the Bible. Isaiah's decision to preserve his testimony, or some part of it, is mentioned in Isa. 8:16-18, but this text does not inform us clearly about the means of preservation or the content of the oracles that were actually recorded on this occasion. Nor is there enough internal evidence in the extant oracles of Isaiah from which to reconstruct the process, although numerous hypothetical reconstructions have been proposed.[2] The structure

---

[2] See, for example, S. Mowinckel, "Die Komposition des Jesajabuches Kap. 1-39," *Acta Orientalia*, XI (1932), 267-92; G. Fohrer, "The Origin, Composition, and Tradition of Isaiah I–XXXIX," *Annual of the Leeds University Oriental Society*, III (1961/62), 3-38; D. Jones, "The Tradition of the Oracles of Isaiah of Jerusalem," *ZAW*, LXVII (1955), 226-46; R. H. Kennett, *The Composition of the Book of Isaiah* (London, 1910); L. H. Liebreich, "The Compilation of

of the book is complex, and few of its strata may be dated with probability. Its richness and diversity suggest that there must have been a vigorous "school of Isaiah" in Judah during the seventh and sixth centuries B.C. while the grouping of oracles and the alternation of threatening and promising sections imply that the book was used liturgically in the later Jewish community. The latest portions of the book (notably 40–66) are exilic (587-539 B.C.) and postexilic. However, they have strong theological affinities with the oracles of Isaiah so there was probably a continuous tradition underlying the book as a whole. This tradition was dynamic. No other book in the prophetic canon gives greater evidence of having been *used* by the religious community of Israel. The original corpus of Isaiah's oracles was augmented, edited, and rearranged in many stages through many generations. We may be quite sure that the chief contributions were made by Isaiah in the eighth century B.C. and the anonymous "Isaiah of the Exile" in the sixth century B.C. However, we are not certain of the exact limits of either contribution. By a critical consensus chapters 1–11 and 28–32 are attributed to Isaiah and 40–55 to Second Isaiah. But scholars disagree about the relation of Isaiah's primary oracles to the rest of the material in 1–39, and 40–55 to 56–66. Many of the critical conclusions reached in the past have been rejected or modified by scholars of the present generation. For example, Isa. 24–27, the so-called Isaiah Apocalypse, was once universally regarded by critical scholars as very late and quite unrelated to the work of Isaiah. However, it has recently been argued that these chapters contain a core of material from Isaiah himself.[3]

---

the Book of Isaiah," *JQR*, XLVI (1955/56), 259-77, and XLVII (1956/57), 114-38; and R. B. Y. Scott, "The Literary Structure of Isaiah's Oracles," *Studies in Old Testament Prophecy*, H. H. Rowley, ed. (Edinburgh, 1950), pp. 175-86.

[3] See John Mauchline, *Isaiah 1–39* (Torch Bible Commentaries; London, 1962), pp. 23-24 and 183 ff.

It is likely that some of the questions concerning the composition of the book and its historical background will never be answered. At least in the foreseeable future scholars will continue to disagree over the chronology of the oracles in 1–11 and 28–32 and over the authorship of the messianic oracles (9:1-7 and 11:1-9), to name only two of the questions most important for the ensuing discussion. Meanwhile the interpreter and the expository preacher will have to be content to expound the meaning and implications of the more obvious strata of the tradition in their present form and qualify every assertion about the prior history of the strata as tentative and partly subjective.

Isa. 6 is a prose narrative set beside a group of oracles which have a prose framework (7–8). All these oracles relate to the crisis under King Ahaz caused by the Syro-Ephraimite threat of 735 B.C. The prose style of the three chapters distinguishes them from the rest of First Isaiah, which is composed almost entirely of poetic oracles. Chapter 6 is broader in scope than 7–8; indeed its implications extend to the whole of Isaiah's message. Further, the date of the vision, in the year of Uzziah's death (6:1), separates it chronologically from the events of 7–8 by at least six years.[4] Nevertheless, the three chapters now constitute a single stratum of the book of Isaiah. It is a loose-jointed biographical (or autobiographical) narrative [5] coming from the earliest known period of Isaiah's

[4] Uzziah's death has been dated by Begrich (followed by Noth, *The History of Israel* [New York, 1960], p. 253) in 747/46 B.C., by Albright and others in 742 B.C. (see, for example, John Bright, *A History of Israel* [Philadelphia, 1959], Chronological Chart V), and by de Vries ("Chronology of the OT," *The Interpreter's Dictionary of the Bible* [Nashville, 1962]) and the editors of the Jerusalem Bible (chronological table, p. 457) in 740 B.C. This range covers the views of most scholars. A few, however, have dated it in 735/34 B.C., e.g., A. Jepsen (*Die Quellen des Königsbuches* [2nd ed.; Halle, 1956], pp. 41 ff.). If the last date were correct, the vision in chap. 6 would probably not have been Isaiah's initial call to prophecy, for already in 734 B.C. (see 7:3) he had a child to whom he had given a prophetic name, and he was expecting another (8:3).

[5] Chaps. 6 and 8 are in the first person and chap. 7 in the third.

career. It contains several of the salient themes of his collected oracles. Chapter 6 has often been regarded as the exemplar of Isaiah's message. It is probably the most significant chapter in First Isaiah.

Isaiah's sense of prophetic vocation reached a climax in an overpowering vision of God. He took from the experience a strange and perplexing commission as God's prophet to Judah. We are given no information whatever about the personal antecedents of this vision. All that we know about Isaiah's life, apart from his oracles, is the name of his father (Amoz, 1:1), and speculation about his life is idle.[6] We have his oracles and the narrative about his vision. There is no way of knowing what led to the vision or what its psychological concomitants may have been other than the visual content which was actually recorded. The narrative conveys information about Isaiah's self-understanding as a man before God and as a prophet commissioned by God. We may analyze it theologically in these terms, but we may not legitimately put it to any other biographical use.

Isaiah 6

I

1 In the year that King Uzziah died I saw the Lord sitting upon a throne, high and exalted, with his train filling the
2 sanctuary. Seraphim stood above him, each with six wings: two for covering his face, two for covering his body, and

[6] E.g., the theory that he must have been of noble birth because he possessed a cultivated mastery of language (in an age of general illiteracy) and enjoyed access to the Jerusalem court. However, his mastery of language was of the same order, for example, as Amos', Hosea's, and Jeremiah's. There is no evidence that he had easier access to the court than other prophets. Inferences drawn from his literary allusions, with respect to his family background, his specific cultural environment, and his secular vocation (if any), are as dubious in Isaiah's case as in that of any perceptive, imaginative person. This kind of inference has been rife in the modern literature on the prophets. At best it is fruitless; at worst misleading.

3 two for flying. One called to another, saying,
  "Holy, holy, holy is Yahweh of hosts.
  The fullness of the whole earth is his glory."
4 The supports of the doorway shook from the sound of
5 his voice, and the building filled with smoke, and I cried,
  "Woe is me! I am lost!
  For I am a man of unclean lips,
  And I dwell among a people of unclean lips,
  For my eyes have seen the King, Yahweh of hosts!"
6 Then one of the seraphim flew toward me carrying a
7 burning coal from the altar with a pair of tongs. He
  touched my mouth with it and declared,
  "Behold, this has touched your lips.
  Your guilt is removed,
  And your sin is taken away."

II

8 Then I heard the voice of the Lord, saying,
  "Whom shall I send?
  Who will go for us?"
  And I said,
  "Here I am. Send me."
9 So he said,
  "Go and tell this people to
  Keep on hearing, but don't understand;
  Keep on seeing, but don't comprehend.
10 Fatten this people's heart,
      and dull their ears,
        and stick shut their eyes,
    Lest they see with their eyes,
      and hear with their ears,
        and understand with their heart,
    And be healed again."
11 So I cried,
    "How long, O Lord?!"
    And he replied,
    "Until cities are desolate, without inhabitants,

149

> And houses, without people,
> And the land is an appealing waste.
> 12   Then shall Yahweh transport the people afar,
> And leave many places deserted in the land.
> 13   Even though a tenth remains,
> It must be burned again,
> Like trees whose stumps remain
> When they are felled.
> The holy seed is her stump."

Isaiah's awareness of the presence of God was expressed in a vision of great simplicity and power. Visualizing this presence as of a mighty king, "high and exalted," he was overcome by a sense of his own finitude. In reporting the event he multiplied metaphors in order to convey his impression of the majesty and power of God. The temple in which the Lord was enthroned was bursting with his presence. His train filled the room. The mighty voice of his attendant shook the foundations. The great sanctuary was filled with smoke. His attendants dared not gaze upon the incandescent splendor of his face but covered their eyes with their wings. Isaiah, beholding the scene with his mortal eyes, was immediately crushed by the dread of inevitable destruction. For no man could look at God and live (Exod. 33:20-23).

All this, of course, was poetic imagery, used to indicate what was essentially subjective and indescribable. But at one point the description passed out of the realm of pure subjectivity, and there the most adequate symbol of the power of God was provided. It was contained in the reverberating acclamation of the seraph, "the fullness of the whole earth is his glory" (6:3). The weight, majesty, honor, and brilliance of God (all this is connoted by the term "glory") could be symbolized adequately only by the totality of the visible world. Indeed, the earth was not a mere symbol of God's glory. It was itself his glory. The world was not holy. Only God was that. But the world was his glory, that is, the visible manifestation of his power. The sense of the seraph's cry is altered slightly when the line is translated in the usual way of the English versions, "the whole earth is full of his glory." The crucial Hebrew word is neither a simple noun nor an adjective, as in these two translations, but an infinitive ("the filling of the whole earth [is] his glory"). It is a noun clause with inverted word order (in Hebrew as in English) to give the proper emphasis.[7] I prefer the first translation above, which equates the world with God's glory. But the traditional translation is acceptable, provided that it is rightly understood. If God's glory fills the whole earth, it is to be found not only here or there, wherever the religious and esthetic sensibilities of particular men happen to dictate. It is everywhere in all creation. The *whole* earth is filled with it. As long as the full significance of this affirmation is recognized, it does not matter greatly whether the distinction between the world and God is thought of in terms of the difference between him and his glory, as in the first translation, or the difference between his glory and the earth, as in the second. In either case the point is clear that God's presence and power are associated intimately with the created order in its totality. The otherness of God in Isaiah's vision was not an otherworldliness. His vision gave him no special access to an otherwise unknown world but expressed his awareness of God's presence in the world of man's usual existence.

This extraordinary consciousness of the presence of the Holy One of Israel, who was acclaimed as the absolutely and uniquely holy one (this is the meaning of the first part of the seraph's cry) in the midst of the ordinary world, is the

[7] See I. Engnell, *The Call of Isaiah* (*Uppsala Universitets Ärsskrift* 1949:4; Uppsala and Leipzig, 1949), p. 36, and the commentary of O. Kaiser, *in loc.*

principal theme of prophetic theology. Its ramifications are many, and its apparent simplicity should not mislead the reader to overlook its difficulty. Like the doctrine of justification by faith, which is its corollary, it is simple to state and almost impossible to appropriate fully and consistently. This affirmation was stated in the famous "Holy, holy, holy is Yahweh of hosts," which was uttered by the seraph, and it was implied in the whole structure of the prophet's vision, for the temple in the vision was a model of the actual Judean temple. The throne corresponded to the ark, and the two seraphim to the two cherubim, in the sanctuary in Jerusalem. The altar and its sacrificial fire were also evident.[8] However, there was nothing distinctively Israelite in this picture. It was duplicated in its essential features in hundreds of temples in the biblical world.[9] It is a mistake therefore to infer from the vision that Isaiah must have been in the temple of Jerusalem when it occurred or that his vision was a reflection of his habitual attendance there. It is even less justifiable to deduce from the vision that he was an official of the Jerusalem temple. The implication of Isaiah's experience was that God's presence might indeed be known in the rituals of the sanctuary, and for his Judean hearers this would have meant the temple of Jerusalem primarily. Nothing in the vision, however, requires this specific setting. Isaiah's model was an ordinary temple just as the world said to be filled with God's glory was the ordinary world. It was any temple. There is no reason to believe that the writer meant to suggest anything more specific than what he described. Every man in

[8] Cf. Exod. 25. On the form of the seraphim, see Karen R. Joines, "Winged Serpents in Isaiah's Inaugural Vision," *JBL*, LXXXVI (1967), 410-15.

[9] Not, of course, the Israelite ark. But Isaiah's term is "seat," which is very general. Seats for the gods, often in the form of royal thrones, were common in ancient Near Eastern temples.

Israel and most men in the ancient world had sufficient knowledge of temples and their rituals to evoke the sort of picture contained in Isaiah's vision. Most of them would not have seen Yahweh in it, but that is another matter.

Isaiah's terror before God was not expressed in terms of his creatureliness and finitude (although these were probably implied) but in terms of the uncleanness of his lips and those of his countrymen (6:5). It was because of his sinfulness, corporate and personal, that he was doomed in the presence of the Holy One. His confession of unclean lips did not restrict his consciousness of guilt to his speech alone, for speech to an ancient Israelite was never mere words. It was the manifestation of his whole being. This was true especially for a prophet. Speech was his life and, in Isaiah's view, the life of his people also. Their life was unclean, and he believed himself to be implicated in their guilt as well as his own. His consciousness of guilt was accompanied immediately by the sense of having been forgiven and made acceptable to God (6:6-7). His lips were burned by the fire from the altar, and thus purified, he was allowed to speak with God. Once again the picture was a simple one. None of the personal antecedents of the event were described, and no exposition of its meaning was given beyond the bare assertion that his sin had been forgiven. Yet for all its simplicity this recollection was of fundamental importance for Isaiah's theology and his proclamation to Israel. His prophetic commission and his existence as a man were anchored in the dual consciousness of his moral inadequacy before God and of God's acceptance and forgiveness of him. This was how he had experienced the holiness of God, and this was therefore the substance of his preaching about God.

The account moves at once to a description of Isaiah's prophetic commission (6:8-13). We may pass over the symbolism of the divine council with its "angelic" servants (i.e., messengers), for although the image is a familiar one in the Old Testament,[10] it has no objective importance in Isaiah's thought. Angelic messengers are to be found in the old narrative sources of the Old Testament, where they are a feature of popular legend.[11] They have no significance in the realistic preaching of the prophets. Even in the psalms they are almost entirely symbolic. The actual world of the writers of the Old Testament, as they described it from their experience, contained no unhuman, personal servants of God. Spiritualism and superstition were incompatible with their faith in God and with their sober perception of the conditions of existence. This dedemonization of the world was virtually unique in the history of culture until modern times. It is one of the qualities of the Old Testament that make it compatible (even more than the New Testament in this respect) with the temper and perspective of modern men.

Isaiah's commission was to harden the hearts of the people of Israel in order to bring about the fall of the nation and thus enable a genuine renewal of their life under God to take place. It was, in short, to effect for the nation the atonement which Isaiah had experienced himself. It was to be achieved at very great cost, but this cost was dictated by the realities of the nation's moral and political situation and not by any dogmatic religious belief. Isaiah had no control over the destiny of the nation. He was an instrument in the hands of God and was called to confound the nation's leaders and to interpret the meaning of her fall in the interest of her eventual renewal.

In the account of the vision the content of Isaiah's preaching is stated somewhat cryptically: "Keep on hearing but don't understand. Keep on seeing but don't comprehend" (6:9). This is nothing more than a paraphrase of the prophet's

[10] Cf. I Kings 22:19-23; Pss. 82; 89:5-8; etc.
[11] E.g., Gen. 16:7-11; Josh. 5:13-15; and Judg. 13.

appraisal of his audience as this is expressed in his oracles of judgment. This statement and the following ones (6:10) may have been influenced by Isaiah's actual experience as a prophet either before the vision occurred or in the interval between its occurrence and the time when the report of it was given its final form. As expressions of personal sentiment they were sarcastic and rather despairing. However, fundamentally they were neither the brooding of a pessimist nor the recollection of a frustrated evangelist. Whatever coloring the narrative may have been given by the writer's knowledge of the people's eventual response to his preaching, nothing in Isaiah's oracles is incompatible with the conclusion that chapter 6 accurately conveys his initial understanding of his mission.

The retrospective interpretation of this commission, that is, the theory that the narrative in its present form reports the result of Isaiah's preaching as viewed from a later point in his career, has been popular among interpreters, partly because of the common conviction that the prophets' mission was to exhort Israel to repent of its sins and be saved from ruinous judgment. This conviction was first promulgated by the sixth-century writers of the books of Kings, the prose portions of Jeremiah, and Ezekiel.[12] However, Amos, Hosea, and Isaiah did not teach it. All three of the great prophets of the eighth century proclaimed from first to last the determinate end of the monarchial state in Israel together with its visible institutions.

One feature of Isaiah's commission is especially perplexing, from any perspective. It is the duty to prevent the people's repentance and consequent healing (6:10). This aim seems diametrically opposed to the prophetic responsibility defined by the sixth-century writers named above. Three interpreta-

---

[12] See, e.g., II Kings 17:13 ff., Jer. 26, and Ezek. 3:16 ff., and also the comments on Amos, above, pp. 43 ff.

tions of it seem possible to me. First of all, Isaiah may have believed this aim to have been God's intention without himself understanding the moral justification for it. The ways of God often defy man's comprehension, and Isaiah was among the first to admit the apparent "strangeness" of God's work (28:21). There was an irreducibly nonrational element in Isaiah's prophecy. This interpretation of Isaiah's statement becomes most plausible if we accept the retrospective view of the origin of the narrative. However, it seems improbable to me. A second possibility to account for this curious statement of the purpose of Isaiah's ministry is to place it within a strictly retributive conception of the judgments of God. In such a view Isaiah's task, at least in part, would have been to give the nation enough rope to hang itself. Its corruption was already far advanced when God called Isaiah to prophesy, but it was not yet sufficient to justify its complete annihilation. Isaiah's preaching would provide the final test, which Israel would fail. Then God might justly demolish the nation. This conception of God's providence is expressed, for example, in Gen. 15:15, and we have previously considered the possibility that it lay behind Amos 2:9-10.[13] To make use of it here one need not define it in rigidly rationalistic terms. Nevertheless, in the context of the whole narrative of chapter 6 it is an inadequate interpretation, and it lacks confirmation in other texts of Isaiah. This understanding of Israel's situation before God might have been one of the factors in Isaiah's prophetic intention, but there was another of equal or greater importance, I believe. Isaiah's intention was to help bring an end to false measures of atonement which were being practiced by the people, both as a judgment against this behavior itself and as an indispensable step toward the achievement of true atonement. The first goal could have been accomplished by the simple fall of the nation and its religious system. It

[13] See above, p. 73.

required no assistance from Isaiah. The second, however, could not have been accomplished without the religious understanding contained in Isaiah's oracles.

Isaiah's first assignment was to "Fatten this people's heart . . . lest they see . . . and be healed again." Israel was familiar with prophets who exhorted them to eschew false gods and repent of their sins, and they had a full and efficient ritual system for dealing with sin and atonement. Their eyes were constantly being opened to their transgressions, and they were accustomed to being healed by sacrificial means. The complex tradition of Judean rites of atonement, which was finally codified in the fifth century B.C. but which derived in many of its features from the earliest days of the monarchy and before, covered both ritual and social offenses. It entailed compensation of loss in civil and criminal cases where this was possible, but it required ritual sacrifice as the means of covering sin in the eyes of God.[14] This sort of practice was not unique in Judah but had its counterpart in the cults of other nations. The healing that Isaiah was to help abolish was this habitual healing. His allusion was not to ritual sin alone, for the conventional Judean religion provided for moral sin as well. The initial goal of God's judgment, of which Isaiah was one instrument, was the frustration of Judah's conventional religion. The disease that Isaiah diagnosed in the body of the nation was incurable by conventional means. A proper cure required the elimination of illusory cures. However, this elimination alone was not enough. The people's sickness was moral so their eventual healing demanded their *understanding* of the futility of their conventional remedy. Besides, the remedy itself was part of their sickness since there was no separation of their ritual obligations under God from their ethical ones. These were fully interdependent.

Thus Isaiah's task was not to preach repentance in the hope

[14] See, for example, Lev. 4:1–6:7.

of atonement and reconciliation. The people would not have done freely what was necessary to bring about true renewal. The indicated cure was too radical. Isaiah's task was rather to be an agent of this radical healing and during the process to bear witness to what was taking place in the hope that it would be morally redemptive and not simply destructive. This interpretation of 6:10 seems to be clearly indicated when the last line is translated "and be healed again." This is the standard meaning of the Hebrew idiom used here.[15] The same idiom occurs once more in this chapter ("it will be burned again," 6:13). The translation "turn and be healed" (RSV, e.g.) is not really wrong since the verb does mean both to turn and to do again, but it gives the wrong connotation in English. The meaning of the line is obscured when it is rendered this way.

There is a direct correlation between the first half of chapter 6 and the second. The prophet's mission was rooted partly in his dual experience of lostness and forgiveness. The key to the relation of his own atonement to that of the people is provided by the motif of burning, which runs through the narrative. Isaiah's guilt was purged symbolically by fire from the visionary altar (6:6). His unclean lips were burned, God's forgiveness was pronounced, and he was accepted into the service of God. The nation to which he was sent was required to submit to a corresponding purification by fire (6:11-13). This was not merely symbolic but the actual destruction of the visible state. Nothing in it would be exempt. Every element would have to pass through the fire, including the tenth that might be left standing after the initial disaster (6:13). Only a burned-over nation would carry within it the possibility of a true renewal of holiness.

Why, if Isaiah had been reconciled to God and forgiven

---

[15] See GK, 120*d*, *g*; Engnell (*op. cit.*, pp. 42-43); Gray; Kaiser; and Eichrodt; among others.

by an act of faith without first having to suffer personal and material desolation, should the people not have been offered a similar opportunity for renewal? The answer lay not in any difference in principle between Isaiah's relationship to God and that of other Israelites. It lay in the difference between the consciousness of one man and the social institutions of a nation. Isaiah's obedience—his vocation—was a product of his faith. As an individual human being it was possible for him to become aware of the true character of his alienation from God and the deep root of his own sinfulness. He could commit himself to God in radical obedience as a result of his awareness of being forgiven and accepted by God. This was impossible for Israel to do as a nation, he believed. Isaiah was not a sociologist or moral philosopher, and he made no analysis in his oracles of the institutional and psychological obstacles to social change. The modern social scientist may show in detail (though not infallibly) that nations are transformed rarely, if ever, without a powerful external stimulus (political, economic, geographical, or climatic). These categories are entirely alien to Old Testament language and thought. However, the realities that underlie them are universal. Isaiah may not have known *why* Israel could not be transformed by a prophet's exhortation and her own act of will. But he was clearly aware that she could not. He called her incapacity hardness of heart, and he realized that the necessary condition of a change of heart was the destruction of her political and religious institutions. His convictions were identical to Hosea's in this respect, and they were fully compatible with Amos', although Amos, unlike the other two prophets, gave little voice to a positive hope for national renewal.

The "holy seed" mentioned at the end of chapter 6 is a much disputed allusion. It is widely regarded as a late scribal gloss. Frequently it has been considered later even than the Greek translation of the Old Testament (approximately the third century B.C.) on the ground that it is missing in that version.[16] However, all but two major Greek manuscripts of Isaiah contain this clause, and the two have perhaps omitted it through a simple scribal error.[17] The variant in the Dead Sea Scroll of Isaiah (IQ Is^A) is a minor one and hardly justifies the emendations that have been proposed by several scholars.[18] In any case, it does not affect the final clause. Another objection to retaining this clause is that it abruptly reverses the direction of thought and thus allegedly betrays the glossator's hand. There is a certain abruptness here, to be sure, but the clause is neither irrelevant to the content nor alien to the style of the rest of the passage. The report of Isaiah's commission is set forth in two parts of almost equal length (vss. 9-10 and vss. 11-13). The first reaches a climax in the final clause "and be healed again." The second also reaches a climax at the very end in a clause of identical length (in Hebrew, three words) : "a holy seed is its stump." Stylistically the two parts, each of which is in the form of a speech of God, are identical. Each is set in poetic parallelism except for the final clause of each, which stands out as the stressed line.

In content the last clause in verse 13 is by no means extraneous. The Lord's second speech is an answer to Isaiah's question "how long?" (vs. 11). How long must the hardening commanded in the first part (vss. 9-10) continue without the people's being healed? The answer is: until every portion

---

[16] See, e.g., Skinner and Scott. Scott deletes all of vs. 13 as an exilic gloss, and Eichrodt cuts out vs. 12 as well. Scott dismisses the effort to preserve vs. 13 as Isaiah's on the ground that it is based on a priori considerations, but his own treatment of vs. 13a, at least, is entirely subjective. Of course if enough of the context of vs. 13b is removed with it, its relevance to the remainder is understandably reduced.

[17] See K. Budde, "Über die Schranken, die Jesajas prophetischer Botschaft zu setzen sind," ZAW, XLI (1923), 166 ff.; Welch, op. cit., p. 206; Engnell, op. cit., pp. 11-15, 47-52; and Kaiser. Engnell's treatment of the textual history of 6:13 is detailed and thorough.

[18] See, e.g., S. Iwry, "Maṣṣēbāh and Bāmāh in IQ Isaiah^A 6:13," JBL, LXXVI (1957), 225-32; and W. F. Albright, "The High Place in Ancient Palestine," Suppl. VT, IV (1957), 254-55.

of the nation has passed through devasting judgment, including the tenth that might be left standing after the initial disaster (vs. 13). Only then may hardening and judgment cease and renewal begin. The whole national tree must fall and its stump be burned. The holy seed—the new sapling—can grow only from the charred stump of the nation. Nothing short of this will suffice. Then the renewal which follows will grow out of humility and chastened obedience. The symbol of the future people of God is a sapling growing from a burned stump. This charred base will be a constant reminder of the cost and condition of reconciliation. Thus the nation will be made truly aware of the nature of its life before the Holy One. Their awareness will correspond to Isaiah's, which was symbolized by his burned lips (6:6-7).[19]

We know too little about the literary history of this chapter to be dogmatic about its original form. It has come to us as a polished interpretation of Isaiah's commission. The framework is prose, and it is studded with sayings in oracular poetry. The whole is balanced in structure and thought. It is a brilliant literary and prophetic achievement. Yet no one knows, or probably will ever know, who wrote it. It may not have been Isaiah himself, though of course it may. In either case it comprises, with the two following chapters, the first stratum of the book of Isaiah. It serves as a touchstone to evaluate other strata, some of which are more problematic than this in structure, significance, and origin. The writer of this chapter and those that supplement it in the oldest sections of the book is the "Isaiah" whose thought is the object of our theological interest. It seems futile to speculate about the prior history of the tradition behind chapter 6, for as it is, it is a deliberate, polished unity and bears no visible marks of revision or growth.

[19] Cf. E. Jenni, "Jesajas Berufung in der neueren Forschung," *TZ*, XV (1959), 337-39.

The prophet's commission issued in a somber word about atonement and renewal. It did not contain a joyful hope. The career that lay before him was terrible in its significance for his contemporaries. He was supposed to witness the collapse of a proud and prosperous nation, which had been founded upon distinguished religious and legal traditions. The final debacle did not occur in his lifetime, and its postponement beyond the time when he expected it made his lot doubly tedious, for it meant that he had to tolerate personal calumny in addition to the torment he experienced in anticipating the nation's destruction. Prophets were human. But Isaiah seems to have made no concession to the human desire for approval and success. He put himself wholly at the disposal of the word of God although doing so required a considerable sacrifice for him and his family. In a sense they were required to pass through the fire to which his oracles testified and to which he ultimately summoned the people of Judah. His obedience demonstrated the quality of his faith in the commanding presence of God in the midst of the world.

Isaiah's designation of God as king (6:5) is the earliest clearly datable example of this usage in the Bible. Scholars once generally thought Isaiah invented the metaphor, and they took it therefore as the key to Isaiah's conception of sin. According to an oft repeated characterization of prophetic teaching, Amos thought of sin primarily as social injustice, Hosea as idolatry, and Isaiah as rebellion against a king. The royal imagery is now widely acknowledged as an ancient feature of worship in the temple of Jerusalem, going back at least to the time of Solomon. The scene in Isaiah's vision is believed correspondingly to have been fashioned out of the symbolism of traditional Judean rituals.[20] Ivan Engnell has treated chapter 6 in detail as an imitation of a purification rite for the Israelite king, in his office as servant of the heavenly

[20] See, e.g., Mowinckel, *The Psalms in Israel's Worship*, II, 147.

monarch, and he has compared it to Mesopotamian texts.[21] W. Schmidt has worked along similar lines but has traced the affinities of the passage to the picture of the Canaanite god El that is found in the Ugaritic mythological texts.[22] His conclusion is that the imagery and much of the language of Isaiah's vision were the result of Judean adaptation of pre-Israelite, Canaanite ideas, which were adopted by the Davidic priesthood in Jerusalem from the pre-Davidic, Jebusite worship of El Elyon.

There were royal features in ritual and mythology all over the ancient world, and sacrifice was of course ubiquitous. It is not difficult therefore to find similarities between Isa. 6 and religious texts from elsewhere. Further, it is probable that the kingship of Yahweh was celebrated in Jerusalem's royal temple from the time of the United Monarchy in association with the rites of the monarchial office itself. The royal psalms (2, 18, 20, 21, 45, 89, 101, 110, 132, 144:1-10) and the psalms of Yahweh's enthronement (47, 93, 95-99) are our primary sources of knowledge of these rites. There is general agreement among scholars today that the royal psalms were pre-exilic. There is no consensus about the date of the enthronement psalms, although a great many scholars assign them also to the period of the monarchy. The conviction that there was a well-established royal theology which was embodied in ritual in Judah in Isaiah's time is at least a serviceable hypothesis which helps to clarify the history of the kingship in Israel, particularly the southern kingdom, during the tenth to sixth centuries B.C. However, the hypothesis should not mislead us into a static conception of Israelite religion. The books of Samuel, Kings, and the pre-exilic prophets indicate that there was considerable variety in the cultic practices of the two Israelite kingdoms and in the estimates of the

[21] *The Call of Isaiah.*
[22] "Jerusalemer El-Traditionen bei Jesaja," ZRG, XVI (1964), 302-13.

monarchy as an instrument of divine order.[23] Of even greater importance for our present purposes is the evidence of tension in Isaiah's time between the official and the prophetic estimates of the monarchy and its rituals, both south and north. This tension erupted into open warfare in the ministries of Amos and Hosea.[24]

The rejection of the royal cultus and its theology by Amos and Hosea does not mean that Isaiah also rejected it or that his proclamation was unaffected by it. On the contrary, Isaiah appears to have endorsed several features of the royal theology in his prophecies of the just king (9:1-7; 11:1-9). But Isaiah's image of the future king differed in crucial ways from the official Judean conception, which was embodied in the royal psalms. His prophecy represented an ethical transformation of the royal office, as I have tried to show in chapter five, below. This evidence of Isaiah's reinterpretation of the kingship as a sacral office should prevent us from inferring too much from Isaiah's use of the royal metaphor in chapter 6.

There is no clear evidence elsewhere in the Old Testament that the Judean royal rituals included a purification ceremony like the one embodied in Isaiah's vision.[25] Nor is there any

---

[23] The difference between the Judean and the north Israelite traditions with respect to the rule of God and to its embodiment in institutions of leadership has been analyzed by Murray Newman in *The People of the Covenant* (Nashville, 1962).

[24] See the discussion of Amos, above, pp. 23 ff., and of Hosea in my book, *Hosea: A Theological Commentary*, pp. 99-101, 134-38, 151-56, 168-70.

[25] It has been argued that the Davidic king submitted to an annual rite of humiliation and reinvestiture similar to that known in ancient Babylon (see *ANET*, p. 334), in connection with the autumnal new year's festival. See, e.g., A. R. Johnson, *Sacral Kingship in Ancient Israel*, pp. 102-4. The only way in which evidence for such a ritual can be secured, however, is to combine various psalms from the Old Testament arbitrarily in just the right order to form the alleged liturgy. This begs the question, of course. It also entails the designation of some psalms as royal, that is, as having their origin in the rites associated with the office of the king, that are not explicitly so. In Ps. 89:46-51 the Davidic king is subjected to humiliation by his enemies, but this is not a purification ritual (see my article, "The Literary Form and Liturgical Background of Psalm LXXXIX," *VT*, XI [1961], 321-39.).

indication that the office of the Israelite king involved prophetic functions. The offices of prophet and king were kept distinct throughout the history of Israel. There were several figures in Israel's earlier history whom the literary traditions endowed with both prophetic and political features, notably Moses and Samuel. In these instances, however, the pictures of the men have been magnified by popular memory, and they have been made the archetypes of several historically distinct offices. This is especially true of Moses, who was ultimately made the model of the political leader, the law-giver, the prophet, and the priest. It is significant that, despite the tendency of tradition to fuse all these roles in depicting the great forebears, kingship stands out in all the sources as a separate office. No effort was made in Israel to amalgamate the royal office with any other either in fact or in the legends of origin. Kingship was introduced in Israel at a relatively late point in her history, when historical records were already being kept, so it was impossible for the biblical writers to lose sight of the actual features of the office and to fuse it with others whose classical form had been partly colored by oral tradition. Furthermore, the continual conflict between the kings and the defenders of Yahwism, who were responsible for the creation of the Old Testament, doubtless motivated the latter to keep the record straight in this respect.

Isaiah's vision apparently was influenced in its imagery and language by the rituals and theology of Judean national religion. However, it was not a mirror image of it. In its total configuration the vision narrative is unique in the extant literature of Israel and in the literature of the ancient world generally. It was the product of Isaiah's ethical insight and his individual experience, and it gave expression to his unique sense of prophetic vocation.

chapter 5

God's Rule in Israel

The oracles concerning Zion, Immanuel, the Messiah, and the remnant continue to be the favorite topics in scholarly discussion of Isaiah. Interest in the predictive aspect of these oracles, which has always been the preoccupation of theologically "conservative" commentators, is matched today by interest in their institutional and traditional background. These topics cover the areas of least agreement among interpreters. The disagreements are due in part to the doctrinal predilections of the scholars, but more to the ambiguities of the texts. Solutions of the exegetical problems are therefore inevitably contextual, and they vary with the interpreter's choice of contexts. Today the inclination of scholars is to employ the history of tradition, in particular the tradition of the Davidic dynasty and the temple of Jerusalem. But there are two serious weaknesses in this approach. First, the tradition itself is obscure at many points. Second, the extent to which Isaiah embraced the tradition is highly uncertain. These methodological difficulties are sufficient, I believe, to disqualify tradition history (*Traditionsgeschichte*) as the primary tool for dealing with these themes in Isaiah's oracles. However, it does have a limited usefulness and need not be abandoned entirely.

The primary context of the debated oracles is the Isaianic corpus itself. The disputed themes must be interpreted within the general framework of ethical and theological thought provided by the unambiguous oracles of Isaiah. According to Isaiah, Zion, the anointed one, and the remnant were agents of the rule of God in Israel and the world. The oracles in which these agents are mentioned are either silent about the concrete aims of God's rule, that is, its actual ethical and religious content, or are of uncertain authorship. Therefore, in order to ascertain their prophetic significance and decide whether they may be included properly in the corpus of Isaiah's oracles, we must first delineate the main features of his general prophetic proclamation. There are uncertainties involved in this undertaking, to be sure, but they are less crippling than those associated with alternative methods.

The paramount feature of Isaiah's preaching was his criticism of man's idolatry and injustice; therefore, the dominant tone of his oracles is negative. There is little positive ethical counsel in them, nor is there much in the way of explicit affirmation concerning the nature of God or the creative prospects of God's activity in nature and history. Isaiah, like others of the canonical prophets, was a relentless critic of human folly and selfishness. There is no relief from the judgmental quality of his declarations. His mission, as it is documented in his recorded oracles, appears to have been largely destructive. This appearance of nihilism is apt to be misleading, however, for the prophet's criticism was wholly in the service of a positive conception of man's good. His criticism was the negation of those aspects of man's life that were themselves destructive. His denunciation of idolatry was preliminary to an affirmation of faith in God. Therefore, it is possible to discern much that was positive and creative in Isaiah's thought although because of the peculiar nature of his prophetic responsibility and because of his literary style it is largely implicit in what he said.

The range of Isaiah's accusations against the men of Israel was broad. His chief target was pride. This theme recurs again and again and constitutes the burden of several entire oracles. The idol against which Isaiah's attack was aimed was man himself. He was less concerned with plastic forms of idolatry, which were ubiquitous in ancient times. Idolatry in this narrower sense was condemned frequently in the oracles of Hosea, Isaiah's northern contemporary. But Judean religion may have been freer than Israelite from the use of images at this time. The evidence of cultic objects discovered in the two regions by modern archaeological excavation seems to support this conclusion. Nevertheless it is strange that there is no definite reference in Isaiah's extant oracles to the Assyrian cultic objects brought into the temple of Jerusalem by Ahaz (II Kings 16:10-16). But the making of plastic images is a relatively superficial form of idolatry even though it may have vicious psychological and moral effects. Isaiah's concern was the fundamental idolatry—man's self-adoration. His scorn for the idolatry of his contemporaries was the corollary of his awe before the absolute power and righteousness of God (6:1 ff.). The masterful poem in 2:6-22 is Isaiah's most powerful treatment of man's arrogance.

2:6 Surely you have forsaken your people, the House of Jacob;
For they are filled with eastern soothsayers like the
Philistines,
And they swarm with alien offspring.[1]

7 Their land is filled with silver and gold,
And there is no end to their treasures.
Their land is filled with horses,
And there is no end to their chariots.

8 Their land is filled with worthless gods:
They worship their own handiwork,
The things their fingers have made.

9 So mankind is humbled, and man brought low.
Do not forgive them.

10 Get behind rocks and hide in the dirt,
From the terrible presence of Yahweh,
And from his exalted majesty.
The lofty countenance of man will fall,

11 And the pride of man bow down.
And Yahweh alone will be exalted in that day.[2]

12 Surely Yahweh of hosts has a day
Against everything proud and exalted,
Against everything lofty and (high [3]),

13 Against all the cedars of Lebanon, exalted and lofty,
Against all the oaks of Bashan,

14 Against all the exalted mountains,
Against all the lofty hills,

15 Against every tall tower,
Against every fortified wall,

16 Against all the ships of Tarshish,
Against all the elegant fleet.

---

[1] The text is obscure in the last two clauses of vs. 6. RSV, Chicago, Jerusalem, and other versions add "diviners" in the second clause and emend "offspring" to "hands." On the meaning of the final verb cf. KBL, p. 928, and Kissane. D. W. Thomas would restore the text to an original "for they are full of enchanters, and soothsayers abound" ("The Text of Isaiah 2,6 and the Word *spq*," *ZAW*, LXXV [1963], 88-90).

[2] LXX adds, "When he rises to shake the earth"; cf. vss. 19 and 21.

[3] MT reads, "And it will be brought low" (*wᵉshaphel*).

17 And the pride of man will bow down,
   And the arrogance of men be made low.
   And Yahweh alone will be exalted in that day,
18 And the idols will vanish completely.
19 Get into caves in the rock and holes in the ground,
   Before the terrible presence of Yahweh,
   Before his exalted majesty,
   When he rises to shake the earth.

20 In that day man will throw away
   To the moles and the bats
   His idols of silver and idols of gold,
   Which he made for himself to worship,
21 To get into holes in the rock
   And cracks in the cliffs,
   Before the terrible presence of Yahweh,
   Before his exalted majesty,
   When he rises to shake the earth.

22 Leave man alone,
   In whose nostrils is breath,
   For of what account is he? [4]

This oracle was addressed first of all to Israel, but it was a characterization of man as man and of his universal destiny before the wrath of God. The oracle sets God, as the spoiler of men's proud designs, over against the gods of divination, wealth, and militarism (2:6-8). Idolatry (2:6-8, 20) and pride (2:12-17) are the two themes of the oracle, and it is marked by a refrain celebrating the terrible wrath of God (2:9-11, 18-19, 21). Verses 12-17 should not be removed from the poem as a separate oracle.[5] The alternation of themes shows the relation of pride to idolatry, as the inner and outer manifestations of faithlessness. Fleeing before the wrath of God, man is humbled and made to realize the futility of his

[4] LXX omits this verse.
[5] See, e.g., Scott.

idols (vs. 20). Thus pride and idolatry fall together. To the discerning eye this humbling does not require the material failure resulting from reliance upon the idols, but is already evident in the idolizing. Man is humbled in the very act of idolatry (2:8; cf. 40:6-8). The supreme idol is man himself, a thing of wind and vanity (2:22).

This ultimate futility of human pride, which is mocked by man's finitude, was a subject of continual interest to Isaiah, and it has a prominent place in his collected oracles (cf. 3:16-24; 5:21; 9:9-10; 10:5-19; 28:1-4). It was to him the root of moral evil, whose fruit was abundant and variegated. It could also be characterized as rebellion against God (1:2-3; 30:1, 9) and unfaith (5:19, 24; 8:9-15; 30:8 ff.). The moral evils that grew from it were manifold: idolatry, in the narrower sense (1:29-31; 16:12-14; 17:10-11; 19:1 ff.; 21:9; 31:6-7); injustice, tyranny, and oppression of the weak (1:21-23; 3:13-15; 10:1-2); selfish abuse of power (28:1 ff.); greed (5:8-9); debauchery (5:11-12; 28:1 ff., 7 ff.); subversion of the judicial process with a consequent denial of the rights of the poor and innocent (5:23; 9:15-16; 29:21); hypocrisy (5:20; 29:13-14); ritualism (1:10-17; 17:7-8); complacency (32:9 ff.); folly and delusion in high places (19:1-15); false sophistication (5:22); militarism (2:7; 10:5-19; 19:19-20); and moral insensitivity (22:1-14). The final evidence of religious blindness was the denial of sonship to God (1:4-9) and the willing acceptance of evil as good (28:15-18). The hardening of man's heart made repentance impossible (22:1-14), thus fulfilling Isaiah's grim presentiment of the outcome of his preaching (6:9-13).

Isaiah's primary audience was the people of Jerusalem and the leaders of the kingdom of Judah. Many of his oracles name them directly as the objects of God's interest and activity in world history, particularly his judgment against the unrighteous.[6] Furthermore, it is reasonable to assume that *all* of Isaiah's public statements were heard in Jerusalem alone and that all of his recorded oracles were meant primarily as a testament for Judeans in subsequent generations. The oracles concerning the Aramean-Israelite alliance against Judah in 735 B.C.[7] and the conspiracy with Egypt against Assyria in 711 B.C.[8] were obviously intended for the ears of the rulers of Judah. On the other hand, the oracles predicting ultimate retribution against Assyria for her world tyranny[9] would have been of interest to anyone among the people of Yahweh but not least for the faithful in Judah. Isaiah's ethical concern was by no means confined to Judah and her rulers although they were the audience for his oracles. The real subject of his prophetic responsibility was the whole people of Israel, the entire community of the House of Jacob which shared the Yahwistic faith. In this sense his oracles were the most universal among those of the eighth-century prophets. Amos and Hosea were concerned with the kingdom of Israel, and Micah with Judah. Although much of what they said would have been relevant to both kingdoms, their deliberate orientation was less often toward the whole people of God than was Isaiah's. The word of Yahweh that Isaiah declared was often explicitly directed to the people[10] or to the whole of Israel [11] (sometimes called "the House of Jacob" [12]). This conscious-

[6] Isa. 1:4-9; 1:10-17 (and probably 1:18-20); 1:21-28; 3:1-15; 3:16-24 (and probably 3:25–4:1); 5:1-7; 7:1-9; 7:10-17; 8:5-8; 28:14-15, 17b-22; 29:1-10; and probably 32:9-14. The leaders of the kingdom are singled out in 3:16-24; 7:1-9; 7:10-17; 28:14-15, 17b-22.

[7] Isa. 8:1-4; 17:1-6; 9:7–10:4 and 5:25-30; and 28:1-6.

[8] Isa. 20:1-6; 30:1-5; 30:6-7; and 31:1-3.

[9] Isa. 10:5-19; 10:24-27; 14:24-27 (if it is Isaiah's); and 30:27-33.

[10] Isa. 1:2-4; 5:13, 25; 6:5; 22:4; 28:5; 32:13, 18. "This people" refers to the Judeans in 8:6, 11, 12; and 28:14, but is indefinite in 6:9; 29:13, 14; and 30:9.

[11] Isa. 1:3; 8:18; 10:17, 20; 11:12, 16; 31:6. "Israel" means the northern kingdom in 9:8, 12, 14. All Israel is referred to in 8:14 as "the two Houses of Israel."

[12] Isa. 2:5 (if it is Isaiah's); 2:6; 8:17; 10:20-21; and 29:22 (cf. 29:23). This

ness of speaking to the whole community of Israel was reflected also in that most characteristic of Isaiah's designations of God, "the Holy One of Israel." [13] The brilliant series of woe oracles in 5:8-24 is universal in its scope, and there are no essential differences between the judgments pronounced upon the Israelite and Judean kingdoms.[14] Thus even where a particular object of God's wrath is mentioned, the implicit subject is the entire Israelite community, and sometimes the reference is nothing less than universal in its scope. The judgment of God upon Assyria for her pride and tyranny (10:5-19) is identical to that upon the "proud crown of the drunkards of Ephraim" (28:1 ff.), and upon their counterparts in Judah (3:1 ff., *et passim*). And all these are comprehended in the great prophecy of the day of wrath (2:6-22).

Against this background the rule of God in history appears first of all as the execution of justice against unjust men and nations. The means of God's justice are both intrinsic, 2:9-22; 3:1-12; 9:18-21) and extrinsic (1:4-9, 18-20, 29-31; 5:1-7; 7:18-25; 9:8-11; 10:3-4, 5-6; 17:9, 10-11), but they are always social. Never in the oracles of Isaiah is a natural calamity adduced as a divine punishment for unrighteousness.[15] The instruments of God's activity are always appropriate to his aims. This is the point of Isaiah's parable of the farmer (28:23-29). Even the means that I have referred to as extrinsic were not entirely so, for they were primarily military conquest and political subjugation (and their manifold consequences), and these were partly the result

---

usage occurs also in the secondary oracle 14:1-2. "Jacob" refers to the northern kingdom in 9:8 and 17:4 as does the phrase "House of Israel" in 5:7.

[13] Isa. 1:4; 5:19, 24; 10:20; 29:19; 30:11, 12, 15; 31:1; and compare "God of Israel," 17:6; 29:23; "Mighty One of Israel," 1:24; "Rock of Israel," 30:29; and "Holy One of Jacob," 29:23.

[14] Compare 9:7–10:4 (plus 5:25-30) and 28:1-6 with the various oracles against Judah.

[15] Isa. 10:17-19 is of course figurative.

of the actions and policies of those nations which were the objects of God's wrath.

The motives of God's action, in addition to his general determination to maintain justice in his creation, were various. At times Isaiah described the judgment as punitive (1:4-9; 2:6-22; 3:1-12), but at other times he made it appear to be redemptive in its ultimate aim (1:24-28; 6:5-8, 13). The oracles which mention the remnant as the bearer of a continuing obedience of the people to God belong in the latter group (1:9; 7:3; 10:20-27; 17:4-6). In other proclamations Isaiah provided no rational justification for God's action but simply left it unexplained (7:18-25; 22:15-25 [an oracle against an individual]).

As with the agents and motives of judgment, so with the specific results. These, too, were various. To some extent, of course, they were identical with the agents, namely military destruction and conquest (1:7-9, 20; 3:25-26; 5:1-7 [implicitly], 24, 26-30; 7:18-25; 8:1-4, 5-8; 17:9, 10-11, 15, 16, 19). But there were other, subtler punishments as well: anarchy (3:1-12; 9:19-21), fear and despair (2:9-22), shame (3:24; 4:1), hardening of heart (6:9 ff.; 29:9-10; cf. 28:15-18), and faithlessness (7:5-8, 9-15; 7:1-9; 8:16-22). In some oracles the content of judgment is unspecified (1:24-25, 28, 31; 5:24; 17:4-6, 10-11, 18). But in none of the prophecies of Isaiah is there anything miraculous or "supernatural." His conception of the operation of divine justice was utterly realistic and rational, or, one might say, pragmatic and empirical. God's justice was not arbitrary or capricious, was visible to the eyes of any discerning man (i.e., it did not move on some "spiritual" or "heavenly" plane which only the religious initiate or the seer might recognize), and extended uniformly into the lives of all peoples, regardless of their peculiar cultic bonds to the Deity.

Isaiah was not the only ancient man to hold such a view.

There were many others in the line of the prophets in Israel. But it is astonishing that there should have been any at all in the ancient world, which was glutted with magic and superstition, gods, demons, and mythological fantasies. The modernity of the classical Hebrew prophets in this respect is a source of wonder. The vast majority of Jews and Christians who have come after them, including some of the writers of the Old and New Testaments, have failed to achieve the same realism and sobriety. And yet, unlike many a modern realist, the prophets were controlled by a passionate faith in God. Indeed, their realism in interpreting the lives and destinies of nations was the result of their faith in God and not an obstacle to it. It was as a consequence of their absolute refusal to compromise their loyalty to the Creator that they were uncorrupted by the fancies of nature mythology on the one hand or spiritualism on the other.

In its direct thrust, Isaiah's proclamation was more negative than positive. When one searches through his oracles for constructive ethical counsel, he is disappointed to find so little. What were the responsibilities of the faithful man of God? Only occasionally is there any indication. He was to seek the welfare of the widow, the orphan, and the oppressed (1:16-17), that is, to use what power he had in behalf of the powerless members of society. In so doing he took up the cause of God as well, for God was understood by Isaiah, as by the prophets generally, to be the champion of the afflicted, whom he would ultimately vindicate against those who oppressed or exploited them (29:19-20). The faithful man's service was defined generally as devotion to justice (*mishpaṭ*, 1:21; 5:7; 28:6, 17; 32:16), by which he proved his righteousness (*ṣᵉdaqah*, 1:21; 3:10; 5:7; 28:17; 32:16-17), which was the fruit of trust in God and God's word (7:9; 28:16; 30:15). In these statements Isaiah used the common vocabulary of covenantal ethics whose meaning was well known to his

Yahwistic audience. "Justice" was defined first of all by traditional Israelite law, which is exemplified in the Pentateuchal codes (Exod. 20–23 and Deut. 12–26, for example), but it meant more than legal rectitude. It also meant the *spirit* of fairness (28:6). It was ultimately synonymous with "righteousness," as Isaiah's constant matching of these terms shows (1:21; 5:7; 28:17; 32:16). Righteousness was that attitude and behavior which produced harmonious, peaceful, productive, and joyful interaction among members of a community, the model for which was the family or intimate tribal unit. Mutual loyalty, affection, active commitment to the common good, selfless support of another in time of crisis, respect for the person and property of another—all this was denoted by this inexhaustible word. The Ten Commandments became the standard epitome of this ethic, but in order to grasp the true meaning of it, one must read not only such lists of injunctions and prohibitions but the narratives of Genesis and First and Second Samuel, for example, where concrete stories of men's righteousness and unrighteousness are related. We may not assume that Isaiah and his audience knew any particular portion of these or other extant biblical writings, but we may assume that they knew some of the traditions that lay behind them and that the cultural viewpoint of the writers of these narratives was fundamentally the same as Isaiah's and that of contemporary Yahwists. Because his audience was well acquainted with the ethical vocabulary of Yahwistic tradition, Isaiah was able to use this vocabulary without having to define it more explicitly than he did.

The number of Isaiah's explicit ethical affirmations is small. In order to give further concrete content to his conception of obedience we must work backward from his denunciations, deducing affirmations by negating the negations. This is the same method we were forced to use in interpreting the thought

of Amos.[16] However, it is not difficult to apply. In place of
the pride repudiated by the prophet the faithful and righteous
man would possess humility, and in place of the other evils we
have cataloged above he would possess generosity, sobriety,
honesty and selflessness in judicial and national affairs, candor,
watchfulness for social injustice, openness to self-criticism,
willingness to change, and a general subordination of his own
demands to the general welfare, but above all, humility before
God and continual acknowledgment of him as the Lord of
life and the source of good.

Isaiah's oracles thus provide no social program or set of
rules. His ethic was wholly religious and personal and almost
naïve in its simplicity. And yet it was far from irrelevant to
practical affairs. Indeed it was universally relevant, for there
was no social situation in which a man, especially a man of
position and power, might not seek justice for the oppressed
and place himself at the disposal of God in the service of the
community. However, the oracles of Isaiah, as of the prophets
generally, prescribe no specific solutions to the concrete problems that beset the men of Israel in his own age, let alone in
other times. There were certain points at which Isaiah challenged the specific decisions of the kings of Judah, as will be
shown below, but for the most part neither his moral criti-
cisms nor the religious convictions that lay behind them constituted a formula for making political decisions.

The rule of God in the midst of Israel and the nations was
not merely a matter of checking the proud and frustrating
the selfish, but this was the aspect of God's rule that Isaiah
believed himself obligated to assert. He also published oracles
of renewal and hope. But these were logically dependent upon
his oracles of judgment. In them he promised God's support
only for those pursuits that were sanctioned (directly or in-

[16] See above, pp. 70-71.

directly) in his oracles of judgment. It was his preaching of God's justice as a threat to the "unclean" people among whom he lived (6:5) that contributed to the hardening of their hearts. Martin Buber's opinion that it was his preaching of salvation that did this, by making the people complacent and oblivious to the disaster course upon which they were moving,[17] is surely wrong. Isaiah's preaching was dominated overwhelmingly by moral criticism and the threat of divine punishment. It was this that his countrymen refused to accept. They might have been willing to accept promises of salvation, but the promises of Isaiah were hard promises. They were not the sort of thing that made men complacent. Far from assuring them of God's satisfaction of their own needs, Isaiah's promises committed them to a repudiation of their special claims upon God. In a word, Isaiah promised to the men of Israel the succor and approval of God in the pursuit of justice. This was the substance of his oracles concerning the remnant, the Messiah, and the future Zion. The hope he offered was the direct complement of the judgment he proclaimed. He bespoke God's judgment against man's injustice, unrighteousness, and faithlessness. He promised God's aid to those who lived by faith and who showed their faithfulness in the quest for justice.

This may seem like a slender contribution to the religion of Israel—and of Israel's heirs. Isaiah was silent after all about the value of worship and the destiny of the individual person. He did not mention the love of God, and he showed little overt compassion for man in his weakness. There was not much warmth or joy in his words. However, it was not the mission of a prophet in pre-exilic Israel to comfort distressed individuals or urge the disciplines of the religious life. Isaiah's audience was the Israelite community, and especially the lead-

[17] *The Prophetic Faith*, pp. 131-32.

ers of the Judean state. He spoke to men of privilege and power about the nature of their obedience in a world ultimately ruled by God. His harsh criticism of them was a reflection of his compassion for the victims of tyranny and corruption. His few statements about public worship were denunciations, for he considered the established church an instrument of pride and self-aggrandizement and therefore an obstacle to true obedience. This was the perspective of most of the canonical prophets, and it was shared by many other writers of the Old and New Testaments. Most men in ancient Israel, as in other places and times, did not need encouragement to be religious. Quite the contrary. The problem, from the prophets' viewpoint, was that they were too religious and that their religion was idolatrous and selfish. For the prophets the test of faith was the doing of justice and the humble acceptance of the blessings of creation, which God had already bestowed. Israel's conventional religion was seen as an effort to improve upon her God-given situation in the world. In Isaiah's eyes it was futile in practice and faithless in principle. The essence of prophecy was a clearing away of the religious and moral obstacles to faith and justice. In part the prophets' preaching was itself the means by which this could be done, at least for those who had ears to hear. But even more it was the witness to the acts of God in the lives of nations, by which the obstacles would be forceably stripped away. By themselves, without the witness of the prophets, these great historical judgments would have been merely vast, impersonal upheavals lacking moral significance. The prophets turned them into occasions for ethical understanding and faithful obedience. Their interpretation of the manner and motive of God's rule in history was indispensable to the creative working of this rule. In this sense they were the very instruments of God's righteousness.

chapter 6

Isaiah's Counsel
to the House of David

The international crisis that shook Syria-Palestine during the third quarter of the eighth century B.C. as a result of the threat of universal Assyrian domination provided a supreme test for two rival conceptions of the rule of God in Israel. One was Isaiah's and the other the Davidic king's. Isaiah failed to persuade the Judean state to accept his teaching as the basis of policy, and yet his teaching did not die with his failure. Because of the fidelity of a small circle of men who preserved his oracles, his teaching outlived the policy of Ahaz and Hezekiah, the kings of Judah in Isaiah's time. The royal policy, which was a reflection of the religio-political syncretism common among the monarchial states of western Asia, at first succeeded, for it helped the Judean state to survive the immediate crisis. However, it contributed to the eventual destruction of the state by Assyria and Neo-Babylonia. The crisis was precipitated for Judah by the Syro-Ephraimite invasion of 735 B.C. The oracles Isaiah published on this occasion are assembled in a small book within the book of Isaiah (chaps. 7–8). Several other oracles in the book also bear upon this situation (17:1-6 and 28:1 ff.). I believe Isaiah's counsel is consistently represented in these oracles and is exactly what might have been expected from one who was given Isaiah's commission (Isa. 6). However, it has been variously interpreted; indeed, this is one of the areas of least agreement in the contemporary study of Isaiah. The fallibility of commentators is nowhere more evident than here. Of course, one advantage of this exegetical situation is that it provides every reader an opportunity to ponder the meaning of the text for himself, free from the tyranny of a scholarly consensus.

Isa. 7 and 8 contain the following major units: (a) and (b) two oracles delivered to Ahaz, each set in a brief narrative framework (7:1-9 and 7:10-16); a series of five additional prophecies of doom is appended to the second of these oracles (7:17, 18-19, 20, 21-22, 23-25); (c) an account of the symbolic naming of Isaiah's son Speedy-Spoil-Quick-Plunder (8:1-4); (d) a parabolic oracle of the two streams (8:5-8); (e) an oracle about Yahweh as the stone of stumbling (8:11-15), which is linked with a brief, enigmatic saying (8:9-10); and (f) an oracular narrative about Isaiah's retreat from prophesying (8:16-18), to which two obscure sayings are attached (8:19-20, 21-22). These materials are best studied in their canonical order.

"IF YOU DO NOT BELIEVE" (ISA. 7:1-9)

1   In the days of Ahaz, the son of Jotham, the son of Uzziah, the king of Judah, king Rezin of Aram and

king Pekah, the son of Remaliah, of Israel, advanced on
Jerusalem to attack it but were unable to make war
2 against it. When it was reported to the House of David
that the Arameans were encamped in Ephraimite territory, they were frightened and so were their people,
shaking like trees in the wind.
3   Then Yahweh said to Isaiah, "Go with your son
A-Remnant-Shall-Return (*she'ar yashûbh*) to meet
Ahaz at the aquaduct to the upper pool, by the Fuller's
4 Field Road, and say to him, 'Keep still and do not be
afraid. Do not be faint-hearted over these two smoking
stubs of firebrands, over the "burning wrath" of
5 Rezin, Aram, and the son of Remaliah. Because Aram
counsels Ephraim and the son of Remaliah to your
6 detriment, saying, "Let us march into Judah, breach
her defenses, capture her for ourselves, and make the
son of Tabeel king in her midst," (therefore) thus says
7 the Lord Yahweh, "It will not succeed; it will not
8 come to pass; for Aram's head is Damascus, and Damascus' head is Rezin [in less than sixty-five years Ephraim
9 will be a shattered people], and Ephraim's head is Samaria, and Samaria's head is the son of Remaliah. If you
do not believe (this), you will not be established." ' "

Isaiah's first oracle to Ahaz ends with the impressive assertion, best known to readers today in the words of the RSV,
"If you will not believe, surely you shall not be established."
Expositors have made capital of this line, often deducing from
it a far-reaching doctrine of faith. Such use is not
demonstrably wrong, but the results are certainly subjective.
Yet Isaiah meant something by the statement, and the serious
reader is not likely to rest until he has discovered a satisfactory
explanation of it.

The writer (or editor) of chapter 7 has provided a historical
introduction to the oracle, which describes the setting as the
threatened invasion of Judah by the joint forces of the

Aramean kingdom of Damascus and the Israelite kingdom of Samaria during the reign of Ahaz, king of Judah (735 B.C.). The attack on Judah had not yet begun, for the Arameans had only arrived in Israel, preparatory to the march on Judah (7:2). The more generalized statement in verse 1 covers also the subsequent development of the conspiracy, for it places the invaders in the vicinity of Jerusalem, and it adds that the invaders were unable to mount a siege although it does not explain why.[1] The immediate occasion of Isaiah's oracle was the receipt in Jerusalem of the news of the threatened invasion. It is commonly inferred from verse 3 that Ahaz was out inspecting the city's fortifications and water supply in anticipation of a siege. In any case, he was outside the city so it was hardly under attack at that moment. However, both Ahaz and his people were thoroughly frightened by the prospect (vs. 2). Small wonder that the king trembled, for he was very young and this was probably his first serious test in international affairs.[2]

Isaiah was accompanied by his son A-Remnant-Shall-Return (vs. 3). Having named the boy this, the prophet obviously believed disaster was coming to someone and a remnant of them would be left. Although this passage does not say who they were, Isaiah took the boy along deliberately, so his prophetic name was apparently meant to be part of Isaiah's message to Ahaz at this time. The rest of the message was plain enough, except for the final remark, which has provoked so much debate. Isaiah told Ahaz not to be afraid of the conspirators because their plan would surely fail (7:4-9a). He gave him this assurance in Yahweh's name (vs. 7). The plan

---

[1] The English versions go beyond the normal meaning of the verb in translating it "conquer." It usually means to engage another in fighting. Whatever connotation the word was meant to have, the editor's point seems to have been that Isaiah's prediction of failure for the plot proved to be correct.

[2] According to II Kings 16:2 he became king when he was twenty. The Syro-Ephraimite conspiracy occurred in the first year of his reign.

as Isaiah understood it was to terrify and conquer Judah and set up a new king in place of Ahaz (vs. 6). Isaiah's reason for confidence was expressed in the sarcasm with which he referred to the two plotters, Rezin and Pekah. To him they were nothing but "two smoking stubs of firebrands" whose flame had already gone out. There was nothing to fear from them. Had the writer said nothing more, our exegetical task would be a simple one. We would want to check the extant historical records to see whether Isaiah's disdain for Rezin and Pekah was justified, and we would want to describe the larger political situation of Judah at the time as well as the outcome of the crisis. This would exhaust the major issues of interpretation. But the prophet's parting word to Ahaz, as it is reported here, complicates everything. What did he mean by "believing" and "being established," and what relationship did these have to each other? The oracle itself seems to raise issues more difficult and complex than the mere fulfillment of a prediction. Do these additional questions arise only in *our* minds by free association with a word taken out of context? To what extent did the writer himself intend to raise these questions?

First of all, we may rule out the possibility that 7:9*b* was an afterthought of the writer. The line is a play on words, a memorable kind of saying and one likely to find its way into the literary tradition. Of all the lines in the recorded oracle this is the one most likely to have been spoken by Isaiah in his meeting with Ahaz. It is the nucleus around which the rest of the oracle revolves. However, this consideration does not justify our reading more into the line than the text will bear. After all, it is a pun, albeit a serious one. The two main words in the saying are different forms of the same verb: "If not *ta'ᵃmînû,* then not *te'amenû.*" The possible connotations of the first form (hiphil) range from "stand firm" or "stand still" to "trust" and "believe" and those of

184

the second (niphal) from "prove oneself faithful" to "be established, lasting, or firm." Thus, if we choose one combination, the line becomes a virtual tautology: "If you do not stand firm, then you will not be firm," or "If you do not hold fast,/ Surely you shall not stand fast" (Chicago). That is to say, the line may be nothing more than a play on words. If that is the case, it is a simple repetition of what is said in the preceding lines of the oracle though it is cast in negative form and made more memorable by the wordplay. The meaning is that if Ahaz wants to be steady, firm, and secure in the circumstances confronting him, all he need do is stand confidently, firmly, and still, for the threat to Judah and to his throne is a hollow one. Conversely, the only thing that can shake him in these circumstances is his own panic, for the northern conspirators have no real power to do so. This interpretation suits the context admirably. Isaiah had gone to the king to give him counsel because the king and his people were shaking with fear (vs. 2). Isaiah began by telling him to be quiet and not fear (vs. 4), and he ended by telling him once again to stand still (vs. 9).[3]

The alternative to this interpretation is to take the first verb in the final line in the sense of believing or trusting. This of course is what most translators and interpreters have done. The question then is what or whom Ahaz was to believe or trust. The simplest and most obvious answer we may give to this question, once we are freed from the bias of a long expository tradition and are willing to judge the statement in its immediate context, is that Ahaz was to believe what Isaiah

---

[3] There is a minor difference between the last line of the oracle and the preceding lines. The one is in the plural form of address, and the others are in the singular. The shift probably indicates only that the whole "House of David," i.e., the royal court, was included in the final admonition, and not Ahaz alone. The difference is unimportant because the king and the court were effectively one. Even if the plural referred to the king and his people (vs. 2), the situation would not be changed materially, for the admonition applied equally to both.

was telling him, namely that the alliance against him was in-
consequential and unworthy of his fear. This meant that he
was to believe the word of Yahweh, for this is the form in
which the counsel was given (vs. 7). But this counsel was the
only word of Yahweh he was here called upon to believe. Any
other signification that we might draw from this statement is
unwarranted and superfluous. This conclusion, that the object
of the verb is the message delivered here by the prophet, is confirmed by the usage of the verb in the Old Testament generally. In the overwhelming majority of the occurrences of
the hiphil of '*mn*—thirty-four in all—the meaning is to believe something that is said, prophesied, reported, or promised.
Very often the words that are believed (or not believed) are
explicitly stated.[4] In other cases it is a person (often God)
who is (or is not) believed with respect to something that has
just been said.[5] Elsewhere the specific content of what is believed is not indicated, but it is clear that it is speech or ideas.[6]
Two of these last passages are especially significant because
they speak of believing God, while the context shows that
what this means concretely is believing his prophets.[7] These
references must therefore be added to the list of those in
which the object of the verb is a particular message brought
from God by a prophet or delivered directly by God himself.[8]
Second Chron. 20:20 is particularly interesting because it is
closely parallel to Isaiah 7:9*b*—"Believe Yahweh your God
and you will be established; believe his prophets and you will
prosper." A serial reading of these thirty-four passages, together with their contexts, should provide persuasive con-

[4] Exod. 4:5, 31; I Kings 10:7; II Chron. 9:6; Job 9:16; 15:22; 39:12;
Pss. 27:13; 106:12, 24; 119:66; Isa. 43:10; 53:1; Lam. 4:12; Hab. 1:5.
[5] Gen. 15:6; 45:26; Exod. 4:1, 8, 9; Deut. 9:23; I Sam. 27:12; II Chron.
32:15; Prov. 26:25; Jer. 12:6; 40:14; Jonah 3:5.
[6] Exod. 14:31; Num. 14:11; II Kings 17:14; II Chron. 20:20; Job 15:31;
29:24; Prov. 14:15.
[7] II Kings 17:14; II Chron. 20:20.
[8] Gen. 15:6; Exod. 4:1, 8, 9, 31; Jonah 3:5; Hab. 1:5.

firmation of the judgment that "believe" in Isa. 7:9 means to believe what Isaiah has just said to Ahaz.

There are a few passages in the Old Testament in which the verb is used in other ways. It may mean to be confident of one's life or, negatively, to despair of it (Deut. 28:66 and Job 24:22). This usage would be like that in Isa. 7:9 if the latter meant simply "stand firm" or "be confident." However, the verb has an explicit object in the other two texts and not in Isa. 7:9. There are not many occurrences of the verb in the sense of trusting a person who is generally reliable, and none of these refers explicitly to faith in God.[9] It is possible that Ps. 116:10 implies such a meaning although the text is difficult and has been variously translated.[10] This lack of a single instance outside Isaiah in which the word is clearly used to mean the general attitude of faith in God reduces the a priori probability of its meaning this in Isa. 7 to zero though, of course, it does not rule out absolutely the possibility that it means this here alone.

I have not yet mentioned Isa. 28:16, where the crucial verb appears again. Unfortunately, this passage offers little help in settling the issue of Isa. 7:9, for it is an equally ambiguous statement. It is possible to read it as a reference to general faith in God. Thus some commentators regard the statement "He who believes will not be in haste" (RSV) as itself the cornerstone which God "is laying in Zion" (28:16) or as a hypothetical inscription upon the cornerstone.[11] However,

---

[9] Job 4:18 and 15:15 (of God trusting the righteousness of his angels) and Mic. 7:5 (of man trusting his neighbor).

[10] RSV ("I kept my faith, even when I said") and Jerusalem ("I have faith, even when I say") make the line denote a general attitude of faith, which the preceding verses make to mean faith in God. However, other translators take the line quite differently. Chicago, "I believe what (*ki*) I say;/I am fully responsible for it," if correct, confirms my thesis, namely that the verb '*mn* (hiphil) usually means "to believe that. . . ." Gunkel (*Die Psalmen, in loc.,* following Gressmann and Buhl) and Kissane (*The Book of Psalms, in loc.*) also treat '*mn* in this way here.

[11] See the protracted discussion in K. Fullerton, "The Stone of the Foundation,"

it is equally possible to interpret the line as an assertion that God is laying a cornerstone and that whoever believes *this assertion* will not be in haste. This is the way the verb is used in the majority of occurrences in the Old Testament. Thus one's decision about 28:16 is likely to correspond to his decision about 7:9.

In the opinion of Gerhard von Rad, Isaiah was asking Ahaz to believe that God would work a miracle on his behalf and thus save him from the power of the invaders.[12] All Ahaz needed to do was stand still and watch it happen. Isaiah was thus allegedly reviving the old tradition of the holy war. But nothing in Isa. 7:1-9 supports this hypothesis. This belief in victory by the miraculous intervention of God without human effort is expressed by the writer of II Chron. 20:13-23, part of which passage (vs. 20) I have quoted above. That statement, which is very similar to Isaiah 7:9*b*, might appear to support von Rad's interpretation. However, the injunction of Jehoshaphat in II Chron. 20:20 is to believe *the message* that God has sent through the prophet, who in this case is the Levite Jahaziel (20:14). Jahaziel had promised the Judeans a miracle (20:15-17). Therefore, in *this* instance they were asked in effect to believe that a miracle would be worked by God. But what they were asked directly by the king to believe was the oracle.[13] In Isa. 7 the oracle which Ahaz is exhorted to believe contains no allusion to a miracle. It asserts simply that the threat to Ahaz and Judah will fail. There is no hint in Isa. 7:1-9 that the reason for the failure is God's impending

---

AJSL, XXXVII (1920), 1-50, in addition to the more recent commentaries.

[12] *Old Testament Theology*, II (New York, 1965), 158 ff.

[13] Buber believed Isa. 7:9 meant faith in God in a general sense, and so he dismissed the reference to the prophets in II Chron. 20:20 as "wrong" (*The Prophetic Faith*, p. 137). Even to say "confide ['*mn*] *in Yahweh*," as is done there, is to weaken the "absolute" meaning of the verb, in Buber's opinion. However, his interpretation goes squarely against the evidence, which shows as clearly as one might wish that there is no "absolute meaning" of the verb in the Old Testament.

action (let alone miracle) on Judah's behalf. On the contrary, the reason explicitly given by Isaiah is that Rezin and "the son of Remaliah" (Pekah) are ineffectual.

Von Rad's thesis is intrinsically improbable. The notion that God worked miracles on Israel's behalf without her effort, in battle, in the exodus from Egypt, or in the trek through the desert of Sinai, is legendary. It is a product of the oral transmission of popular memories over hundreds of years.[14] It was not and could not be the basis of policy for the leaders of Israel regardless of how pious they were. Similar ideas may be found in prophetic oracles in the Old Testament, but these are eschatological and therefore figurative. Unless there is clear evidence of such a belief in an oracle dealing with contemporary affairs, it is incorrect to attribute it to the writer (speaker). There is no such evidence in Isa. 7:1-9.

The same objection cannot be made to the thesis that Ahaz was being asked by Isaiah to believe that God would fight *alongside* him and his people in defending themselves against an invasion by Rezin and Pekah. This interpretation has been proposed recently by several scholars.[15] The basis of Isaiah's assurance was supposedly his acceptance of the Judean belief in the everlasting endurance of the Davidic dynasty (II Sam. 7:12-16; Ps. 89:19-37) as well as the ancient tradition of the tribal holy war.[16] His oracle to Ahaz, then, had the same

---

[14] In Ps. 78:22 and Num. 20:12 the verb '*mn* (hiphil) means trusting Yahweh in virtue of the wonders he has worked in the wilderness trek, etc., but the context alone supplies the specific content of the verb in this case as in almost all of its occurrences.

[15] E. Würthwein, "Jesaja 7, 1-9 . . . ," *Heim Festschrift* (Hamburg, 1954), pp. 47-63; H. Junker, "Ursprung und Grundzüge des Messiasbildes bei Isajas," *Suppl. VT* (1957), pp. 181-96; and M. Saebø, "Formgeschichtliche Erwägungen zu Jes. 7:3-9," *Studia Theologica*, XIV (1960), 54-69.

[16] The verb "established" is used in Isa. 7:9*b* and II Sam. 7:16, but these occurrences are a frail basis for supposing that Isaiah was alluding to this dynastic tradition. There are other verbs in II Sam. 7:12 ff. and related texts, particularly Pss. 2, 89, and 110, referring to God's establishment of the Davidic House. There is no evidence that the verb '*mn* had a technical association with

purpose as the priestly oracle mentioned in Deut. 20:3-4, namely to inform the leader of Judah's forces whether Yahweh would fight on their side in an ensuing battle. There can be no a priori objection to this interpretation of Isa. 7:9. It is true that the verb *'mn* is actually used only once in the Old Testament in reference to a *battle* oracle (II Chron. 20:20), but this infrequency is fortuitous. The verb is often used in reference to oracles, and the specific content of the oracle may vary widely. The weakness of this interpretation of Isa. 7:9 is that Isaiah's oracle says nothing about Judah's fighting. Isaiah's admonition is not to fight confidently but to be quiet and have no fear. I infer that Isaiah believed no fighting would be necessary because no invasion would take place. In a sense this oracle was a battle oracle; however, unlike the usual battle oracle, which was an answer to a commander's inquiry whether God would give him victory in an ensuing fight, Isaiah's oracle was unbidden by Ahaz, and it seemed to suggest that no fight would be necessary.

Isaiah's warning to Ahaz was that he would not remain steady in the present crisis unless he believed the message Isaiah had just delivered from Yahweh. In this instance he did not attempt to tell the king what action ought to be taken, nor did he enjoin him from taking any action at all.[17]

---

this tradition or that its use in a royal context would suggest *ipso facto* the dynastic promise. After all, this is a common word in the Old Testament. Isa. 7:9b is a *pun*, not a cryptic allusion to Nathan's oracle.

[17] The injunction to Ahaz to "be quiet" (Isa. 7:4) does not in itself mean he was to remain inactive, contrary to the opinion of Buber (*op. cit.*, pp. 135-36) and von Rad (*op. cit.*, pp. 159-60). It means only that he was not to be afraid. Whether one who is quiet (*šqṭ*) is also outwardly passive must be indicated by an auxiliary verb (cf. Isa. 18:4). Exod. 14:13, therefore, is not parallel to Isa. 7:4-9, for in the former passage (on which von Rad's case rests largely) it is explicitly said that Israel is to "fear not, *stand still*, and *see* the salvation of God." The verb "to stand still" here is *yṣb*, not *'mn*, and its primary meaning is *stand* or take a stand, unlike the latter verb. The verb "be silent" (*ḥrš*) in Exod. 14:14 means to speak not so it too is different from Isaiah's word (*šqṭ*), which refers chiefly to an inner quiet. Exod. 14:31 reads, "The people feared Yahweh,

He merely expressed an opinion (which he believed was inspired by Yahweh) about the true context of action. This is all he did. He obviously wanted to save Ahaz from taking the wrong action, but he did not say what he thought such an action might be. His oracle gave the premise of action, not its content. On the other hand, it did not constitute a general teaching about the meaning or consequence of faith in God although it was fully consistent with Isaiah's other declarations on this subject. When a prophet addressed the Davidic sovereign in the name of Yahweh and asked him to believe his counsel as the word of God, his exhortation presupposed the king's knowledge of Yahwistic tradition and at least a nominal commitment to it. Therefore, to believe this word entailed believing in God also—I do not wish to deny that there is this much general teaching about the meaning of faith in God contained in Isa. 7:9. But it is mistaken exegesis, I believe, to extend the particular assertion made here ["If you do not believe, you will not be established"] to cover other particular situations in which the historical circumstances and ethical options are quite different.

THE IMMANUEL SIGN (ISA. 7:10-16)

10 Once again Yahweh spoke to Ahaz, saying, "Ask for
11 yourself a sign from Yahweh your God—from the depths of Sheol or the heights above."
12 But Ahaz replied, "I will not ask and put Yahweh to a test."

---

and believed Yahweh and his servant Moses." This statement, however, does not mean they had a general belief *in* Yahweh and Moses (as the RSV, for example, translates it) but that the people now believed what Moses had previously told them about his meeting with Yahweh at the burning bush and his commission from Yahweh to take Israel out of Egypt (4:1). Everything Moses had done from his departure from Sinai to the crossing of the Sea of Reeds had been aimed at persuading the people to believe this *word* of Yahweh (Exod. 3:7-10).

13   So he said, "Listen then, House of David. Is it too small a thing to try the patience of men, that you
14   must try also the patience of my God? Therefore the Lord himself will give you a sign: Behold, the maiden is pregnant and about to bear a son, and she
15   will call him God-Is-With-Us (*'immanû 'el*). He will eat curds and honey until he knows (enough) to re-
16   fuse the bad and choose the good. For before the boy refuses the bad and chooses the good, the territories whose two kings you dread will be deserted.

Apparently Isaiah was rebuffed by Ahaz when he delivered his first oracle to him (7:4-9) so he delivered another (7:12-16). This second oracle was an annoucement of the birth of a child who would bear a symbolic name, that is, would be a sign to Ahaz and his house (vs. 14). But before Isaiah made this announcement, he invited Ahaz, who had already refused to accept the counsel the prophet had brought from Yahweh, to try himself to obtain a sign from Yahweh. Since he had not accepted *Isaiah's* representation of Yahweh's word, let him find out in some other way what Yahweh's counsel was—any way at all in heaven or earth! This is the only interpretation of 7:10 that makes sense to me. It is preposterous to think Isaiah offered to provide Ahaz some external sign, chosen by Ahaz at will from among the endless possibilities in heaven and earth, to confirm the truth or authority of his (Isaiah's) prophetic word. Yet this is perhaps the most common interpretation of the line.[18] If it were correct, we would be forced to dismiss the report as a pious legend, for no sober prophet of Yahweh, either in the eighth century B.C. or any other time, could have thought himself able to fulfill such a request. But this interpretation is wholly unnecessary, especially since it involves an incorrect reading of the line.

[18] See, e.g., Gray, where it appears in its baldest form.

The English versions omit the most important word in the line and consequently give it a distorted connotation. They read, "Ask a sign of the Lord your God; let it be deep as Sheol or high as heaven." [19] It must, however, be translated, "Ask *for yourself* a sign from Yahweh your God." [20] Isaiah was not offering proudly (and magically) to produce any sign Ahaz might suggest but was challenging *Ahaz* to produce some sign of Yahweh's will, any sign at all, since he had refused to accept Isaiah's representation.[21]

Ahaz declined the invitation, naturally. What need had he to disprove Isaiah's word? He needed only to disregard it. Isaiah was only a prophet, and Ahaz was the king. Neither on this nor any other occasion, as far as we know, did he pay the slightest attention to Isaiah. He did not have to. He did not even have to answer him. However, on this occasion he did condescend to give him a reply, according to the writer, and it was theologically correct. He said, "I will not ask and put Yahweh to a test" (vs. 12). Commentators have read pious cant into this reply, but it is perhaps nothing more than a refusal. *We* may take Ahaz as a hypocrite and Isaiah as the voice of God, but this is simply our opinion and a rather easy judgment after the fact. Isaiah *claimed* to be speaking for God. Ahaz rejected his claim. This was not necessarily hypocrisy. Many men in Israel claimed to speak for God, and they very often spoke against one another! Ahaz would have been a fool to accept a prophet's advice solely because it was represented as the word of Yahweh.

[19] RSV. Cf. Chicago, KJV, and ASV.

[20] The pronoun is correctly indicated in Jerusalem and Kissane, and cf. Fohrer, Eichrodt, and Kaiser (the translations, not the interpretations).

[21] Isaiah might have challenged Ahaz instead to produce some other *oracle* since there were other prophets around. The writer's choice of the term *sign* here appears to have been dictated by what followed in his narrative (Isaiah's sign of Immanuel) and not by what preceded (Isaiah's previous oracle). The failure to see this contrast between Ahaz's sign (which he did not, refused to, probably could not, produce) and Isaiah's sign (which he promised and would soon produce in the flesh) has misled many commentators.

Naturally, Isaiah had not finished. He accused the Davidic house of trying the patience both of men and of God (vs. 13). The first was a fact (Isaiah's patience was tried and so, probably, was that of others in Judah) and the second an opinion, once again. And then Isaiah offered his own sign, this, too, as if from God (vs. 14), like the oracle already proclaimed (7:4-9).

Behold, the maiden is pregnant and about to bear a son, and she will call him God-Is-With-Us (*'immanû 'el*).[22] He will eat curds and honey until he knows (enough) to refuse the bad and choose the good. For before the boy refuses the bad and chooses the good, the territories whose two kings you dread will be deserted.

(7:14-16)

The traditional Christian interpretation of this prophecy is well known. It arose from the (pre-Christian) Greek translation of Isaiah, in which "the maiden" (*ha'almah*) became "the virgin" (*parthenos*) and from the consequent Christian belief that the virgin birth of Jesus had been predicted by the prophet (Matt. 1:23). It is a moot question whether the early Christians searched the scriptures (i.e., the Old Testament) for a prophetic confirmation of a belief in Jesus' virgin birth that had already taken form, or formed the belief out of Isaiah's prophecy; but this is beside the point of Old Testament exegesis. The Christian messianic interpretation of Isa. 7:14 has dominated the history of exegesis, but today it no longer commands the assent of a majority of commentators, in the sense that they believe Isaiah intended the oracle mes-

[22] The first two verbs are participles and the third a consecutive perfect. Cf. Jerusalem, RSV Marg., ASV Marg., Chicago, Moffatt, Gray, Kaiser, Eichrodt, and Fohrer, among others. Cf. also the announcements in Gen. 16:11 and Judg. 13:5, 7, which use the participial form. Kissane insisted that all these participles expressed the future. However, BDB and KBL list them as adjectives. GK cites Gen. 16:11 as a present (116*n*) and Isa. 7:14 as a *futurum instans*, i.e., "as imminent, or at least near at hand (and sure to happen)" (116*p*).

sianically.[23] But it continues to exact tribute from some who believe this theory must be disproved in order to clear the way for an alternative or who are willing to affirm that Isaiah's original oracle pointed beyond the circumstances and possibilities of his own time even though it was primarily intended as a word to Ahaz in the crisis of 735 B.C. This concession may be made in regard to the royal oracles in Isa. 9 and 11, but it is entirely unnecessary in the case of 7:14. There is nothing royal or messianic in Isa. 7:14-16, and it has nothing to do with a virgin birth. The writer of Matt. 1:23 was simply wrong. He used a single word in the Greek version of the Bible as the pretext for a Christian dogma.

Isaiah's initial counsel to Ahaz not to fear the Syro-Ephraimitic threat to Judah and therefore, implicitly, not to act out of that fear, had obviously been disregarded since the prophet considered it necessary to speak on the subject a second time, again as Yahweh's spokesman. He challenged Ahaz to produce some sign of God's will in the situation and when Ahaz declined, announced one of his own, in confirmation of the oracle he had already delivered. Isaiah's promise of a sign from "my Lord himself" meant that he, Isaiah, would deliver the sign. What else could it have meant? Isaiah understood himself as Yahweh's messenger and representative, and his words and signs to Judah were represented as Yahweh's. Most of his deliverances were spoken oracles. Some were signs, like naming A-Remnant-Shall-Return and Speedy-Spoil-Quick-Plunder, his sons, and walking naked in public for three years (7:2; 8:1-4; 20:1-6). The signs were always provided with verbal explanations, and thus they became incarnate oracles (10:20-21; 8:4; and 20:3-6).

Isaiah had no supernatural control over events in the world.

[23] There is, however, a vigorous minority. See, e.g., J. Coppens, "L'Interpretation d'Is., VII, 14, a la lumiere des études les plus récentes," *Lex tua Veritas. Festschrift für H. Junker*, H. Gross and F. Mussner, eds. (Trier, 1961), pp. 31-45 (with full bibliography).

The only signs from God he could ensure were those he himself performed. The only words from God he could promise were those he himself proclaimed. If we take any other approach to the sign in Isa. 7:14, we are taking the line of magic or legend.[24] According to the narrative, Isaiah was certain the sign would be given, that a child would be born, would be named a particular name, out of an infinite number of possibilities, and would be fed a particular diet during the first months (or years) of his life, this from a limited but still considerable number of possibilities. How could he be so sure that this name would be given and this diet maintained? He was sure because the pregnant woman was his wife, and because he himself would choose the name and food.[25] Thus God-Is-With-Us would be another of Isaiah's prophetic signs, which would be suggestive though not entirely self-explanatory, like naming A-Remnant-Shall-Return and Speedy-Spoil-Quick-Plunder and walking naked in public. Each sign required clarification. The explanation was simple in all four instances, involving only a few words, but it was indispensable to a right understanding of the meaning of the sign.

The child is referred to as a boy, but the sex of the still unborn child, over which of course Isaiah had no control, was not a factor in the sign. A Hebrew father would naturally refer to an unborn child as a son. Also, it is not impossible that the narrative has been influenced at this point by the writer's subsequent knowledge of the actual sex of the child who was eventually born. The child would soon be born and would be named God-Is-With-Us.[26] He would be fed an unusual

---

[24] See the legendary account of Isaiah's oracle and sign to Hezekiah in Isa. 38:4-8.

[25] See N. K. Gottwald, "Immanuel as the Prophet's Son," *VT*, VIII (1958), 36-47.

[26] The woman is the subject of the verb, but this is unimportant. The terse announcement merely runs three verbs together ("is pregnant and about to bear

(but adequate) diet from the time of his birth until he was able to express his own likes and dislikes. This would be a short period, probably not more than a few months or a year (as any parent can testify!). It would be only until he could "choose" what he liked or disliked and make this preference known. This communication would not require articulate speech but would take place long before the child was able to talk. This immediacy of the sign's fulfillment was completely consistent with Isaiah's previous promise that the threatened conquest of Judah would never take place (7:7). The second promise, incorporated in the sign, went somewhat beyond that contained in the previous oracle, for it said not only that the plot against Judah would fail but that the ploter's lands would soon be forsaken. The sign went further than the initial oracle in another respect also. It indicated that God would be present throughout the crisis. This might have been assumed in the case of the first promise since it was a word of God, but it was said explicitly only in the second.

The period of time involved in the symbolic action would be longer—though the prophet's point would be essentially the same—if "refuse the bad and choose the good" (7:15-16) meant to discriminate morally. But Deut. 1:39 and II Sam. 19:35 confirm the interpretation we have adopted here. In the former text little children are described as those who do not yet know good from bad, which seems to me to mean that they are too young to discriminate in anything. Isa. 7:14-16 specifies the realm of discrimination, at least by association, namely food. As the youngest child lacks taste, so does the oldest man. Barzillai at eighty had lost what God-Is-With-Us would not yet have gained, according to Isaiah, that is, the

---

and will call"). It was irrelevant whether the naming was first done by father or mother, since both would call him by this name in any case. The identification of the child does not hinge on this point, as has sometimes been asserted.

power to tell "good" from "bad." Consequently, he had become indifferent to food (II Sam. 19:35).[27] In any case, Isaiah's point was that the boy would not have attained the age of discernment before the collapse of Syria and Israel took place. It had little to do with the quality of the discernment itself. He made exactly the same point in 8:4 in connection with the inability of the infant Speedy-Spoil-Quick-Plunder to speak. *What* he spoke, when he eventually spoke, was irrelevant, though "Daddy" and "Mama" served to make the point. *What* God-Is-With-Us eventually chose was in one sense equally irrelevant, but in his case Isaiah deliberately narrowed the realm of his choosing by relating it to the curds and honey, which were part of the whole symbolic action. Isa. 7:14-16 is hardly concerned with the quality of the boy's eventual ethical discernment and is thus to be distinguished from the oracles concerning the just king in 11:1-9 and 32:1-4.

We must not deduce too much from the name God-Is-With-Us. The writer did not say the presence of God in Judah's midst was a guarantee of physical protection for the land or the city of Jerusalem or that it was an assurance of success in Judean military efforts. He said only that the kingdoms whose rulers now planned to subjugate Judah would soon be forsaken themselves and that, in the meantime, "God is with us." He did not even explain specifically to whom the "us" referred! The deliverance from the present threat might therefore be interpreted as a gift of God. But the gift might not be taken legitimately as a general guarantee of support for Judean policy. It might, however, be taken as a God-

---

[27] To discern between good and bad (evil) often means to discern morally in the Old Testament (e.g., I Kings 3:9; Isa. 5:20; Mic. 3:2), but "the good" itself is used non-ethically 107 out of 135 times and "the bad" (evil) 50 out of 126, according to BDB (pp. 375a and 948b). The phrase "to know good and evil" seems to connote universal knowledge in Gen. 2:9, 17; 3:5, 22; and II Sam. 14:17; but "until he knows (enough) to refuse the bad and choose the good," in Isa. 7:15, hardly refers to this kind of comprehensive knowing.

given opportunity. This is not said in 7:10-16 itself, but it is the burden of all Isaiah's preaching. Every oracle was a call for decision. Every word of Yahweh was an opportunity for obedience whether it contained a threat or a promise. In the events transpiring in 735 B.C. God was present in the same sense in which he was always present, as the Lord who demanded obedience and offered "blessing" in the doing of justice. Nothing more than this need be inferred from the symbolic name of the child, as it is explained in chapter 7, and nothing more may be inferred from it when it is set in the larger context of Isaiah's oracles.

The curds and honey which the child was to be fed have perplexed the commentators. Some have argued that they were the typical pastoral food of the wilderness and therefore a symbol of deprivation. Others have taken the opposite side and interpreted them as a sign of abundance. The writer of 7:21-22 took the curds and honey as the sign of abundance for a few in the midst of general deprivation. But no agreement has been reached over the meaning of this choice of foods in the original sign to Ahaz. If the sign is viewed as one that Isaiah himself was to perform, the difficulty vanishes. The curds and honey were enigmatic in exactly the same way as most prophetic signs, including Isaiah's.[28] Feeding the child curds and honey until the threat against Judah had finally disappeared, an event that would happen by the time the child was able to make his own choice known, was strange and provocative. As in the case of other prophetic signs, the public had no way of discovering the meaning of the sign until it was explained by the prophet. It lacked any reference, any object, until the verbal clarification was made. None of the symbolic actions of the prophets was self-explanatory, and feeding the baby curds and honey was just such an action.

[28] Compare Jer. 4:1–5:6; 13:1-11; 16:1-3; 19:1-15; and Hos. 3.

But what was the significance of the food according to the prophet's explanation? Deprivation or abundance? Neither, so far as the primary pericope (7:10-16) is concerned. In this pericope no meaning is attached to the foods themselves but only to the length of time the child would be kept on this particular diet. The curds and honey would not automatically suggest to an observer a certain set of external circumstances, but the exclusive feeding of these two foods for the period indicated would show that there was an ulterior motive on the part of the parent. What this motive was would have to be explained, exactly as in the case of every other prophetic sign, and so would the significance of the baby's name. In itself the phrase "God is with us" may signify many things, indeed almost anything that might be predicated of God. It is therefore a mistake to take either the name or the food as an explicit prophecy of weal or woe. Both are ambiguous and demand an accompanying explanatory oracle. The sense they were meant to have, on the evidence of the pericope itself, was that the Syro-Ephraimite kingdoms were soon to be destroyed.

Isa. 7:21-22 is a separate oracle having nothing originally to do with 7:10-16. It is one of a series in 7:17-25 that treats the day of God's judgment upon Judah, a subject never raised in the Immanuel oracle. Isa. 7:21-22 makes use of the motif of curds and honey. Here the food is described as the food of abundance, eaten by the few survivors of a devastated kingdom. But this meaning is not attributed to the foods in 7:10-16. It is possible that curds and honey were generally considered to be luxurious fare. Their use in the symbolic feeding of Immanuel would then have attracted people's attention. In any case, the two pericopes have nothing in common except the motif of curds and honey.

This interpretation of the sign of Immanuel makes full sense of every element in the situation of Isaiah and Ahaz and of every feature of the extant narrative except one, namely the choice of the word *ha'almah* to designate the prophet's wife. However, this theory is no more inadequate at this point than the alternative interpretations, for none of them provides a fully satisfactory explanation of the reference. We may ask why the writer did not say "my wife" or "my *'almah*" if he was referring to the wife of Isaiah, but a similar question arises on any interpretation of the sign. Indeed, this failure of the writer to identify the woman explicitly is less an obstacle to the thory that she was Isaiah's wife than it is to any other alternative, for a similar, unclarified allusion ("the prophetess") appears in the narrative about the prophet's begetting Speedy-Spoil-Quick-Plunder (8:3). "The prophetess" perhaps comes closer to indicating the prophet's wife than "the maiden" does, but it is still ambiguous. Nowhere else in the Old Testament is the term used to designate the wife of a prophet. However, 8:1-4 does not require further identification of the woman, for it is clear here that the child is Isaiah's and equally clear that it is he who gives the symbolic name. Had 7:10-16 said that Isaiah had begotten the child, the reference to "the maiden" would have provided no problem for us, for there is no evidence that the word *'almah* might not be used of any young woman past puberty, whether married or not, and no reason why the writers of Isaiah should not have referred to Isaiah's wife by different terms in different narratives.[29] Indeed, he

[29] It has been assumed by some scholars that *'almah* designates a girl past puberty who has not yet borne a child, but there is no biblical evidence to support this theory. All efforts to limit the scope of the term to a specific phase of a girl's sexual development or experience fail for lack of evidence (i.e., that it meant a virgin—married or unmarried; or a sexually mature but unmarried girl—virgin or not; or a sexually mature girl prior to childbirth—whether married or not, virgin or not). All that may be concluded legitimately from the available evidence is that the term designated a girl in the prime of life. Therefore, on the basis of present knowledge, the word *'almah* may not be used in support of or opposition to any interpretation of the sign of Immanuel, though it would seem to rule out the possibility of a prophecy of birth to an aged mother (cf. Gen. 18:9 ff.).

201

may have had more than one wife. Polygamy was acceptable in ancient Israel, and there is no indication in the book of Isaiah that all his sons had the same mother.

We know Isaiah had at least two symbolically named sons. When, therefore, in the immediate context of references to these sons (7:2 and 8:1-4) the writer of Isaiah mentions another child with a symbolic name, the obvious and simple assumption is that he means another son of Isaiah. "*The* maiden" provides no obstacle to this conclusion. This term (*ha'almah*) might have designated equally well (and equally incompletely) the wife of Ahaz or any other specific young woman known to Isaiah and his audience.[30] It is on other grounds that these possibilities must be rejected. The term "*the* maiden," however, is a direct obstacle to any theory which makes the mother of Immanuel indefinite or unknown, including the messianic interpretation.[31] Had the writer been referring to a king or savior in an indefinite future time, whose mother was therefore unknown, he would surely have said "*a* maiden." This is not the most serious weakness of the messianic theory, but it is a weakness.

The decisive weakness of the messianic interpretation is that it lifts the sign out of the historical situation in which the writer has clearly and explicitly placed it. If Immanuel was the Messiah, he was not a sign to Ahaz and his contemporaries. This is a prohibitive obstacle to the hypothesis. There is simply no way around it. The only way the dogmatic belief in Isaiah's prophecy as a prediction of the Messiah may be preserved without doing violence to the Old Testament text is to suppose that Isaiah himself *meant* the sign to be fulfilled in the immediate future but that it did not turn out that way, or that it was fulfilled partly in the immediate future but com-

---

[30] Ahaz was probably twenty so his wife was certainly young.

[31] The corporate theory, i.e., that the maiden symbolized many mothers responding to the national circumstances in which their babies were born, is another in this category. It is implausible for many reasons and has had few advocates.

pletely only in the coming of the Messiah. Both assumptions presuppose that Immanuel was a royal or soteriological figure. Nothing in Isa. 7 suggests either. The name "Immanuel" is no more royal than any of the theophoric names in the Old Testament, nor is it necessarily soteriological. The presence of God in the midst of his people was for the eighth-century prophets primarily a source of judgment and destruction.

The assumption that Isaiah's announcement of the sign was not fulfilled in the time specified by the narrative is wholly unwarranted. Nothing in the book prevents our concluding that the child was born, named, and fed in the manner described. The use of the name in 8:8, in the general context of the Maher-shalal-hash-baz ("Speedy-Spoil-Quick-Plunder") pericope, also suggests that there was someone among Isaiah's contemporaries who actually bore it. There is nothing "left over" to require or justify a supplementary messianic interpretation if the sign is seen as Isaiah's son, born, named, and fed in the manner described. If Immanuel were Ahaz's son, however, a messianic interpretation in the futuristic, soteriological sense, would be partly justified as a supplementary application of the sign since a royal prince of Judah would have become the Messiah ("anointed one"), in the empirical sense, at his coronation. This interpretation of Immanuel as the king's son thus places 7:10-16 alongside 9:1-7 and 11:1-9 as a "messianic" oracle. It has had many advocates in recent times.[32]

The prohibitive obstacle to the conclusion that Immanuel was Ahaz's child, who was soon to be born, is that Isaiah in this case would have had no control over the naming and feeding of the baby.[33] He could not have assured that the

---

[32] References given in Coppens, loc. cit., in addition to the standard commentaries and introductions.

[33] The theory that Isaiah prophesied not merely a new royal child but an heir to the throne requires that the child should have been a boy. The difficulty of this theory is thus compounded in this particular form.

sign from the Lord would actually be given. The name and the diet would have had only figurative significance. The announcement would have been nothing more than a parable. The *sign* would not then have been an actual child named Immanuel who was to be fed real curds and honey but the parabolic oracle given here in the form of a hypothetical birth announcement. Sign and oracle would then have been identical. The sign would have *been* Isa. 7:14-16.[34]

[34] The theory that the child was Ahaz's leads inevitably to the figurative interpretation of the naming and feeding. Certainly Ahaz would not actually have named and fed his child in this way. Once Isaiah had predicted this, he could be certain this would be the *last* thing Ahaz would do! So this name and diet were not to be the real name and diet but ones that might be appropriate to the occasion. But why would they be appropriate? The only adequate reason would be that the danger to Judah would already have disappeared by the time the child was born. But according to 7:15 this was to happen later, after the child was several months old, at least. This objection applies whether the Immanuel sign was single (pure promise) or double (promise and threat). It has often been considered double by commentators. Thus the prophet is supposed to have been saying that the birth of the child would coincide with the release of Judah from the threat of a Syro-Ephraimitic invasion so he would be named "Immanuel" as an act of gratitude and faith (vs. 16). But unbeknown to the parents, the name would have a second, sinister significance, which would be disclosed when (in a few years at most) Judah was overrun by Assyria (vs. 17) as a judgment of the God who was in their midst. This interpretation violates the clear indication of the text that the naming and feeding would point toward a still future event, and it leaves the curds and honey unexplained. If we suppose the reason for the naming was the parents' joy over the successful birth, as has sometimes been suggested, we are right back again to the theory that the name "Immanuel" would actually be given. Otherwise, the parents' joy over their new baby would have no conceivable connection with the national crisis. This connection would depend upon the meaning of this particular name and the significance of this particular food. The name God-Is-With-Us would be a fine name for the child of grateful parents, relieved from anxiety over the dangers of childbirth. And it might also be construed to have a hidden significance, pointing to a national deliverance from danger. The curds and honey would then have to be recognized as luxurious food (which of course it would not be unreasonable to give to a prince), symbolizing the coming blessedness of Judah. But this name and this food would have to be given actually to the child. We have come full circle and made a diviner of Isaiah again. There is no way out of this web of impossibilities. One advocate of the theory tried to get out by supposing the sign itself was the prediction that the royal child would be a boy (K. Fullerton, "Immanuel," *AJSL*, XXXIV [1918], 256-83). We might as well suppose Isaiah was willing to cast lots with Ahaz to decide whether the prophet's original oracle was reliable!

The only way around this conclusion is desperate. We would have to assume that Isaiah was merely *predicting* a birth, a naming, and a feeding (or, if the mother were known to be pregnant, the naming and feeding alone) without having any direct control over these acts himself. He would then have been saying that when and if this prediction were fulfilled, Ahaz should accept it as a sign from God that confirmed Isaiah's original message. The sign would have been separate from the oracle(s) which it confirmed.

This theory makes Isaiah a diviner and forces us to imagine him staking the validity of his message upon the wildest sort of speculation. It has nothing to commend it. The parabolic interpretation is vastly superior in every way. However, the parabolic or figurative view is equally inferior to the conclusion that Immanuel was the prophet's son. The Lord was about to give the House of David a sign in action, like other prophetic signs, as an embodiment of Isaiah's counsel to the king as this was expressed both in his initial oracle (7:4-9) and in the now accompanying explanation (7:16). This sign, again like other prophetic signs, was not to be "fulfilled," that is, proved true, independently of the fulfillment of the message in Isaiah's oracles. The two would be fulfilled simultaneously. There is no instance in the books of the prophets where an acted or tangible sign from God was meant to be fulfilled extraneously as a kind of temporary proof that the prophet's prophecies of God's future acts were true. All the signs of the literary prophets were *acted* oracles though, as I have said, they all required verbal clarification by the prophet in order to become fully intelligible. If Isaiah's sign were a *prediction* of a symbolic action, it would be unique among the signs of the canonical prophets. But there is no need to assume that it was. The most natural way to read Isa. 7:10-16 is to regard the sign as the action itself. This action was not predicted; it was promised. It lay in the future only because the baby was not yet born. But the birth was imminent and so, therefore, was the symbolic action.

Prophetic signs pointed toward God's historic judgments concerning Israel; they added nothing substantially to the content of the prophets' oracles. They were simply a different kind of oracle, often a more memorable kind. They did not "confirm" the oracles or make them more credible prior to the fulfillment of the oracles themselves. Neither did Isaiah's sign of Immanuel. Isaiah was not a diviner or a magician, in spite of the picture of him given in chapters 36–39. The only ground upon which he might have been sure (as the narrative clearly indicates he was) that the Lord would give the sign of Immanuel was that the child was his own and soon to be born. *No* other interpretation meets this essential requirement. On the other hand, the messianic and figurative interpretations fail utterly to meet the other essential requirement, namely that the sign should have been a sign to Ahaz in the circumstances described by the narrative.[35] But these theories are superfluous in the light of the simple adequacy of the view that Immanuel was the prophet's son. The objection to this view that it does not do justice to the quality of mystery and ultimacy in the announcement is baseless. There was as much of these qualities about the sign of Immanuel as about any other prophetic sign, and no more. It is incorrect to call the sign a "mystery." The sign was merely arbitrary, like all prophetic signs. It made sense once it was explained, but not before, like all prophetic signs.

The interpretation of Immanuel as the Messiah is contextual since 7:10-16 itself contains no clear messianic note. It depends on the assimilation of this prophecy to 9:1-7, in which

---

[35] It was necessary for Ahaz and his advisers to *know* the sign had been given, but this would be accomplished in the same way in the case of Immanuel as in that of Shear-yashubh and Maher-shalal-hash-baz, i.e., the sign would quickly become a matter of common knowledge.

the birth of a royal child is announced, and, unfortunately, it owes too much to older Christian tradition, which was based on the Greek Bible and on a mechanical view of the nature of prophetic prediction. The view that Immanuel was the child of Ahaz is also contextual. It entails the assumption that Isaiah shared the official Judean estimate of the empirical dynasty of David and that 7:10-16 should be interpreted in the light of the explicitly messianic oracles in the book. However, it is not purely contextual, for it makes much of the term *ha'almah* as an alleged designation of a royal or a royal-cultic figure. However, there is no Old Testament evidence to support this allegation with respect to the word itself. This is now acknowledged by most advocates of this theory. Therefore, their case is based upon the assumption that a reference to "the maiden" which was made in the palace of the king would probably have been to the queen. But this opinion involves the prior assumption that because the "House of David" was addressed in the announcement (7:13), the scene must have been the palace. This assumption is improbable. Isa. 7:1-9 refers also to the House of David (vs. 2; though this is not in the oracle itself), and it uses the same plural form of address as 7:13-14 (i.e., in the actual oracle, 7:9*b*). And the scene of 7:1-9 was obviously not the palace! The foundation of this argument is thus precarious. Nevertheless, the conclusion that "*the* maiden" referred to the wife of one of the principal participants in the dialogue is sound.

There are contextual elements in the theory that Immanuel was Isaiah's son, notably the observation that the other two children with symbolic names in the book were sons of Isaiah. But this theory, more than any other, rests upon a serious regard for the explicit emphases of the text itself. It alone does justice to all of these. At the same time, it is the most natural and straightforward interpretation, and it creates no difficulties that must be rationalized away, unlike every alternative proposal.[36]

Isaiah spoke a second time to Ahaz to reaffirm his conviction that the conquest of Judah and the deposition of Ahaz by Aram and Israel would not succeed and thus, implicitly, to advise Ahaz to act on the basis of this assurance. This was God's word to the House of David in this national crisis. Isaiah's first proclamation of this word had been in the form of a standard prophetic oracle (7:4-9). The second was in the form of a standard prophetic sign, that is, an acted oracle. Isaiah's wife was soon to give birth to a child. They would name him God-Is-With-Us and would feed him nothing but curds and honey until he himself was able to let them know what he liked. The name and the arbitrary diet would be testimonies to Isaiah's belief that the invasion of Judah would fail and the invaders themselves be destroyed. They would be such a testimony because Isaiah himself was telling his audience they would be. These arbitrary actions would serve as continual reminders of the prophet's prediction until the time when the prediction was fulfilled. This would happen, Isaiah believed, by the time the child was able to make his own choices. Then the king would know the prophet had counseled him correctly, had spoken truly for God.

The episode of Immanuel is a classic example of a symbolic action by a prophet. It lacks nothing that was standard or essential to this kind of action, and it contains nothing superfluous to it. And the narrative of Isa. 7:10-16 is a model of the literary form developed to record such an act.

---

[36] The interpretation creates no problems with respect to the meaning and relevance of the passage itself. There is, however, one contextual problem, that is, the chronology of the births of Isaiah's sons. See the discussion of 8:1-4, below, pp. 217-18.

SUPPLEMENTS TO THE IMMANUEL SIGN
(ISA. 7:17-25)

17   Yahweh will bring for you and your people and your father's house times unlike any since Ephraim revolted from Judah [the king of Assyria].

18   In that day Yahweh will whistle for the fly from the
19   Delta in Egypt and the bee from Assyria, and they will all come and settle in the stream-beds and rock-crevices, and in every thornbush and every pasture.

20   In that day the Lord will shave with a razor hired in Mesopotamia [the king of Assyria] both head and body, and will stroke off the beard as well.

21   In that day each man will raise a cow and two sheep.

22   But there will be too much milk. He will eat curds—for, "He will eat curds and honey"—everyone left in the land.

23   In that day there will be briars and thorns where there
24   used to be a thousand vines of great value. One will go there with bow and arrow, for the whole land will be
25   briars and thorns. And one will not go to the hills that were cultivated, for fear of briars and thorns. It will become grazing ground for cattle and sheep.

An adequate explanation of the sign of Immanuel is given in the single sentence of 7:16. In form it corresponds exactly to the one-sentence explanation of the prophetic sign in 8:1-4, and in substance it agrees completely with the oracle in 7:4-9. The series of additional comments in 7:17-25 therefore seems superfluous. On the other hand, verses 17-25 are not a self-contained pericope, for if they were separated from what precedes, there would be no antecedent to the pronouns in verse 17. Verses 18-25, in turn, depend upon verse 17 for an antecedent to their introductory formula ("In that day," vss. 18, 20, 21, 23). Thus, whatever may have been the prior literary history of these five short sayings—and we may only speculate about this—they are now well connected to the foregoing narrative. With the exception of the two glosses in verses 17 and 20 ("the king of Assyria") this material has every right to be included in the primary stratum of the Isaianic corpus. The chief exegetical question, then, is whether the sign of Immanuel was originally intended to have a single significance (the collapse of Aram and Israel) and was subsequently extended editorially to symbolize the collapse of Judah as well or whether the sign was meant to have a double significance from the beginning.

This question cannot be answered with absolute assurance. The other oracles of Isaiah, as well as the vision narrative (Isa. 6), prophesy the destruction of both kingdoms of Israel. These materials make clear that Isaiah's preaching was not predicated upon the hope of Judah's continued political independence; however, these oracles may be partly the result of Isaiah's later reflection on the outcome of the crisis of 735 B.C. Therefore, they provide no adequate control for judging the possible stages of development in chapters 7 and 8. Numerous chronological arrangements of his oracles and reconstructions of the development of his thought have been proposed, but each of these is subjective, circular, and unconvincing. The conclusions are always presupposed in the premises. There are a few allusions to specific historical events that may of course be dated. But an oracle in which one of these allusions occurs does not necessarily reflect the prophet's viewpoint at the time of the event even when it gives the impression that he was speaking contemporaneously with it. There was ample opportunity between the speaking and the recording of the oracle for retrospective conclusions to color the original declaration, and additional opportunity during the process of collecting and transmitting.

Isa. 7:18-25 prophesies the devastation of an unspecified

land by an invading army of Assyrians (vss. 18 and 20 [37])
and Egyptians (vs. 18). The first two threats are strikingly
metaphorical and the last two graphically literal. If they had a
prior literary history, the object of their original threat is
unknown. In their present place they are directed against
Judah, for verse 17 links them to the Immanuel sign. This
connecting statement is itself ambiguous. It might be either a
threat or a promise, and naturally it has been interpreted in
both ways. Were the coming days to bring a restoration of
the empire of David and Solomon or a disaster comparable
to the great schism under Solomon's son Rehoboam? Isaiah
could hardly have believed the destruction of Aram and
Israel, which could only have been accomplished by Assyria,
would open the way for Judah's annexation of their territories. A prophecy of the restoration of the Davidic empire is
therefore ruled out here. But the point of the comparison may
have been any number of other things, good or bad. The significance of the prediction in 7:17 depends upon the context.
It is threatening in its present place because of 7:18-25. But
what if it once stood apart from these threats as the conclusion of the Immanuel oracle (7:10-17)? [38] It would then
have been ambiguous. Its meaning would have been that the
devastation of the lands of Aram and Israel (vs. 16) would
create for Judah an opportunity unlike any she had had since
the division of the kingdom of Solomon. But it would not

---

[37] "The River" means the Euphrates (cf., e.g., Gen. 31:21; Exod. 23:31; and
Jer. 2:18) so the gloss is correct—and gratuitous.

[38] The commentators usually consider 7:10-17 to be one literary unit and
7:18-25 to be supplementary threats (generally believed to have been added by
Isaiah or an editor). Vs. 17, however, is as closely linked to 18 ff. as it is to 13-17.
The pronouns in 17a are singular, like the one in 25 ("you"), while those in 13-17
are plural ("ye"); and the "day" in 18, 20, 21, and 23, refers to the "days" in
17. There is a conjunction between 17 and 18 but none between 16 and 17. Vs. 17
may well have been written as a means of linking 18-25 to 13-16. I do not deny
that it has links to 10-16 (e.g., the plural pronoun in vs. 11, which, however,
is outside the oracle itself [13-16]) but only that these are stronger than the
links to 18 ff.

have specified the ends for which the opportunity might have been used.

Many interpreters assert that Isaiah's original oracle was deliberately ambiguous. He promised Ahaz an opportunity that might be used well or badly and thus lead either to Judah's welfare or to her ruin. In doing this he invited Ahaz (or rather he declared the situation prevailing when Immanuel reached the age of first willfulness would be an opportunity for Ahaz) to decide the destiny of Judah. He had already invited Ahaz to act on the basis of the *assurance* of the collapse of Aram and Israel (7:1-9). He now proposed a sign which would be a reminder of this invitation and predicted that within a short time Ahaz would be forced to act on the basis of the *actuality* of this collapse. But whether the same opportunity would exist then to turn the situation to Judah's welfare depended on Ahaz's decisions in the interim. It was therefore not a matter of indifference whether Ahaz accepted the prophet's counsel now or waited until then, for by then it might be too late. Ahaz might have sealed Judah's fate for evil by then. If so, the coming "days" would manifest the judgment and not the blessing of "God-Is-With-Us." The symbolic name of the child might be either a threat or a promise. Everything depended upon Ahaz's decision.[39]

One alternative to this approach is to assume that all of 7:10-25 comprised the original oracle. In this case the sign of Immanuel was the threat of an Assyrian conquest of Judah which was to take place within a year or two. The placement of this narrative immediately after the oracle in 7:1-9 would have shown that Isaiah's original promise of deliverance from the Syro-Ephraimite threat (1-9) was re-

---

[39] The curds and honey may have been meant also to signify this dual possibility (rich food for all, or for only a few, cf. 7:22). But the choice of particular foods was probably irrelevant since what mattered for the effectiveness of the sign was that the diet be arbitrary and be maintained consistently until the child expressed his own wishes.

affirmed (16) but was coupled now with the threat of an Assyrian invasion. This juxtaposition, then, would suggest that Ahaz had made a decision (perhaps even embodied in action) between the time of Isaiah's first oracle (7:1-9) and that of his second (7:10-17) and that this decision had led Isaiah to prophesy the Assyrian conquest of Judah. This interpretation has often been made. Ahaz's decision is presumed to have been requesting Assyrian aid against Israel and Aram, an action reported in II Kings 16:5-9. This policy entailed the diplomatic importation of part of the Assyrian cultus (II Kings 16:10-18), and it marked the beginning of Judah's assimilation into the Assyrian Empire.

A third possibility is to interpret the Immanuel sign as an unambiguous promise of relief from the Syro-Ephraimite threat (corresponding exactly to the substance of the first oracle, 7:1-9), to which was added subsequently the series of threats against Judah (7:18-25). This theory, too, has had many advocates. Actually, the whole of 7:10-25 may be read as pure promise to Judah once the gloss in verse 17 ("the king of Assyria") has been removed. For the treats in 18-25 say only that a land will be despoiled, without saying what land it will be. These lines might be a simple expansion of the promise that Israel and Aram would be forsaken (vs. 16).

In none of these lines (7:10-25) is it suggested what Ahaz was to do or not to do in the light of Isaiah's prediction.[40] They describe the context for decision but define no specific policy for the king to follow. Isaiah's understanding of the proper goals of royal policy was expressed in other oracles, and we must look to them for an answer to the question what he hoped Ahaz would do. They do not reveal the concrete acts Isaiah had in mind on this occasion, if any, but

---

[40] Isaiah's complaint that Ahaz was "wearying" God and men meant that the king had refused to accept Isaiah's assurance of the Syro-Ephraimite failure, but it implied nothing in particular with respect to the king's own political decisions.

they indicate the general objectives toward which he believed the Davidic king was obliged to work. These objectives may be characterized as the maintenance of justice and the resistance of idolatry in Judah.

SPEEDY-SPOIL-QUICK-PLUNDER (ISA. 8:1-4)

1 Yahweh said to me, "Take a large seal and inscribe it in ordinary script, 'Speedy spoil, quick plunder' (*maher*
2 *shalal ḥash baz*)." So I secured reliable witnesses, namely
3 Uriah the priest and Zechariah ben-Jeberekiah. Then I went to the prophetess, and she conceived and bore a son. And Yahweh said to me, "Name him Speedy-Spoil-Quick-
4 Plunder, for before the child knows how to say 'Daddy' or 'Mama' the wealth of Damascus and the spoil of Samaria will be carried away before the king of Assyria."

The meaning of this prophetic sign is clear, but the chronology is not. There are actually two signs mentioned, the inscribing of the tablet (or cylinder-seal) and the naming of the child. Both the inscription and the name consist of a single line of four words. Like all symbolic prophetic acts, these were not self-explanatory, for they did not name those who were to be despoiled. The explanation, made here in the usual way, supplied the missing datum. The victims would be Damascus (Aram) and Samaria (Israel) (vs. 4). The plunderer would be Assyria. Once again, the sign embodied a prophecy that Isaiah had declared to the Judean kingdom in several other ways. According to the present account the tablet was inscribed and then witnessed by two "reliable witnesses," Uriah and Zechariah, before the child was conceived. This was done in obedience to a command from Yahweh (vs. 1). Did Isaiah himself not know the significance of the inscription at that time? Had this command been received in the form of a general foreboding of disaster without a specific object? When the child was born, again according to the narrative, a second command was received to use the inscription as a name for the child, and this time the explanation of its meaning was given. Had the prophet intended to use the inscription as a name for a child from the beginning? The answer is, "Yes," if the meaning of the Hebrew in 8:1 is *"Belonging to* Speedy-Spoil-Quick-Plunder." [41] The answer is, "Not necessarily," if the preposition here is merely a sign of the accusative case (i.e., indicating the object of the verb "write"). [42]

Why had Isaiah required witnesses? It must have been because he wanted to fix publicly the *date* of the original inscription. Later he would not need affidavits to prove such an inscription existed, for all he would have to do would be to produce it. He would, however, need the witnesses to verify the time when it had actually been made. But why did he wish to be able to verify the time? Once the child was born and the name given, what would it add to the prophet's message to be able to say that he had declared this word as an oracle of Yahweh many months before? Surely he did not want merely to use this inscription as a means to publish the word while he was waiting for the child to be born. In that case he would have needed no witnesses, but might simply have displayed the seal (tablet) to the public (he could have worn it on a string around his neck, for example). He seems to have wanted to prove that he had *prophesied* the despoiling of Damascus and Samaria at a time when this was not expected by his countrymen. By the time the child was born and named the situation might have changed so that such a

---

[41] E.g., ASV, RSV, Gray, and Kaiser.

[42] E.g., Chicago, Jerusalem, Scott, and Kissane. This seems to be the more popular translation among scholars today. However, if the *gillayôn* was a cylinder-seal (cf. Jerusalem, footnote), the inscription was probably meant to indicate ownership, for such seals were used to stamp clay jars with the owner's name.

prospect was obvious to all and a special *prophetic* announcement of it gratuitous. In this case, he was concerned to establish his reliability as a prophet. As it turned out, however, the situation had not altered materially by the time the child was born so Isaiah proceeded to carry out his original intention and gave the symbolic name to the child. Of course, he might have done so even if the situation had changed, in order to confirm the original prophecy.

The reported sequence of events may be altered by rearranging the narrative,[43] but this is a subjective enterprise. The implication of the prophet's act was discernible whether the inscribing of the seal came before the conception of the child, as the present text indicates, or after it, as Lindblom has asserted. However, if the inscribing of the seal, like the naming of the child, occurred after the birth, as Kissane has argued, the significance of the double publication of the sign and that of the "reliable witnesses" is not evident.

The change in the political situation to which I have referred would have been the Assyrian advance upon Syria-Palestine, which led to the investment of Damascus and the annexation of two thirds of the territory of the kingdom of Samaria. The latter occurred in 733 B.C. Damascus fell in 732 B.C., completing the Assyrian conquest of the kingdom of Aram. The city of Samaria and its immediate environment were left in the control of a puppet Israelite government, and their full assimilation into the Assyrian Empire did not take place until 722 B.C. Since Isaiah 8:4 seems to be a prediction of the plundering of Damascus and Samaria, Speedy-Spoil-Quick-Plunder was probably named before 733 B.C. The fulfillment of Isaiah's prophecy of Samaria's fall was delayed well beyond the child's age of first speech (8:4) but not beyond the end of Isaiah's public career.

[43] See, e.g., Kissane, and Lindblom, *A Study on the Immanuel Section in Isaiah* (Lund, 1958), pp. 28-29.

The relation of the birth of Maher-shalal-hash-baz to the birth of Immanuel is an important historical question. Both signs point to the same end. This duplication is no problem in itself, for the whole series of prophecies in this collection (chaps. 7–8) points to the same end. The difficulty is in ascertaining the sequence of the births in relation to the international events referred to in the two symbolic names. Which child was born first? Did they have the same mother? Was there sufficient time while the crisis lasted for both signs to be performed in the fashion described? For our purpose the important question *exegetically* is whether or not the chronology of events precludes the interpretation of Immanuel as Isaiah's son.

The *terminus ad quem* for the birth of Maher-shalal-hash-baz is 732 B.C., for Damascus was still standing when the child was named (8:4). The *terminus a quo* for the announcement of Immanuel's impending birth (7:14) is the time when the threat of a Syro-Ephraimite invasion of Judah became known to Ahaz and Isaiah. The exact time of that event is unknown, but it is generally assumed to have been about 735 B.C. Even if it occurred somewhat later, there was ample time for both of these children to be borne by the same wife of Isaiah. The exact chronology of political events in the period 737-732 B.C. is uncertain. Furthermore, the precise relation of the words and acts of Isaiah to these events is at many points unspecified by the text. Add to this the possibility that the relationship has been confused in the retrospective reporting of the oracles, and the result is a fugitive set of exegetical data. Yet insofar as the facts are discernible, they do not in the least prohibit the conclusion that both Immanuel and Maher-shalal-hash-baz were Isaiah's children whether or not they had the same mother. Perhaps the least elusive datum of all in this connection is the reference in the annals of Tiglath-pileser III of Assyria to campaigns against Damascus in both the years 733 and 732 B.C.[44] If the conquest of the city took two years, there was plenty of time between the first Syro-Ephraimite action against Judah and the fall of Damascus for Isaiah to announce, beget, and name two children by the same wife. But he did not have to do all of these, for the first child was about to be born at the time of that first action (7:14). The minimum period of time required by our interpretation is about one year.[45]

THE PARABLE OF THE TWO STREAMS (ISA. 8:5-8)

5, 6   Yet once more Yahweh spoke to me saying, "Because this people has refused the waters of Shiloah that flow gently—and melts before Rezin and the son of Remaliah;

7   therefore, behold, the Lord is raising over them the waters of the great and mighty River—the king of Assyria and all his glory. And it will rise over all its

8   channels, and go over all its banks, and sweep into Judah, flood, and pass over, rising to the neck. And his outspread wings will fill the width of your land, Immanuel."

Here for the first time in this small collection of oracles on the crisis of 735-733 B.C. (Isa. 7–8) we find an explicit and unambiguous prophecy of the devastation and conquest of Judah by Assyria. The editor of 7:10-25, probably, and the glossator, certainly (7:17), interpreted the Immanuel oracle as a prediction of Judah's ruin; but the original oracle had not pointed clearly in this direction. Isa. 8:5-8 does. The major issue in interpreting this pericope is explaining *the refusal*

---

[44] See *ANET*, p. 283, and the discussion in M. Noth, *The History of Israel*, p. 260.

[45] The biological minimum is ten months, if the birth of Immanuel was imminent when Isaiah announced the first sign to Ahaz (7:14), assuming that Maher-shalal-hash-baz was not born prematurely. The reasonable minimum, however, is twelve to fourteen months.

adduced by Isaiah as the cause of the coming destruction (vs. 5). The usual view is that the waters of Shiloah symbolize faith in Yahweh and that the refusal was Ahaz's reliance upon Assyrian protection in place of trust in God.

If this opinion were correct, it would set religious faith and military alliance over against each other as alternative political policies. It would not necessarily set faith in God over against all military action but only against the dependence upon foreign aid. I believe this interpretation goes beyond the requirements of the text, however, and raises ethical questions which are not directly relevant to it. It also involves a conjectural interpretation of the symbol of the waters that seems forced and unsatisfactory. There is no evidence outside this passage that the waters of Shiloah were a symbol of trust in Yahweh. The pool of Siloam in Jerusalem and the stream which flowed into it from the Gihon (or Virgin's) spring had no direct connection to the temple that we know of. The only cultic act known to have had an association with them was the anointing of Solomon at the spring (I Kings 1:33). The name Shiloah appears nowhere else in the Old Testament; however, New Testament references and the famous Siloam inscription, which describes the construction of Hezekiah's tunnel,[46] make it probable that Isaiah's "waters of Shiloah" were these waters, which supplied Jerusalem. Therefore, they were an everyday object of his hearers' experience. We may assume the waters were near at hand and well known to Isaiah's audience. We may not assume they were a common symbol of cultic life or religious faith, or would be understood in this way by the audience. Nor does the oracle itself suggest this was the prophet's meaning. It has been read into 8:6 from 7:9, but this is dubious exegesis. Actually, the oracle is entirely self-explanatory without the need to resort to unverifiable assumptions.

[46] See John 9:7 and *ANET*, p. 321.

The oracle is a kind of parable, or double metaphor, of the two streams. "This people" (Judah, vs. 8) has refused the quiet waters of Shiloah; therefore, Yahweh will bring upon them the mighty waters of the River (i.e., the Euphrates).[47] Everyone in Judah knew exactly which streams these were and would have understood instantly the contrast made here between the size and power of the two. But what did the comparison mean? The commentators have erred in thinking the *application* of the comparison would have been obvious from the mere use of the two terms. Some have gone so far as to say the references to Rezin and Pekah ("the son of Remaliah," vs. 6) and to the king of Assyria (vs. 7) are both explanatory glosses. The second may be a gloss, but the first is indispensable to the meaning of the oracle. The point is simply that Judah has refused to endure the threat of Aram and Israel and will be forced as a consequence to endure a far more terrible threat, namely Assyrian conquest. The power of Rezin and Pekah was to the power of Assyria as that of the stream of Shiloah to that of the Euphrates.

The meaning of verses 7-8 is fairly obvious even without the naming of Assyria (if this is a gloss). "The River" was Assyrian at that time, and the image of it flooding Judah to the very borders could have had only one meaning in 735 B.C. Incidentally, the reference to the outspread "wings" of the river (vs. 8) is a mixed metaphor which has bothered interpreters. But it may refer to the common Assyrian symbol composed of the head of a king (or god) flanked by outstretched eagle's wings. The quietly flowing waters of Shiloah contrasted perfectly with the raging Euphrates in flood stage. However, the parable was not self-explanatory. Most prophetic parables were not, including those embodied in the symbolic actions of Isaiah. Therefore, it was necessary to specify Rezin

[47] See above, p. 211.

and the son of Remaliah. Refusing the waters of Shiloah (vs. 6) is synonymous here with trembling before Rezin and the son of Remaliah.[48] This simple construction (6a is to 6b as 7a is to 7b-8) has been overlooked by commentators.[49] Apparently they have been preoccupied by the assumption that the waters of Shiloah were a popular religious symbol in Isaiah's time.

Does the parable of the two streams, then, have no bearing upon the Judeans' faith (or faithlessness)? It has an indirect bearing, of course. Their refusal to abide the threat of Aram and Israel must have taken shape in some political action. We may accept the usual opinion that Ahaz's request for Assyrian intervention against Damascus and Samaria, together with his acceptance of the terms of vassalage to Assyria (II Kings 16:5-16), lay behind Isaiah's prediction of Judah's "inundation." To the prophet this would have been an act of idolatry. Also, according to the testimony of the preceding oracles, it would have been unnecessary. It therefore involved a total displacement of Judah's proper religious objectives for the sake of momentary dynastic security. It was a godless policy in this sense. However, this conclusion is an implication of an implication of the oracle. It is not what the parable signifies primarily. The waters of Shiloah in this oracle are not the symbol of the quiet power of God, in which Israel was supposed to trust, but of the harmless power of Rezin and Pekah, which Judah was not to fear.

[48] MT reads "rejoices," but nearly everyone now assumes the word was originally "melts" (trembles). The Hebrew words are homophonous. If the original oracle read "rejoices," then "this people" must have meant the Israelites and not the Judeans. In this case the flood was to cover Israel first (vs. 7) and then move on into Judah (vs. 8). The parallel to 7:10-25 is obvious.

[49] Gray cited the opinion of F. C. Burkitt (JTS, XII, 294) to the effect that the waters of Shiloah symbolized the Syro-Ephraimitic invasion. This is the only supporting modern opinion I have found for this view. The alternative has led to considerable speculation about the reason why these waters should have symbolized God's power. The conclusions, as one might expect, are not uniform.

THE STUMBLING-STONE AND THE TESTIMONY
(ISA. 8:9-22)

9 "Know this, O peoples, and be dismayed.
 Listen, all distant parts of the earth.
 Arm yourselves, yet be dismayed.
 Arm yourselves, yet be dismayed.

10 Plan a strategy, but it will be checked;
 Speak a word, but it will not succeed;
 For God is with us."

11 But thus said Yahweh to me
 In the grasp of (his) hand,
 And turned me from walking
 In the direction of this people, saying,

12 "Do not call conspiracy
 All that this people calls conspiracy,
 And do not fear what they fear,
 Nor be in dread.

13 It is Yahweh of hosts
 Whom you shall count holy,
 And him you shall fear,
 And him you shall dread.

14 And he will become a sanctuary—
 And a striking-stone and a stumbling-block—
 To the two Houses of Israel,
 And a trap and a snare
 To the inhabitants of Jerusalem.

15 And many will stumble over it,
 Fall and be broken,
 Be trapped and taken captive."

16 Bind up the testimony,
 Seal the teaching among my disciples,

17 And I will wait for Yahweh,
 Who is hiding his face from the House of Jacob,
 And I will hope in him.

18   Behold, I and the children
      Whom Yahweh has given me,
      Are signs and symbols in Israel
      From Yahweh of hosts,
      Who dwells in Mount Zion.

19   And when they say to you,
      "Consult the spirits
      And the whispering, mumbling soothsayers—
      Should not a people resort to its gods,
      To the dead for the sake of the living?"

20   (Then) to the teaching and the testimony!
      Surely they will speak such words,
      For which there is no dawn!

21   And they will traverse the land,
      Hard-pressed and hungry.
      And as they grow hungry,
      They will become enraged,
      And they will curse their king and their gods.
      They will look upward,

22   And then to the ground;
      But, behold, distress and darkness,
      Oppressive gloom,
      And unrelieved blackness.

In Isaiah's eyes the purpose of God often contravened the purpose of men. The arrogant ambition of men was frustrated ultimately in spite of temporary triumph while patient obedience to the demand of God was vindicated in spite of apparent failure. The first tangible result of an action is a poor measure of its rightness; therefore, the servant of God must be prepared to wait for history's (and God's) deliberate judgment. One of the difficulties in waiting, however, is that there is no absolute assurance that obedience will ever be vindicated in the eyes of men. Righteousness (social justice and love of neighbor) and faith (trust in the Creator and disavowal of idolatry) are partly self-authenticating. One must act, finally, on the basis of the intrinsic worth of the goals of action. This insight is perhaps obvious to all thoughtful persons, and it might have been obvious to Isaiah's contemporaries, the leaders of Judah. But Isaiah's responsibility was not the formulation of original ideas.

This conviction about the consequences of action lay behind Isaiah's counsel to Ahaz. But what was true for kings was also true in principle for prophets. So when Isaiah failed to persuade the leaders of Judah to choose his goals and reject their own, there was nothing left for him to do but wait in silence for the judgment of God. Concretely, this meant waiting for the failure of Ahaz's policy and the surrender of Judah's freedom to Assyria. One outcome of Ahaz's decision in the crisis of 735 B.C. was the loss of his right to decide. In this sense it was a manifestation of God's justice. But Ahaz's vassalage was Judah's also, and its corollaries were the further paganizing of her forms of worship and the displacement of her own standards of justice by those of Assyria. In practice this last meant a further subversion of the rights of the private citizen, for state tyranny was far more complete in Assyria than Judah. Furthermore, the welfare of a subject people is always subordinated to that of the conquering nation. The prospects for Yahwistic teaching, law, and worship were dim. By the time the events of 735-733 B.C. had passed, it was evident the Judean tree was falling and its stump about to be burned (Isa. 6:11-13). How would the teaching survive, the testimony to God's sovereign holiness be maintained, if the Judean kingship and cultus were put into the service of the Assyrian Empire? Isaiah's answer was to create a circle of disciples, beginning with his own children (8:16-18). They would preserve the teaching among themselves by whatever means were required (perhaps in written form). And they would wait.

Isa. 8:9-10 states the theme of the final section of this

small book of oracles, indeed of the book of Isaiah itself: the purposes of the nations will not stand against the will of God. On the surface this declaration places the nations over against "us" ("for God is with us," vs. 10). But it is not a simple promise of Judah's triumph against her enemies. It is not even a promise of national success on the condition of obedience to God. Isaiah never made such a promise to Ahaz or any other king. Obedience to God was not the guarantee of overt success as Isaiah's own failure demonstrated. He could hardly promise to king and nation what he knew nothing about himself. His entire counsel to Ahaz presupposed the perpetual contradiction between appearance and reality with respect to the vindication of faith and righteousness. Isa. 8:9-10, therefore, must be interpreted in its context. "God is with us" is not a nationalistic slogan. Isaiah's theology was not the reactionary propaganda of Israelite tribalism, with its holy war. All that was guaranteed among men by the power of God was the fulfillment of the word of God, manifested negatively in the frustration of idolatry and arrogance and positively in the establishment of the rights and welfare of individual men and in the continued existence of a worshiping community of the "Holy One of Israel." The king of Judah had spurned the fragile security given by fidelity to this word. He had preferred the more tangible security of the royal office despite its prospect of restricted freedom. A limited sovereignty was better to him than none at all, and Isaiah's policy involved the risk of losing it all. To Isaiah the kingship was a means of God's righteousness; to Ahaz it was an end that justified any means; therefore, the conflict between Isaiah and Ahaz was insoluble.

Isaiah found himself and the small group gathered about him to be the trustees of a conception of corporate responsibility unlike that of the established guardians of Judah's national life. In effect the group was required to adhere to a counsel with respect to the nation that Isaiah had urged upon the nation with respect to the other powers involved in the international crisis of 735-733 B.C. They were to stake their lives upon faith in God's righteousness and reject every alternative principle of action. The admonition to trust in the triumph of God's righteousness over the unjust schemes of the nations is expressed in Isa. 8:9-10 in the form of a word of God spoken to Isaiah. It is applied to the situation of his prophetic circle in 8:11-15. They had become an embattled "opposition party" in the midst of Judah, obligated to stand firmly by their teaching (7:9) and not to sanction the policy of the establishment or the ethical and religious conceptions which it presupposed. The world powers which the nation feared were not to be feared by Isaiah's circle (8:12). They were to fear only the Holy God, who was the ultimate sanctuary and source of life but who was to those who set themselves against him a stumbling-stone and cause of destruction (8:13-14).[50]

God had now "hidden his face" from the House of Jacob (vs. 17; that is, both Israel and Judah, vs. 14) in the sense that the power of his holiness and the counsel of his word were no longer available to them creatively. Israel under Pekah had shown its false conception of God's justice and of man's obedience by invading Judah, and now Judah showed that her principles of action were identical to Israel's. They were playing the same game, and they were playing against each other. Isaiah's obligation was to preserve the record of God's counsel until it might become a guide for obedience once more and a means of access to "the face" of God. This

---

[50] There is a play on words in 8:12-14 between *qesher* ("conspiracy"), *taqdîshû* ("revere"), and *miqdash* ("sanctuary"). The last two are derived from *qdš* ("be holy"). The older critical habit of emending *qšr* to *qdš*, or vice versa, has been abandoned generally by scholars during recent years. There is no textual basis for an emendation, and the MT makes good sense.

word of God, embodied in Isaiah's oracles, was the same word that had hardened the hearts of his people (6:9 ff.). It was the proclamation of the judgment of God against pride, idolatry, and injustice, as well as the approval of God of every act of justice and faith. During the collapse of the kingdoms those who were still blind to the demands and judgments of God might come to the little prophetic group to use them as diviners and necromancers (8:19), but in reply the group would appeal, as always, "to the teaching and the testimony" (20a). The last lines of the chapter (8:20-23) apparently describe the final despair of morally blind Judeans amid the ruins of the nation.

chapter 7

Zion in the Oracles of Isaiah

There is nothing more difficult to evaluate in the prophecy of
Isaiah than the Zion motif which runs through it. Of all
the themes in his oracles this one was most subject to secondary coloration by postexilic users of the growing Isaianic
collection. Jerusalem (Zion) had already come to dominate
Judean affairs in the pre-Isaianic era because it combined the
political and religious capitals of the southern kingdom.
After the assimilation of the kingdom of Israel by Assyria in
732-722 B.C., Judah alone remained as the chief bearer of
Yahwistic tradition. There may have been enclaves of faithful
Yahwists in territories that had once been Israelite, and there
were probably some among the Israelite exiles who continued
to teach the faith of the fathers to their children in spite of

the pagan environment in which they lived. Jer. 30–31 is addressed to the heirs of the northern kingdom, and it seems unlikely that the writer was speaking to them only hypothetically. Nevertheless, the institutions of the north disappeared as primary bearers of Yahwism, and it fell to Judah to maintain the worship of Yahweh and to promulgate covenantal teaching and law.

Yahwism suffered an official eclipse during the reign of Manasseh (687-642 B.C.) but enjoyed a splendid revival under Josiah (640-609 B.C.). Josiah's great religious reform in 621-609 B.C. (II Kings 22–23) exalted Jerusalem and its temple to an unprecedented height as the focus of Israelite piety. Zionism persisted during the exile and was given further impetus by the rebuilding of the temple of Jerusalem in 520-516 B.C. The book of Isaiah was probably completed in substantially its present form before the time of Nehemiah and Ezra a century later, so their work in Jerusalem had little if any impact upon its development. But the events of Jerusalem's history, from the fateful failure of Sennacherib to destroy it in 701 B.C., through Josiah's reform, to the rebuilding of the temple in 516 B.C., were sufficient stimuli to Zionism for it to become prominent in Judean prophetic tradition.

The book of Isaiah contains several forms of Zionism, and it is debatable which of these belong to the teaching of Isaiah himself. Some interpreters deny that Zion played a positive role in his preaching at all. Others assert it had fundamental importance. The scholarly debate over this issue has persisted through several generations and has not been resolved by form or tradition criticism. Since there is little immediate prospect of achieving a consensus on this basic question, we must continue to expect a variety of interpretations of Isaiah's theology. We may illustrate the gulf separating scholars on this issue by referring to two recent books dealing with Isaiah's thought. They are Sheldon Blank, *Prophetic Faith in*

Isaiah,[1] and Gerhard von Rad, *Old Testament Theology*, Vol. II.[2] In Blank's view, Isaiah predicted the destruction of Jerusalem by Assyria throughout his career, even during the siege of Sennacherib in 701 B.C. (1:4-8) and following the sudden Assyrian withdrawal from Judah, which saved the city and proved the prophet wrong (22:1*b*-14). The belief in Zion's inviolability as the place of God's earthly abode, which is expressed in Isa. 36-39, is a later reaction to the event of 701 B.C. The picture of Isaiah contained in these chapters is purely legendary. The legend, together with the belief in God's continuing protection of Zion, has filtered back into the genuine oracles of Isaiah in the form of glosses and expansions (e.g., 7:8*b*, 9*b*, 13, 15; 8:4; and 31:5). Even the meaning of "faith" in the oracles of Isaiah differs from the meaning in the legend. In the first it means righteousness, in the second belief in the wonder-working power of God.[3]

In von Rad's interpretation, Isaiah was profoundly influenced by an old Judean dogma of God's theophany upon Mount Zion, which was celebrated ritually in the Jerusalem temple along with rites pertaining to the sacred office of the Davidic king (the messiah or anointed one). The theophanic tradition was based on the memory of God's intervention on Israel's behalf in the crossing of the Sea of Reeds during the flight from Egypt. It is best exemplified by Exod. 14:13, where Israel is admonished simply to stand still and watch the act of God. This quietistic belief was the antecedent of Isaiah's teaching about the meaning of faith. It was expressed in worship at the Jerusalem temple in the dogma of God's descent, first to judge his own people for their sin and then to destroy their pagan enemies. Isaiah adapted this dogma to Judah's historical situation in the eighth century. He

[1] New York, 1958.
[2] New York, 1965.
[3] Blank, *op. cit.*, pp. 9-39.

prophesied the punishment of Judah for her sins through the agency of foreign invasion, but he also prophesied God's ultimate intervention on Mount Zion to defeat the invader. Thus the heathen armies would be punished for their godlessness, and Zion would be restored as the purified mountain of God (7:1-9; 10:27*b*-34; 14:28-32; 17:12-14; 29:1-8; 30:27-33; 31:1-8). Isaiah admonished the kings of Judah to act upon this belief. When Hezekiah paid tribute to Sennacherib in 701 B.C. and thus saved Jerusalem in the wrong way, that is, without simple reliance upon God's miracle, Isaiah's hope for the people was dashed, and his last prophetic word became a lament (1:4-9; 22:4).[4]

In von Rad's analysis Isaiah began as a prophet of salvation and ended as a prophet of destruction. A related theory which deserves mention is that Isaiah began as a prophet of Judah's destruction (at the hands of Assyria) and ended as a prophet of Judah's deliverance. The turning point came when he realized that Assyria, the rod of God's anger, was more wicked than Israel, against whom God had first wielded the rod. At the end of his career, then, he came to believe in God's protection of Zion. The belief was exaggerated by editors of the book but was essentially Isaiah's.[5] One of the advantages of a developmental interpretation of Isaiah's message is that it permits the attribution of Isaianic authorship to materials that are otherwise contradictory. However, several different theories of change have been proposed so this approach has not solved all the problems.

The conclusion to which I am led, and which I shall defend

[4] Von Rad, *op. cit.*, pp. 166-77. The theory that Isaiah urged the kings of Judah to wager the entire destiny of the nation upon sheer belief in the protective power of God has been expounded also by Eric Voegelin in *Israel and Revelation* ("Order and History," Vol. I; Baton Rouge, 1948), pp. 448-52. See, further, J. H. Hayes, "The Tradition of Zion's Inviolability," *JBL*, LXXXII (1963), 419-26.

[5] See, e.g., A. Lods, *The Prophets and the Rise of Judaism* (London, 1937), pp. 106-7.

in the following pages, is that Isaiah never proclaimed the military or political inviolability of the city of Jerusalem, either in the present or the future, but that he did prophesy the support of God for the continued existence of that community formed by faith in Yahweh and characterized by zeal for justice. Those who pursued justice among men and bore prophetic witness to the justice of God were assured of God's aid in this pursuit and this witness whether they were Isaiah himself and his children, the reigning king of Judah, the remnant left after the destruction of Judah, or any future king. This kind of Zionism is an essential ingredient of Isaiah's proclamation. Other forms of Zionism in the book are a reflex of Jerusalem's survival in 701 B.C. or an expression of later Jewish piety.

Jerusalem/Zion is prominent in the first group of Isaiah's oracles, 1:2–5:24.[6] The conclusion I have just stated is confirmed by everything here, including even those portions of the text that have been suspected of secondary origin. Chapter 1 is a composite poem on the destiny of Zion. It has been regarded by some scholars as an epitome of the preaching done by Isaiah at various times in his ministry.[7] Some of the seams in it are evident, but it is impossible to reconstruct the original components. The editorial unity of the chapter has even led some critics to consider it a single oracle.[8] The importance of the central section can hardly be exaggerated, for it is Isaiah's fullest statement about the Jerusalem cultus, which was the chief factor in the development of Zionism. This section pro-

[6] Except where the term is used metaphorically (14:32; 28:14-16; 29:8), Zion is synonymous with Jerusalem in the book of Isaiah (1:21; 2:3; 3:16; 4:2-6; 8:18; 10:12, 24, 32; 16:1; 31:4-6, 9; 33:20). The city is occasionally called "the daughter of Zion" (1:8; 4:4-6; 10:32; 16:1). "Mount Zion" means the temple in the late text 18:7. The meaning of the term is uncertain in 12:6, 30:19, and 33:5, 14 (all of these are late), though it seems to mean the Jewish religious community.

[7] E.g., R. H. Pfeiffer, *Introduction to the Old Testament*, p. 431, and G. Fohrer, "Jesaja 1 als Zusammenfassung der Verkündigung Jesajas," *ZAW*, LXXIV (1962), 251-68.

[8] E.g., Kissane.

vides the best evidence we have of Isaiah's evaluation of worship in Judah and serves as an excellent point of departure for a study of the significance of Zion in his teaching. The subject of the central section (1:10-20) is false and true atonement.[9] Ritual modes of access to God are wholly rejected (vss. 11-15), and the active pursuit of justice is upheld as the sole legitimate means of appropriating God's blessing (16-20).

Isaiah 1:10-20

10 Hear the word of Yahweh,
Rulers of Sodom!
Listen to the teaching of our God,
People of Gomorrah!

11 "What is the wealth of your sacrifice to me?"
Says Yahweh.
"I am sated with burnt rams
And cattle fat,
And I have no taste
For the blood of bulls and goats.

12 When you come to appear before me,
Who seeks this from your hand?
Trampling through my courts,

13 Bring no more useless offerings.
I loathe the smoke of sacrifice.
New moon and sabbath, calling assemblies—
I can't stand fasting [10] and sacred assembly!

14 Your new moons and stated feasts
I thoroughly despise.

---

[9] Procksch, Kissane, and Kaiser, among others, have acknowledged the unity of 1:10-20. Other commentators divide it in two between vss. 17 and 18. However, 1:10-17 has no conclusion, formally or logically. Vss. 18-20 make sense by themselves, but they make better sense as the conclusion to 10-17. The unit extends from "Hear the word of Yahweh" (1:10) to "The mouth of Yahweh has spoken" (1:20). The phrase "says Yahweh" no more indicates a division of units in vs. 18 than it does in vs. 11.

[10] Cf. LXX, Chicago, Jerusalem. MT reads "guilt and sacred assembly."

They weigh me down;
They are a tiresome burden to me.
15 When you stretch out your hands,
I turn my eyes away.
Even when you heap up prayers,
I am not listening.

"Your hands are full of blood.
16 Wash! Be clean!
Take your evil deeds
Out of my sight.
Stop doing evil;
17 Learn to do good.
Seek justice;
Restrain oppression.
Champion the orphan;
Plead the widow's cause.
18 Come now, and let us debate the case,"
Says Yahweh.
"Though your sins are like scarlet,
They shall be as white as snow;
Though they are as red as crimson,
They shall be as white as wool.
19 If you are willing and obey,
You shall eat the good of the land;
20 But if you refuse and rebel,
You shall be devoured by the sword;
For the mouth of Yahweh has spoken."

It has been denied by many Old Testament scholars in recent decades that the eighth-century prophets repudiated Israel's sacrificial cult outright. In their view, the prophets condemned the debased cult of their own time but not the Israelite cult per se. What they most objected to in the behavior of their contemporaries was the failure to balance ritual zeal with zeal for social justice. They would probably have given their approval to a purified cult, according to this interpretation.

However, the theory is entirely inferential. There are no explicit statements in the oracles of Amos, Hosea, Micah, or Isaiah to support it. Every reference to the sacrificial cult in these oracles is negative. The only modes of communion with God that they acknowledge positively are confession of guilt, faith, the fostering and teaching of justice, and the praise of God (Hos. 14:1-3; Mic. 4:2; 6:7). Isaiah's repudiation of ritual as a means of becoming accepted by God could not have been more complete than it was, judging by the present oracle. It covers the entire system built upon offerings, including prayer (1:15).

This apparent rejection of prayer cuts to the core of all religion so it is not surprising that commentators have sought ways to reduce the force of Isaiah's words. In one of the latest commentaries on Isaiah, for example, Hans Wildberger asserts without argument that Isaiah would not have questioned prayer in principle. Actually, however, there is no objective reason why he should not have done so. In dealing with the pre-exilic prophets all a priori judgments are precarious, particularly those which tend to accommodate prophetic utterance to the norms of popular religion, either ancient or modern. Of course, to ask whether the prophets rejected the cult, or prayer, in principle is to obscure the real exegetical question, which concerns the nature and function of the concrete religious acts repudiated by the prophets. There are various motives and modes of prayer. A prayer of petition for moral insight and the power to work for justice would have been consonant with the prophetic intention of Isaiah's oracles. However, even this prayer, as *prayer*, would have been unavailing to qualify a man to stand in God's presence, according to the standard defined by Isa. 1:10-20. Only *doing justly* could qualify him to do that. If he were a doer of justice,

then, might he also pray? Isaiah did not say. His oracle, however, excludes the possibility that prayer itself, or any other
ritual act, might increase a man's acceptability to God. In
this sense Isaiah put prayer in question *in principle*.

If we hew closely to the explicit wording of the oracle, we
find no explanation of this denunciation. The following lines
in the text are an admonition to champion the rights of the
oppressed (1:16-17), but it is not said whether the failure
to do this has made the offerings and prayers unacceptable to
God or whether doing it will make them acceptable. What
is said is that God does not want their offerings and prayers
but does want them to seek justice. What will happen if they
seek justice? Two things. First, and surely more important,
their "sins" will be purged away (1:18). This will be true
partly by definition, for their sin is injustice (1:16*a*). This
is another way of saying that the goal and reward of doing
justly are the act itself. Secondly, they "shall eat the good of
the earth" (1:19). Correspondingly, if they fail to pursue
justice they will be devoured by the sword (1:20). This is not
a promise of special favor in return for obedience but a statement of the general condition for continuing in possession of
the land. Had the writer wished to add that the fulfillment of
this condition would also make their offerings acceptable to
God, he would have done so, presumably. His silence on this
issue is indicative. The good of the earth is to be enjoyed by
the people, not by God, on condition of the maintenance of
justice. This affirmation stands in direct contrast to the
vehement denial that God desires any part of their offerings,
or the rituals built upon them, and as such it constitutes a
repudiation in principle of such a cultus.

Nothing in the other oracles of Isaiah mitigates the force of
1:10-20. The cultic symbolism of chapter 6 does not, although
it has occasionally been construed as an implicit endorsement

of a sacrificial cult. Taken as a whole, chapter 6 represents a radical transformation of Israel's worship into a ritual of the prophetic word. Its implications are fully consistent with the public oracles of Isaiah that bear on the present and future of Israel's worship. The symbol of the burned tree stump in 6:13 is as applicable to her worship as to other aspects of her corporate life. The form of the future plant was not to be a simple repetition of the old but something quite different. However, its form is not defined in the passages we have cited so far. For this we must look elsewhere.

Atonement, that is, the elimination of the effects of sin and the reestablishment of communion with God, could not be achieved by ritual means, in Isaiah's view. The only sin that meant anything was moral, and it could be repaired only by moral means. The guilt of the Israelites ("Your hands are full of blood," 1:15) was cultic, to be sure, but only in the sense that they used the cult as a means to effect atonement and not in the sense that they neglected some proper cultic act. Their fault was having too much cultus, not too little. "Wash yourselves!" (1:16) means "be rid of the sacrificial cultus" as much as it does "seek the welfare of the oppressed" (1:17). Worship in the Jerusalem temple was not only futile; it was also pernicious. This oracle undercut the very foundation of cultic Zionism. We should be surprised to find other oracles of Isaiah that endorsed it. Had Isaiah repudiated only the Assyrianized cultus of King Ahaz (II Kings 16:5-16), it would have been possible for him to endorse the purged cultus of King Hezekiah (II Kings 18:1-7). However, what he condemned was the "pure" Israelite cultus. His attack was radical. Therefore, it is impossible to reconcile an alleged later endorsement of Zion's sanctity by Isaiah with an earlier repudiation of it, on the ground of Hezekiah's intervening reform. Isaiah, like Amos and Hosea, rejected the sacrificial cultus itself.

This repudiation of all ritual means of effecting atonement does not presuppose a simple moralism in religion. On the contrary, Isaiah affirmed the reality of God's forgiveness of those who were willing to obey (1:18) and thus transcended moralism (legalism). Forgiveness meant putting behind them their former acts of injustice (or the neglect of justice) and idolatry, and acting justly and in faith. This forgiveness was what Isaiah experienced in his vision (6:7). It was something to be accepted in faith, not engineered by a ritual act. Significantly, in the vision there is no offering made by the prophet, indeed no ritual act performed by him or by a priest in his behalf. The symbolic burning of his mouth by the angelic ministrant represents a transformation of the service of the altar. It symbolizes God's accepting him without his doing anything except acknowledging his relationship to the Holy God of all the earth and obeying the commission to speak.

The rest of chapter 1 complements the teaching in 1:10-20 although some of it (1:26-31) may be by a later writer. Isa. 1:4-9 is not an expression of prophetic teaching but a description of the visible desolation of the land of Judah, either after the Syro-Ephraimitic invasion in 735 B.C. or (more likely) after the Assyrian invasion of 701 B.C. However, the latter part of the chapter contains further prophetic reflections on the quality of life in Zion. Following a characteristic criticism of the present moral degradation of the city (1:21-23), the judgment of God is prophesied (24-25) in terms reminiscent of 6:11-13, and the promise is made that God will one day give Zion new judges like those of old, and the city will be "redeemed by justice" (1:26-27).

Isaiah 1:2-9

2 Hear, O heavens, and listen, O earth,
   For Yahweh has spoken.

"Sons have I raised and nurtured,
But they have rebelled against me.
The ox knows its owner,
3 And the ass its master's stall.
Israel does not know;
My people does not understand."

4 Woe, sinful nation,
People heavy with guilt,
Evil brood,
Perverse sons!
They have forsaken Yahweh,
Despised the Holy One of Israel,
Alienated themselves from him.[11]

5 Where would you be beaten again
That you repeatedly rebel?
The whole head is bruised,
And the whole heart faint.
From head to foot
6 There is not a healthy spot:
Black and blue;
Open sores.
They are neither cleaned out,
Nor salved, nor bandaged.

7 Your country is a desolation,
Your cities charred remains.
Foreigners despoil your land,
While you stand by,
And it is ruined,
Like Sodom overthrown.
8 And the daughter of Zion is left
Like a hut in a vineyard,
Like a watchtower in a cucumber-field,
Like a city under siege.
9 Had Yahweh of hosts not left us
A few survivors,

[11] Reading *me'ach°râw* for *'achôr*, with Budde (cf. KBL, p. 253*b*, *zwr* II).

239

> We would be another Sodom,
> We would now be like Gomorrah.

Isaiah 1:21-31

21 What a whore she has become,
   The "faithful city"!
   She was filled with justice;
   Righteousness lodged in her,
   But murderers do now.
22 Your silver is badly tarnished;
   Your wine is watered-down;
23 Your princes are rebels,
   The accomplices of thieves.
   Everyone loves a bribe,
   And chases a gift.
   But no one seeks justice for the orphan,
   And the widow's cause never comes to trial.

24 Therefore, here is the utterance of the Lord,
   Yahweh of hosts, The Mighty One of Israel:
   "Ho, I am incensed by my adversaries,
   And wreak vengeance on my foes.
25 I shall turn my hand against you,
   Burn away your slag in a furnace,
   And rid you of all impurities.
26 Then I shall restore your judges as of old,
   And your counsellors as they used to be.
   And then at last you may be called
   'Righteous City,'
   'Faithful Town.' "

27 Zion will be redeemed by justice,
   And her repentant ones by righteousness,
28 But transgressors and sinners are doomed,
   Everyone who forsakes Yahweh.
29 For you will be ashamed of the sacred trees
   That you adore,

> And regret the gardens
> That you favor.
> 30 For you will be like a tree
> Denuded of leaves,
> Or a garden desperate for water.
> 31 And the strong will become tinder,
> And his deeds a spark,
> And they will burn up together
> With nothing to put out the fire.

The closing lines of the last poem contain a note that sounds strange among the oracles of Isaiah. The sharp distinction between the sinner and the righteous suggested here (1:27-28) presupposes a simpler understanding of the depth and ubiquity of sin than is expressed elsewhere in the book, especially in 6:5. Thus it corresponds to the simple ethical dualism found in some of the late psalms (e.g., Ps. 1). However, the assurance that Zion would be redeemed by justice (1:27) is fully Isaianic in spirit. This is not an affirmation of Zion's sanctity or inviolability nor a promise of extraneous reward for righteousness; it is simply a declaration that the proper concern of the people of God is justice, that the "salvation" of Zion is the doing of justice, and that God himself acts in her life to pull down leaders who have failed in this and to give her leaders who may not. Whoever composed this oracle (1:21-27) understood Isaiah's theology. There is no mention of the cult here in reference to the future Faithful City (26), only justice—and recognition of the necessity of Zion's purgation (25). This is exactly what the prophet's commission (6:9-13) should lead us to expect in his oracles.

There is no indication who were the just leaders of former times (1:26), and little is to be gained therefore by our speculating about their identity. It is enough to note that the writer distinguished the ethical competency of the leaders of a previous age from the incompetency of the city's contemporary rulers and held out the hope of proper leadership in the future. Thus the prophet's criticism of Israel's life was not a universal leveling-down in the light of an impossible ethical ideal. On the other hand, since it is always easy to glorify the past and exaggerate the evils of the present, there may be a measure of unintentional distortion in the oracles of Isaiah, as in the prophetic books generally.

There are Zionistic promises in Isa. 2:2-4 and 4:2-6. The latter is universally regarded as a postexilic supplement to the book, and the former is so regarded by many scholars. We may accept the consensus concerning 4:2-6, and therefore need not discuss the passage in detail. Nevertheless, it is an interesting poem which has at least one important affinity to the oracles of Isaiah.[12]

Isaiah 4:2-6

2   In that day Yahweh's shoots
     Will become lovely and glorious,
     And the fruit of the land the proud ornament
     Of Israel's survivors.

3   Zion's remnant, Jerusalem's few,
     Will be called holy,
     All those marked down to live in Jerusalem.

4   When the Lord has washed the filth
     From the daughter of Zion,
     And cleansed the blood
     From the midst of Jerusalem,
     By the breath of judgment,
     By the breath of fire,

5   Then Yahweh will create
     Over the whole settlement on Zion's hill,
     And over those assembled there,
     A cloud of smoke by day

---

[12] Whether the passage is prose (BH, RSV, Chicago, JPS) or poetry (Jerusalem, Moffatt) is difficult to decide. It manifests poetic parallelism but no clear or consistent meter.

And a blazing fire by night.
For over all the glory there will be
6 A covering and a shelter,
For shade from the heat by day,
And a refuge and cover
From the storm and the rain.

Like Isaiah, the writer of this poem acknowledged the vulnerability of the empirical Jerusalem. Far from proclaiming the inviolability of the old Davidic city, he made capital of its destruction. He interpreted it as a purgation by fire, thus reminding us of Isa. 6:13. The new Zion would arise out of a mere remnant of the old population, those few who were marked down for survival. The imagery in the latter part of the poem is so figurative that we may hardly form any sure conclusion about the writer's concrete hope for the city. He seems to have been concerned with its ritual purity more than its righteousness. The covering that God would provide for the place would be as much a shield for the glory (*kabôd*) of the holy place as a protection for the assembly gathered there. The language recalls the separatist orthodoxy of the period following the reform of Ezra (about 400 B.C.), and it is thus conducive to formulation of a doctrine of the inviolability of a purified Jerusalem.

No fantasy of Zion's inviolability is expressed in Isa. 2:2-4, a great eschatological poem that has influenced profoundly the hopes of Jews and Christians. The question of its authorship will doubtless never be answered objectively and finally. It appears again in Mic. 4:1-4 with a fuller conclusion. It may have been written by Isaiah, or Micah, or by a third person earlier or later than they. There are no clear indications of its origin or date. The opinion that it is postexilic, which has been common among critics during the past century, is based upon the undemonstrable assumption that all eschatological prophecies in the Old Testament are late. Actually this one may embody a pre-Isaianic, Judean tradition that has found its way into two different prophetic books.[13] We have no choice but to treat it as an anonymous poem of indeterminate date. Our task here is to assess the prophetic content of the poem, in relation to other oracles in the book.

Isaiah 2:2-4

2 In the latter days the mountain of Yahweh's house
   Will be established at the head of the mountains,
   And be exalted above the hills;
   And all nations will stream to it,

3 And many peoples will come, and say,
   "Let us climb the mountain of Yahweh,
   To the house of the God of Jacob;
   So he may teach us his ways,
   And we may walk by his direction."
   For the teaching will go forth from Zion,
   And the word of Yahweh from Jerusalem.

4 And he will judge among the nations,
   And adjudicate for many peoples.
   And they shall beat their swords into plowshares,
   And their spears into pruning hooks.
   Nation shall not lift up sword against nation,
   Neither shall they learn war any more.

5 [O House of Jacob, come,
   Let us walk in Yahweh's light.] [14]

---

[13] This theory has been argued in H. Wildberger, "Die Völkerwallfahrt zum Zion. Jes. II 1-5," *VT*, VII (1957), 62-81, and H. Junker, "Sancta Civitas, Jerusalem Nova," *Wehr Festschrift. Trier Theol. Studien*, XV (Trier, 1962), 17-33.

[14] This poem appears also in Mic. 4:1-5, with the following lines in place of Isa. 2:5:

> But each man will sit beneath his vine
> And beneath his fig tree
> With nothing to fear,
> For the mouth of Yahweh of hosts has spoken.

It is apparent at once that the temple hill of Yahweh in Jerusalem stands at the center of this imaginative vision of a future age of universal peace and justice. The positive estimate in this poem of Zion's role in the new age contrasts sharply with the radical denunciation of Judean worship in 1:10-20 and the grim prophecy of the nation's destiny in chapter 6. However, there is no direct contradiction between 2:2-4 and these other oracles, for it is plainly eschatological and they are not. In itself this oracle presupposes neither the continuation of the existing temple and its cultus nor their definite destruction, and it is therefore compatible with either eventuality.

The oracle is framed in the grammatical future and refers to "the latter days." This is not an apocalyptic phrase here, denoting the end of present history and the in-breaking of a new world. It denotes an indefinite future time. No doubt the writer meant it as a genuine future in the temporal sense, believing that God would one day actually fulfill his righteous purpose for all the nations of the world. At the same time, his oracle is eschatological in an ethical sense in that it expresses the ultimate goal of all God's activity in the midst of the nations, past, present, and future. What the writer was saying in effect was that whenever the conflicts of peoples are adjudicated peacefully, on the basis of law, the will of God is done, and that all God's judgments in history are directed toward this goal.

The temple of Yahweh stands at the center of the writer's vision (2:2-3). However, the function of this temple is different from that of the temple of Jerusalem in Isaiah's time. There is no allusion here to the sacrificial cultus or any of its attendant activities. The function of the temple is wholly prophetic. The *teaching* (*tôrah*) of Yahweh is to be published, nothing more. The prophetic *word* has triumphed here over the ritual of the altar. The nations shall stream to Zion to learn "the ways" of God so that they may "walk in his paths." This language is ethical and has little to do with the conventional sacrificial cultus. Further, the emphasis here is entirely theocentric. The peoples are put at God's disposal. They are to come to Zion to learn obedience to God's teaching. And the goals of their obedience are justice and world peace. All peoples will be "served" in this way, but none will be accorded the privilege of a materialistic, self-indulgent system of public worship. The service of the word, which is mentioned only too briefly in this oracle, has no relationship to the service of the altar described and repudiated in 1:10-16. Here by implication the prophet of the word of God has displaced the sacrificial priest as the primary mediator between God and man.

The writer envisioned the achievement of universal peace without recourse to arms, through the intervention of God (2:4). The image is again theocentric and omits all reference to instrumentalities. In this it is poetic, even unrealistic. But we must not be misled by this quality of the oracle to think of it as exhibiting an otherworldly idealism. The poetic exaggeration merely serves to heighten the theocentricity of the proclamation. The practical instrument of divine justice in the midst of the nations is the *tôrah,* the teaching, the prophetic word. It is to the place of this teaching that all the peoples will come.[15] They must come willingly, since true obedience and justice are inconceivable apart from freedom. Coercion is inadmissible. It is ruled out on the part of the nations (2:4b), and it is ruled out also on the part of God (2:4a). The fulfillment of justice for man means the fulfillment of man. It must therefore express his own will as well

---

[15] Wildberger's opinion that Isaiah here extended the old Zionism beyond the limits of the Palestinian peoples to comprehend *many* peoples, and thereby moved a step closer to universalism, is inadequate. The text of Isa. 2:2-4 plainly says *all* the peoples (vs. 2b). The scope of the vision is unrestricted; it is truly universal. See, *op. cit.,* p. 71.

as the will of God. Instruction, not force, is the proper medium of this justice.

Zion is the place of prophetic teaching in this picture, but prophetic teaching is not bound to a place. Merely as place, Zion is dispensable in the vision. But it is also the symbol of the continuity of prophetic teaching, that is, the proclamation of the ways of the God of Jacob (2:3). The unbroken Yahwistic tradition is an indispensable ingredient of man's knowledge of God. So the old center of tradition and worship continues as the symbol of the new. There were other centers of tradition in Israel, of course, but by Isaiah's time most of these had been engulfed by the Assyrian Empire. And, in any case, for the Judeans to whom the oracles of Isaiah and his disciples were addressed, Jerusalem was the "city of the soul."

The eschatological vision in Isa. 2:2-4 is quite different from that in 4:1-6. It is universalistic while the other is separatistic. It is a prophecy of justice and peace while the other is a prophecy of ritual purification. Neither mentions the sacrificial cult of the old temple, but the spirit of 4:1-6 is the spirit of the holy place and the sacrificial ritual while these things are remote from the interest expressed in 2:2-4. The word *tôrah* ("teaching," 2:3) does not itself denote prophetic as against priestly instruction since it is often used in the Old Testament in the latter sense, but here the connotation of the word is unmistakably prophetic. The writer's vision of the new Zion represents the transformation of Israel's worship from the service of the altar to the service of the prophetic teaching. The man who wrote the oracle shared the theological perspective of Isaiah.

The alternate version of this oracle, which appears in Mic. 4, has a better conclusion, in my opinion, than that in Isa. 2. In the longer version it is said that after the nations have all converted their weapons into agricultural implements (Mic.

4:3, Isa. 2:4), every man shall be secure materially beneath his own vine and fig tree and shall have no fear of other men (Mic. 4:4). Some such conclusion is already implied in the change of weapons to tools, but it is not explicitly stated in the present text of Isa. 2:2-4. The ending in Mic. 4 links the oracle more closely to Isa. 1:10-20 in one respect. It is made clear in Mic. 4:4 that the purpose of God's historical judgment is to secure the natural blessing of everyman. This blessing includes enjoyment of the fruit of the earth and freedom from fear of others. Thus the goal of history is the fulfillment of creation, and the goal of international justice is the welfare of individual men. The condition of blessing is moral, that is, learning obedience to the ways of God. This affirmation complements the one in Isa. 1:19-20, where obedience is made the condition of natural blessing and disobedience the agency of social disaster. Incidentally, the affirmation does not imply a simple doctrine of material retribution, for there is no promise here of a tangible, extraneous reward for individual virtue. What is affirmed in these oracles is that the good of a nation cannot be achieved without justice (1:20) and that justice is measured by the well-being of everyman (Mic. 4:4). These affirmations should not be confused with the notion that God rewards the righteous man with health and wealth and withholds them from the sinful.

Our thesis that Isaiah preached "Zionism" in a unique way is strengthened by the brief but significant biographical statement in 8:16-18. This passage concludes a collection of oracles, set within a narrative framework, that were delivered during various phases of the crisis caused by the Syro-Ephraimite invasion of Judah in 735 B.C. These oracles have been treated in detail in chapter six of this book so I shall refer here only to the passage that bears upon our present subject. During the extended crisis brought about by the invasion of Judah, Isaiah sought in a series of confrontations to dissuade the

Judean king Ahaz from any national policy that would prevent the fulfillment of his and his people's proper responsibility to God. Isaiah failed. Ahaz pursued an opposite course to what Isaiah counseled. Therefore, the outcome could only be to precipitate the disaster for Judah that had been anticipated in Isaiah's commission (6:9-13). Ahaz's response confirmed Isaiah's conviction that his mission would harden the heart of the nation and thus contribute to its judgment at the hand of God.[16] However, it did not relieve him of his own continuing responsibility but made it doubly urgent that he fulfill it. For Isaiah, together with his children (7:3; 8:1-4) and his disciples (8:16), was the best sign in Israel of the presence of "Yahweh of hosts, who dwells on Mount Zion" (8:18).

Ahaz and the people of Judah undoubtedly believed that God's presence was assured by the rituals of the temple of Zion and that his power was available to the anointed Davidic king. To Isaiah's mind, however, God's presence (his "face," 8:17) was hidden to the whole House of Jacob. This meant that God's distinctive dwelling "on Mount Zion" was confined to Isaiah's prophetic witness. This witness was embodied in the circle of those gathered about him and the oracles which they preserved (8:16). God was the ultimate source of both judgment and renewal. Neither of these was understood by Ahaz or the adherents of the temple. Renewal could not take place without understanding because it was a matter of personal faith and obedience. The destruction of the nation did not depend upon understanding, but if it were to be recognized as the judgment of God, it required prophetic interpretation. Thus, to be truly effective, the presence of God, in judgment and reconciliation, required a witness like Isaiah's. Apart from this testimony the face of God would have been utterly hidden in Israel. This prophetic testimony alone dis-

---

[16] The viewpoint expressed in 6:9-13 is consistent with the implications of 8:16-18 whether or not chap. 6 in its present form contains retrospective coloring.

tinguished God's dwelling in Zion from his presence in the world as a whole (6:3).

The kingship and the cult, those two bulwarks of Judean national piety, had become obstacles to God's dwelling in Zion. Neither was essential to it, and both were marked for the coming purge. The only remaining bearer of sanctity, that is, witness to the holiness of God, was Isaiah's teaching— not the man himself, nor his children, nor his disciples—only the teaching. This alone made Zion the present sanctuary of God, and this alone, according to the writer of 2:2-4, would give it special significance in the time to come. Where the prophetic teaching was, there was the "dwelling" of Yahweh. Everything else was dispensable. Thus in principle the old Zionism was abolished in Isaiah's theology. As it happened, the old Zionism received new impetus in Judah from the events of the following century and virtually eclipsed the teaching of Isaiah until the prophet Jeremiah once again challenged the cultic optimism that pervaded the Judean religious community (cf., e.g., Jer. 7 and 26).

In order to interpret the remaining Zion oracles of Isaiah properly, it is necessary to take account of his conception of Assyria's role in the historic purposes of God. He was convinced that none of the powers of the Middle East could check Assyria's advance or prevent her temporary mastery of the Semitic world in the eighth century B.C. and that this conquest was a judgment of God, especially against Israel and Judah. But he was equally certain of Assyria's finitude and temporality. Her sway in history would eventually cease, and her fall would also be an act of God's justice against pride and folly. Isaiah's understanding is most fully conveyed in the great oracle in chapter 10.

Isaiah 10:5-19

5   Woe, Assyria, the rod of my anger,
    And the staff I wield in my fury.

6 I send him against a godless nation,
  And command him against the people of my wrath,
  To plunder the spoils and carry off booty,
  And to trample them down like clay in the streets.
7 But he is not disposed to this,
  And does not plan this way;
  For his will is to demolish,
  And cut off nations not a few.
8 For he asserts,
  "Are not my officers the equals of kings?
9 Is Calno not like Carchemish?
  Is Hamath not like Arpad,
  And Samaria like Damascus?
10 As my hand has reached
  To the kingdoms of the idols,
  Whose images surpass Jerusalem and Samaria,
11 Shall I not do likewise
  To Samaria and her idols,
  And perform in equal fashion
  Against Jerusalem and her images?"

12 When the Lord has finished his work
  In Mount Zion and Jerusalem,
  He will punish the arrogant boasting
  Of the Assyrian king, and his vainglorious pride.
13 For he asserts,
  "By my own strength have I achieved,
  And by my wisdom, for I have understanding.
  I have altered the boundaries of nations,
  And plundered their stores,
  And brought down their inhabitants to the dust.[17]
14 My hand has found like a nest
  The wealth of the nations,
  And gathered like untended eggs
  The treasures of the world.

[17] Cf. BH, Chicago, and Jerusalem, among others.

> Not a wing fluttered.
> Not a mouth chirped."

15 Does the ax vaunt itself over him who wields it,
    Or the saw exalt itself over him who saws?
    As if a rod might wave its bearer,
    Or a staff lift what is more than wood!

16 Therefore, the Lord, Yahweh of hosts,
    Will send a wasting sickness among his stout ones,
    And light a blaze beneath his glory,
    Like a consuming fire.

17 The Light of Israel will become a fire,
    And his Holy One a flame,
    And it will burn and devour
    His briars and thorns in a single day.

18 The glory of his forests and gardens,
    Both form and substance, will it consume.
    It will be like a sick man's wasting away.

19 The remaining trees of his forests will be so few
    That a child may record their number.

It is crucial to a right understanding of Isaiah's proclamation to observe that Assyria's fall was to follow the completion of Yahweh's work in Mount Zion and Jerusalem (10:12). This was Yahweh's "strange work" of punishment against his own people (28:21). Thus in Isaiah's view the city and temple of Jerusalem were highly vulnerable to Assyrian power, though this power would not cut off the community of Zion without a trace. It would endure to profess its faith in Yahweh and give refuge to the poor and oppressed (14:32). The oracles in 10:24-27 and 14:24-27 promise deliverance from the *yoke* of Assyria after it has been forcefully and effectively imposed (10:27; 14:25). The second of these oracles does not refer to Zion or Jerusalem but widens the range of concern to include the whole of Yahweh's (i.e., Israel's) land (14:25). However, it is a close companion to the first, which does specify "my people who live in Zion" (10:24). These oracles differ from those we examined earlier in omitting any explicit ethical justification for either the Assyrian oppression of Israel or the eventual Assyrian collapse. It is reasonable to think of them as having been composed at a time when Judah was actually under Assyrian domination, when such a word of reassurance was called for in the face of the people's threatened despair. Although they lack the obvious ethical content of most of Isaiah's oracles, they stop short of the vindictive nationalism expressed in 11:10-16, which is an addition—and an ethical contradiction—to the messianic oracle in 11:1-9. When in 14:24-27 the writer declares Assyria's ultimate fall to be a part of Yahweh's "fixed plan against all the world" (vs. 26), the premise of his conclusion is the universal operation of God's justice among the proud nations of the world and not the inviolability of Jerusalem.

In Isaiah's vision of the future there was no miraculous divine intervention at the last moment to save the holy city, but a captured city whose people would subsequently be offered another opportunity for obedience in new historical circumstances. Zion was a refuge for the faithful community in this sense; indeed, it was the faithful community insofar as it maintained the prophetic tradition. This is the meaning of Isa. 28:14-22. The new foundation being laid for Zion (vs. 16) was to be measured by justice and righteousness (vs. 17), the tested and perennial standards of the Yahwistic community. This foundation, embodied in those who believed the prophet's testimony,[18] would endure—though we certainly need not

---

[18] This statement is based on the conclusion that the line "he who believes will not stumble (or, be in haste)" (28:16) is not itself the cornerstone. As I have argued above, pp. 186 ff., "believe" is more likely to mean here "believe the foregoing assertion" than it is to mean "have faith," in a general sense. However, the larger argument here hardly requires this conclusion; indeed, it would be strengthened by the other, namely that the statement "he who believes will not stumble" is itself the cornerstone of Yahweh's new Zion.

assume this meant all those individuals would be miraculously protected against personal hazard or material loss—while those who gambled the fortunes of Judah in the deadly game of military alliance and counteralliance, conspiracy and revolution, would be swept away (vss. 14-15, 18-22).

This oracle is generally dated during the first half of the reign of Hezekiah (715-687 B.C.), which was marked by several threatened and actual rebellions against Assyria by various coalitions of Syro-Palestinian powers, including Judah.[19] Philistia took part too, and Isaiah was as quick to proclaim her hope futile as he was to challenge his own Judean leaders (14:28-32). This oracle does not set Philistia's vulnerability over against the invulnerability of Yahweh's nation of Judah, as has sometimes been supposed,[20] but sets the durability of the community bent on justice for the poor and oppressed, and the divine sanction of this community, against the futility of contemporary international politics, this time in its Philistine version.

Yet another oracle from this period is Isa. 22:1-14. This fascinating but partly enigmatic piece is usually regarded as Isaiah's comment upon Judean behavior during and after the Assyrian siege of Jerusalem in 701 B.C. Apparently he scorned their frantic military preparations (22:8b-11), the cowardly behavior of their leaders during the attack (2b-3), the fatalistic revelry of some on the eve of capture (13), and the careless rejoicing of the multitude after the siege was lifted (1b-2a). Shortsighted, selfish, materialistic, and superficial—a people bent on destruction (22:4), which was really self-destruction. To Isaiah's mind such blasphemy was unforgiveable (vs. 14).

[19] The principal rebellions took place in 712 B.C., led by Ashdod (cf. Isa. 20), and 705 B.C., led by Ashkelon (cf. II Kings 20:12-19; Isa. 30:1-5; 31:1-3).

[20] E.g., by Scott. The occasion for the Philistine conspiracy was probably not the death of Ahaz, which is here used to date the oracle (14:28), but a change of ruler in Assyria.

The promise of Zion's deliverance from siege is made, finally, in several oracles at the end of the Isaianic collection (29:1-8 and 31:4-9). It is possible to read these as prophecies of God's last-minute intervention to save the beleaguered—and properly chastened—city from the arrogant, heathen tyrant. It must be admitted that they are the most susceptible to this reading of all the Zionistic materials commonly credited by critical scholars to Isaiah.[21] But several considerations should prevent our abandoning an otherwise massive case against Isaiah's having taught the inviolability of Jerusalem on the basis of this exhibit. Both 29:5-8 and 31:8-9 may just as well be read as reflections of the actual events of 701 B.C., when Assyria withdrew from Judah without having captured Jerusalem. This happened because Hezekiah capitulated and paid a heavy tribute (II Kings 18:13-16), although there may also have been other factors that influenced the Assyrian decision. The historical records are not fully coherent so a clear picture of the event is not available.[22] Furthermore, 31:4-5 is not a simple guarantee of Yahweh's protection of Jerusalem. The oracle contains two metaphors. The first is the lion who won't be driven from his prey by noisy shepherds (31:4). The poet compares Yahweh coming down against Jerusalem to this lion coming upon his prey.[23] He goes on to say (31:5):

> Like a flight of birds
> Will Yahweh of hosts surround Jerusalem,
> Encircle and snatch away,
> Dart over and help to escape.

[21] Isa. 30:18-26 is almost universally regarded as postexilic. Isa. 30:31-33 is sometimes attributed to Isaiah (along with 30:27-30), but I do not see how one can reconcile the approval given there to the gaiety of Israel after Assyria's defeat with the condemnation of similar rejoicing in 22:1-14.

[22] See the thorough discussion in B. S. Childs, *Isaiah and the Assyrian Crisis* (SBT, Second Series, No. 3; Naperville, 1967), pp. 69-103.

[23] To fight *against* (ʿal) Jerusalem (so Childs, *op. cit.*, pp. 57-59).

This metaphor does not suggest to me the idea of Jerusalem's material inviolability.[24] It suggests the rescue of some of the inhabitants from the power of the attacker. Is this not essentially the idea of the remnant proclaimed elsewhere by Isaiah? Nor does 29:1-8 advocate reliance on a divine guarantee of protection. It really advocates nothing at all on the part of the people. It is morally neutral. It proclaims the wrath of Yahweh against Jerusalem and the ultimate passing of the agent of his wrath, just like the great oracle on Assyria (10:5-19).

We have two choices. We may read these oracles as declarations of Jerusalem's inviolability, a notion that besides being untrue would have been morally destructive to Isaiah's contemporaries. Or we may read them in the light of the other oracles of Isaiah, which are less figurative in their language, less susceptible of secondary coloration in the hands of later editors, and filled with the ethical counsel and criticism of the prophet. There is no doubt in my mind that this is the better choice. One happy consequence of this interpretation is that it makes Isaiah's "Zionistic" oracles ethically relevant to us as well as to his fellow Judeans of the eighth century B.C.

---

[24] The verb *gnn*, to encircle or enclose, is taken by the RSV to connote protection, but it seems to me to be more neutral than that. How might a flight of birds around a city be conceived as a protective shield? Are they not rather visualized as flying over the beleaguered city and carrying out some of the defenders to safety?

chapter 8

The Remnant and the Future King

There was a time not long ago when a great many Old Testament critics, indeed the majority of those who accepted the principles of historical and literary criticism, believed that most, if not all, the oracles of hope, particularly the so-called messianic oracles, had been composed after the Babylonian exile and added to the books of Amos, Hosea, Isaiah, and others in order to balance their original prophecy of doom. The supposition upon which this conclusion was based was that the prophets prophesied affliction in times of prosperity and salvation in times of adversity. Accordingly, Isaiah's messianic oracles were regarded as late additions to the book (9:1-7; 11:1-9; 32:1-5).

The situation is different today. Many, if not most, critical scholars regard these oracles as Isaiah's own and take them as expressions of a venerable Judean belief in the sanctity of the Davidic king as God's vicegerent amid the nations. Some have gone further and interpreted other oracles of Isaiah that are not explicitly royal or messianic in the light of Isaiah's alleged endorsement of this dynastic belief. I have noted in an earlier chapter the effect this approach has had on recent criticism of Isa. 7–8.[1] Thus, interestingly, contemporary critics have restored the dogma of the everlasting kingship of the Davidic line to the status it had among precritical interpreters as one of the two foundations of Isaiah's theology. The other foundation, which has received corresponding recognition, is the dogma of the sanctity of Zion. However, neither of these was characteristic of Isaiah's thought. The messianic and Zionistic motifs were used in his oracles, but both were transformed radically.

It is a mistake to read Isaiah's nonmessianic oracles in the light of the dynastic traditions of Judah. At most they may be read in conjunction with his own messianic oracles, if 9:1-7, 11:1-9, and 32:1-8 are his. It cannot be demonstrated that they are, but at least they now stand in close proximity to the primary oracles of Isaiah and have a claim to be included among them. If they are secondary, they represent the thought of those who were closest to Isaiah in the prophetic tradition. If these oracles do not reflect Isaiah's messianic teaching, then none of the royal/messianic materials in the Old Testament do so. Therefore, if these may be shown to exhibit a new dimension in Judean Messianism, there is every reason to reject the notion that Isaiah himself embraced the crass old dogma of Davidic nationalism. It is one of the aims of the present chapter to show that the messianic oracles in Isa. 9, 11, and 32, represent a prophetic transformation of the Judean royal ideology. The other aim is to discuss the prophecies of

[1] See pp. 188-89.

the remnant in Isaiah. The materials revolving around these two themes will be seen to be further manifestations of Isaiah's fundamental prophetic insights, which were at odds with the ideas regnant in Judah in his time. Furthermore, I believe this discussion will confirm the conclusions reached above with respect to the significance of Zion in the oracles of Isaiah.

The conviction that Yahweh had chosen David and his direct descendants as a perpetual dynasty in Judah and had promised them a wide dominion among the nations of western Asia is expressed in the oracle of Nathan (II Sam. 7:4-16) and in the royal psalms (Pss. 2, 18, 20, 21, 45, 72, 89, 101, 110, 132, 144:1-10). It is impossible to date precisely the stages in the development of this belief and of its ritual embodiment. However, it is probable that it became well established in Judah during the latter half of the tenth century B.C. in the decades following Solomon's erection of the Jerusalem temple and consolidation of David's empire.

The first premise upon which the Judean royal theology was based was the recognition of David's great military and political success. He had created a permanent kingdom where Saul had failed. He had done so partly by displacing the heirs of Saul as sovereigns of the north Israelite territories, so that the fall of Saul's house had been one of the preconditions of David's rise (II Sam. 3:6-21). But then he had crushed the Philistines (II Sam. 5:17-25), who had destroyed Saul (I Sam. 31), and extended his kingship over all Israel as well as the neighboring peoples (II Sam. 8).

David's achievement naturally affected Judean historical perspective, so that the editors of the patriarchal traditions were able to interpret his leadership of Israel as the fulfillment of an ancient tribal blessing (Gen. 49:8-12; cf. Num. 24:15-19). However, Judah's tribal pride and David's military success were not enough to produce the royal theology found in the psalms. It required also the adoption of religious rites of kingship that were standard practice among the nations of the ancient Near East. There were many models to follow, but that of the pre-Israelite, Canaanite city-kings was closest to hand and least incompatible with Yahwism. There is evidence in the Bible that David adopted the style of the Jebusite priest-kings of Jerusalem after he had made the city his capital (II Sam. 5:6-10; Ps. 110; cf. Gen. 14:17-24). What was decisive for the formation of Davidic Messianism was not the peculiar features of the Jebusite model but the features it shared with monarchial institutions generally. These were belief in the sanctity of the king and acceptance of the hereditary character of the royal office. These made the kingship absolute and distinguished it from the charismatic Israelite judgeship, which had been the instrument of central authority, insofar as there was any, among the Israelite tribes in the premonarchial era.

David established a hereditary dynasty in Judah at great cost to his family, because of the inevitable struggle for the succession (II Sam. 9-20; I Kings 1-2). Official sanction was provided for the dynastic principle by the Yahwistic religious establishment in the form of a doctrine of divine election. Tradition assigns the initial publication of the doctrine to the prophet Nathan (II Sam. 7). The oracle in II Sam. 7 shows marks of later modification, but there can be little doubt that the basic idea incorporated in it was endorsed by the leaders of the Judean religious community at an early date, if not at the beginning of David's kingship. The royal establishment was reinforced by the installation of the ancient ark (the battle-palladium of Yahweh) into the sanctuary of Jerusalem (I Sam. 4-6; II Sam. 6). The rituals in which the kingship was celebrated and renewed thus became an amalgam of foreign and native elements (Pss. 2, 89, 110, and 132, especially).

The dynastic principle was never as fully accepted in north Israel as it was in Judah. There were doubtless many reasons why this was so, not all of which may be clearly deduced from the extant sources. In Judah the native forms of leadership may have been more autocratic, and the "federalism" inherent in the Yahwistic amphictyony less important, than among the northern tribes.[2] David was himself a Judean, of course, and therefore a greater hero to Judeans than to others. (His rivalry with Saul, which is described with a Judean bias in the Bible, surely produced lingering hatred toward him among Saul's tribesmen.) The territory of the kingdom of Judah was smaller than that of Israel, and its populace probably more homogeneous. These and other factors combined to give the House of David strong control over the political and ecclesiastical destiny of Judah. Its empirical importance in the nation's life was reflected in the belief in God's promise of perpetual sovereignty to the dynasty.

The rebellion of the northern territories from the kingdom of Rehoboam in 922 B.C. occurred before the dynastic claim of the Davidic House could be established among the people of the north. However, the schism may have saved the Davidic establishment in the south. The rebels were content to leave Judah to the line of David and form an independent state for themselves. Had they chosen to carry Judah with them in their reaction against the tyrannical Rehoboam, they might well have destroyed the Davidic dynasty then and there. The dynastic dogma must have been accepted fully in Judah by the middle of the ninth century, for the destruction of the usurper Queen Athaliah, who was an Israelite princess and wife of the Judean king Jehoram, was followed not only by the restoration of native Judean rule but by the restoration of the Davidic line (II Kings 11). The story of Joash's narrow escape from Athaliah and his eventual ascension to the throne, if it is historical, indicates the effort Judeans would exert to

[2] See M. Newman, *The People of the Covenant* (Nashville, 1962),

maintain the Davidic line, or, if it is legendary, the depth of the Judean need to validate the young king's Davidic lineage. In either case it testifies to the triumph of the belief in the divine election of the line. By the time of Isaiah, a century later, the conviction had been long established in the Judean imagination.

There were elements of propaganda in the Judean royal theology, but it incorporated also the ideal of a universal and peaceful dominion of God, which was to have increasing importance in Israelite religious thought. The dynasty's claim to sanctity was qualified by the demand for obedience to God (II Sam. 7:14; Ps. 72:1-4, 12-14; 89:31-34) and was thus brought under the discipline of the covenantal ethic, which was at the heart of Mosaic tradition. This qualification, however, was severely limited. The Davidic monarchy was not constitutional. Individual kings might be "punished" by God for their evil acts (II Sam. 7:14), but this condition was nothing more than a general condition of human existence. It was not a special restriction upon the will of the king. The dynasty itself was sacrosanct. The practical effect of the doctrine of divine election was to give the Judean kings absolute authority by "divine right." The possibilities of abusing this authority were infinite, and the king's subjects had little, if any, means of redress. A permanent army of mercenary soldiers gave the monarch all the power he needed to quell any popular rebellion.

Amos and Hosea regarded the monarchy as an expendable instrument of God's rule in Israel even though they had nothing to say about the morality of monarchy itself. Hosea explicitly denounced the Israelite institution as godless (Hos. 8:4-10), and both prophets prophesied its determinate end (Amos 5:1-3; 7:7–9:8a; Hos. 10, et passim). However, the fall of the northern kingdom in 722 B.C. did not shake the Judean belief in the perpetuity of their own royal house. For some it strengthened it because it was proof to them of God's opposition to the non-Davidic kingdom of Israel. Judean additions to the books of Amos and Hosea have made these prophets appear to be advocates of the Davidic doctrine (Hos. 1:7; 3:5; and perhaps 1:10–2:1; and Amos 9:11-12). These additions were probably made during the seventh century, when the doctrine was still being kept alive by an existing Davidic kingship. Among the prophetic writings of the exilic era (587-539 B.C.) the doctrine plays no significant role. There are only faint echoes of it in the books of Jeremiah, Ezekiel, and Second Isaiah.[3]

The most important royal oracles in the prophetic corpus of the Bible are Isa. 9:1-7 and 11:1-9. These, like the related oracle in Mic. 5:1-4, presuppose the Davidic doctrine of election by God. They are comparable therefore to the Zion oracle in Isa. 2, which presupposes the Judean belief in God's choice of Jerusalem as the central Israelite sanctuary. On the other hand, there is no oracle in Isaiah as critical of the kingship as 1:10-17 is of the Jerusalem cult. It is easier therefore to accommodate the messianic oracles (9:1-7 and 11:1-9) to the so-called undisputed utterances of Isaiah than it is to accommodate the Zionistic oracles, although the latter is not impossible and the former is not without its difficulties.

Isaiah 9:1-7 (Hebrew 8:23–9:6)

1 But there is no more darkness
   For her who is oppressed.
   As in time past he humiliated
   The land of Zebulun and the land of Naphtali,
   So in time to come he will glorify
   The Way of the Sea, Transjordan, Galilee of the Nations.

---

[3] Jer. 23:5-6; 33:14-16 (both passages belong to the secondary, deuteronomic source of the book); Ezek. 34:23; and Isa. 55:3.

2 The people who walk in darkness
　Have seen a great light.
　Those who dwell in a land of blackness,
　Upon them a light has shone.

3 You have magnified its gladness,
　You have increased its joy.
　They rejoice before you,
　As men rejoice at harvest,
　As they are glad when they divide the spoil.

4 Because the yoke for his burden,
　And the staff for his shoulder,
　The rod of his oppressor,
　You have broken as on the day of Midian.

5 Because every boot of the battle march,
　And every coat rolled in blood,
　Will be for burning and fuel for fire.

6 For a child is born to us,
　A son is given to us.
　And dominion will be upon his shoulder.
　And they will name him
　Wonderful Counsellor, Godly Hero,
　Enduring Father, Prince of Peace.

7 Dominion and peace will increase without end,
　For David's throne and for his kingdom.
　To establish this and make it sure,
　In justice and righteousness,
　From this time on, forever,
　The zeal of Yahweh of hosts will accomplish it.

Isaiah 11:1-9

1 A branch will grow from Jesse's trunk,
　And a shoot from his roots will bear fruit.

2 And the spirit of Yahweh will rest upon him:
　The spirit of wisdom and understanding,
　The spirit of counsel and valor.

3 And he will delight in the fear of Yahweh.
He will not judge by appearances,
Nor arbitrate by hearsay,

4 But he will judge the weak righteously,
And arbitrate fairly for the poor of the land.
He will strike the ruthless with the rod of his mouth,
And execute the wicked with his breath.

5 Righteousness will clothe his waist,
And faithfulness his loins.

6 The wolf will live with the lamb,
And the leopard lie down with the kid.
The calf and the lion will feed together,
And a little child will lead them.

7 The cow and the bear will be friends;
Their young will lie down together.
The lion will eat straw like the ox.

8 A baby will play beside the hole of a cobra,
And an infant put his hand upon a young viper.

9 They will not hurt nor destroy throughout my holy mountain,
For the land will be filled with the knowledge of Yahweh,
As water fills the sea.

The occasions when the messianic oracles were published cannot be deduced from the text although many suggestions have been made. For example, the oracle in chapter 9 has been interpreted frequently as an announcement of Hezekiah's birth. Albrecht Alt proposed a variation of this theory, interpreting the oracle as an announcement of the coronation of a new Davidic king, delivered to the survivors of the fall of Samaria (722 B.C.).[4] But the collectors of Isaiah's oracles neglected, or were unable, to describe the original historical setting. It is evident here, as in the books of the prophets gen-

---

[4] "Jesaja 8, 23-9, 6. Befreiungsnacht und Krönungstag," *Festschrift für Alfred Bertholet* (1950), pp. 29-49 (reprinted in *Kleine Schriften*, II [Munich, 1953], 206-25).

erally, that the writers were more interested in the contents of the oracles than the specific events that called them forth.

The purpose of the royal psalms, as we have noted, was to exalt the Judean king and secure fulfillment of God's alleged promise of universal and perpetual dominion. Only in Ps. 72 is there any stress upon the responsibility of the king to secure justice among his people, and even there it is matched by the wish for Davidic hegemony among the nations (72:8-11, 15-17). Thus in the royal cultus the ethical responsibility of the king was subordinated to his divine right. However, this order of emphasis was reversed in the messianic oracles of Isaiah. Indeed, in Isa. 11:1-9 there is no stress at all upon the prerogatives of the Davidic king. It is clear that the righteousness and justice which he was to champion would be universal, but there is no mention here of the privileges claimed in the royal psalms. Isa. 9:1-7 ascribes to a newly born (or newly crowned) [5] king the wide and enduring sovereignty celebrated in the royal psalms, as well as a series of majestic titles (vss. 6 and 7). But the climax of the oracle is the proclamation of the king's responsibility for peace, justice, and righteousness. In these two oracles the king is the servant of God and his people, and the champion of the poor and oppressed (cf. Isa. 32:1-2). There is no necessary contradiction between the image of the king in these poems and that in the royal psalms, for all kings and their courtiers were able to conceive of themselves as the champions of justice; but the emphases are different. In reading the royal psalms one is impressed by the writer's concern for the continuation of the Davidic line. In reading the messianic oracles of Isaiah he is impressed by the

[5] The birth of the son may be figurative here, implying God's adoption of a a royal "son" as his vicegerent at the time of his anointing and coronation. The physical birth of a royal prince did not necessarily mean the birth of a future king even if he were the firstborn, for the succession was not automatically determined by primogeniture.

concern for the king's fulfillment of his moral responsibilities. In the first case Yahweh is the supporter of David. In the second, David is the servant of Yahweh.

The ethic of power suggested by Isa. 11 is fundamentally different from that suggested by the royal psalms. The psalmists took for granted that the king was the wielder of coercive authority in Israel, and they invoked God's support of his military enterprises, by which this absolute rule was maintained (especially Pss. 18, 20, and 21). In Isa. 11:1-9 the king is envisioned as ruling only by the intrinsic authority of his wisdom, integrity, and devotion to the common good, without resort to force. The picture is less clear in Isa. 9:1-7. It is said there that the rod of oppression will be broken and the boot of the warrior burned (vss. 4-5), but the writer may have meant only that the power of Israel's oppressors would be checked and not that all use of force would be eliminated. Isa. 11:1-9 is eschatological, for all nature is pictured here as a realm of peacefulness, free from conflict and violence (vss. 6-9). Therefore, as a royal prophecy it expresses an ethical ideal and not a pragmatic norm. By placing the prophecy of a restored Davidic monarchy (11:1-5) alongside that of a transformed nature (11:6-9), the writer implicitly acknowledged the impossibility of achieving a non-coercive state in the existing world. The very proclamation of messianic oracles precluded a radical criticism of monarchy on the part of the writer. Nevertheless, he completely subordinated the doctrine of dynastic privilege to the Yahwistic ethic proclaimed by the classical prophets.

Both of these oracles presuppose the occurrence of a dire calamity in Israel. Isa. 9:1-7 offers hope to a people who "walk in darkness." These may have been the victims of Assyria's conquest of Galilee and Gilead (733 B.C.) or of Samaria (722 B.C.). They need not have been Judeans. Isa. 11:1-9 speaks of a "shoot from the stump of Jesse," suggesting the beginning of a new era in the Davidic monarchy. In itself this does not necessarily imply a disruption of Judean sovereignty, but it does so in its present context. The Assyrian conquest of Judah is prophesied repeatedly in Isa. 1–11 and 28–32, not least in the lines immediately preceding 11:1-9. Similarly, 9:1-7 follows the prophecy of Judah's destruction in 8:5-8 and 8:16-22. Therefore, the new David prophesied in the messianic oracles was intended to be the ruler of a new Israel, which would arise from the remnant of the old. The messianic oracles should be read, then, in relation to Isaiah's prophecy of the remnant.

Isaiah's initial prophecy of a remnant was probably the naming of his son A-Remnant-Shall-Return (Shear-yashubh, 7:3). The boy appears first in the book (the only time by name) on the occasion of his father's meeting with Ahaz during the Syro-Ephraimitic invasion. The oracle delivered then (7:4-9) concerned the failure of the conspiracy of Rezin and Pekah. It is natural in this setting to take the boy's presence as a tacit allusion to the remnant of the kingdoms of Israel and Aram. But the range of the prophet's intention must have been broader than this in one direction and narrower in another. The boy had obviously been named at a time some months or years before the invasion of Judah occurred so his name had not been meant originally to signify the collapse of the anti-Assyrian alliance. On the other hand, the boy was clearly included among those to whom Isaiah later referred as the symbol of God's impending judgment against the House of Jacob (8:18). The name is therefore to be interpreted as an oracle pertaining to the kingdoms of Israel and Judah, that is, the whole people of Yahweh, and not to the kingdom of Aram. It is irrelevant to debate whether the name was a counsel of despair ("*only* a remnant shall return") or a counsel of hope ("a remnant *shall* return"), as has often been done, because it is not strictly either of these.

Whether one despaired or took courage over the national conquest depended upon who one was and what he believed the causes and consequences of the conquest to be. The name Shear-yashubh itself is neither an exhortation to hope for the best nor an assertion of the futility of action. It is a simple prediction of the conquest of the nation.

The short poem in Isa. 1:7-8 is apparently a retrospective description of the result of the Assyrian invasion of Judah in 701 B.C., and it too depicts the conquest without drawing a moral from it.

Isaiah 10:20-27

20   That day will come when the remnant of Israel and the survivors of the House of Jacob will depend no longer upon the one who struck them, but will depend truly
21   upon Yahweh, the Holy One of Israel. A remnant will return, a remnant of Jacob, to the Mighty God.
22   Although your people, Israel, are like the sand of the sea, only a remnant of them will return. Disaster is decreed;
23   justice flows on. For the Lord, Yahweh of hosts, is making a determinate, full end throughout the whole land.
24   Therefore thus says the Lord, Yahweh of hosts, "My people, who dwell in Zion, do not fear Assyria when she strikes with a rod, or lifts a staff against you, as Egypt
25   did. For in a very little while, wrath will be exhausted,
26   and my anger will be at an end. Then Yahweh of hosts will whip the lash against him, as he struck Midian at the Rock of Oreb, and as he smote the Sea and the Egyptians.
27   And that day will come when his burden will be lifted from your shoulder, and his yoke from your neck.

This oracle contains both a counsel of despair (vss. 20-23) and an exhortation to hope (24-27). The apparent contradiction may be resolved by considering the dual perspective from which the fall of the nation was viewed. The circumstances assumed in the first part, namely those of Israel before her conquest by Assyria, are displaced by others in the second, namely those of the survivors of the event. The issue was whether the survivors would accept the fall as God's punishment and as the occasion for a renewal of obedience. The "full end" (vs. 23) is the end of national independence, the end of an era, but not the end of life for all Israelites. The prophet naturally hoped that those who "returned" from the fall, that is, those who were left, would "return" to God in faithful obedience. The double meaning contained in the verb is thus expounded. The same ambiguity resides in the image of the burned stump in Isa. 6:13. The prophecy of the remnant, then, is implicit in all the oracles of Isaiah. It was not an optimistic afterthought to the prophecy of national conquest but an essential ingredient of Isaiah's message form the outset.

Isaiah deemed it certain that Judah and Israel would be conquered by Assyria, but he knew that life would go on in the land of the two kingdoms when the conquest had been completed. He was equally confident that the minds of some of the men of Israel would be opened by the event to consider the word of God, which he (Isaiah) had declared. The opening of their "blind eyes" would result in a renewal of faith in God and a new zeal for social justice. If the messianic oracles are Isaiah's, then he believed the Israelite monarchy would not be permanently cut off by the Assyrian conquest but that a new "son of Jesse" would arise, filled with the spirit of righteousness, through the zeal of the Lord, to lead the new community of Israel. The old militancy and arrogance of the Davidic court would be replaced by a humble dedication to civil justice. Anxiety over the preservation of the dynasty and the privileges of the court would disappear, and the new king would be preoccupied with the rights and needs of the people. Essentially the same affirmation is contained in 32:1-8, but there is a slightly different emphasis there. The future king and his court will show their righteousness by protecting the rights of the people and by maintaining candid and open dealings with them (1-4) rather than by exploiting them and trying to conceal their motives behind pious and patriotic affirmations (5-8).

Isa. 32:1-8 is not necessarily messianic in the usual sense but may be regarded as a comment on the nature of good government generally. The style of the piece recalls the wisdom literature.[6] The contrast drawn in verse 3 between blindness and sight, stammering and articulate speech, binds this poem to others of Isaiah (cf. 6:9 ff.; 28:7-22) and exhibits the writer's intention to portray the prospect of a new administration to displace the present one.

Isaiah 32:1-8

1 Behold, a king will reign for righteousness,
   And princes rule for justice.
2 Each will be a shelter from the wind,
   And a refuge from the flood,
   Like streams of water in an arid place,
   Like a shady boulder in a weary land.
3 Then eyes that see will not be stuck shut,
   And ears that hear will heed.
4 Rash minds will discern with knowledge,
   And stammering tongues will speak quickly and clear.
5 A fool will not be called noble,
   Nor a scoundrel said to be generous.
6 For fools speak only foolishness,
   Their minds devise vain things:
   To work godlessness,
   And speak nonsense about Yahweh,

---

[6] Scott even attributes its composition to one of the teachers of wisdom, citing the similarity to Prov. 8:15-21; 16:10-15; 20:8, 26-28; and 25:5.

> To frustrate the need of the hungry,
> And deprive the thirsty of drink.
> 7 So the scoundrel's wiles are devious.
> He counsels schemes,
> To deprive the weak by crooked words,
> Though the claim of the poor be just.
> 8 But the noble counsels nobly,
> And by noble things he stands.

One major question remains to be considered before we may reach any final conclusion concerning the political dimension of Isaiah's oracles on the kingship. It is the significance of Assyria in Isaiah's prophecy. His oracles dealing with the political situation in Palestine in 711-701 B.C. are among the materials that bear on this issue, in addition to the oracles on Assyria itself. The latter have already been considered in our discussion of Zion. When Isaiah told Ahaz in 735 B.C. that the plan of Rezin of Damascus and Pekah of Samaria to conquer Judah and depose Ahaz in favor of their own ally, "the son of Tabeel," was bound to fail, he gave as the reason for his assurance the manifest insignificance of the two plotters (7:4-9). Later, when Ahaz purchased aid to rid Judah of the attackers (II Kings 16), he obviously credited them with a greater capability than Isaiah had done. Of course Isaiah may have evaluated their power against that of Assyria and been persuaded that their ambitions would be frustrated by the tightening of Assyria's control over her western vassals and her continued expansion toward the Mediterranean. However, he had not said this to Ahaz. Nowhere in his oracles is there an explicit word concerning Ahaz's policy toward Assyria. Commentators have surmised that Isaiah's counsel to Ahaz to be quiet (7:4) was occasioned by the knowledge that Ahaz had already taken the first steps toward securing Assyria's intervention, or was about to do so, and that Isaiah's eventual prediction of Judah's inundation by Assyria (8:7-8 and perhaps 7:18-25) was a response to Ahaz's unyielding resolution to solve his international problems by resort to Assyrian arms.

This is a reasonable conjecture although it is not absolutely necessary in order to make sense of the oracles in Isa. 7–8. Isaiah might have been advising Ahaz to do nothing at all, not even to resist the invasion by the force of Judean arms. The temptation is great to read these chapters in the light of subsequent events and oracles. The subsequent events were Ahaz's request for Assyrian aid and his prostitution of Yahwistic worship in the cause of diplomacy (II Kings 16). The subsequent oracles were those condemning pro-Egyptian conspiracies among Judah and other Assyrian dependencies in 713-701 B.C. Here are the oracles themselves:

Isaiah 20:1-6

1   In the year when the commander sent by the Assyrian king, Sargon, came to Ashdod and besieged and took it,

2   Yahweh spoke through an act of Isaiah son of Amoz, saying, "Go, take the sackcloth from around your waist and take off your shoes." And he did so, going naked and

3   barefoot. Then Yahweh said, "Just as my servant Isaiah has gone naked and barefoot for three years, as a sign

4   and symbol to Egypt and Ethiopia, so will the Assyrian king lead away the captive Egyptians and deported Ethiopians, young and old, naked and barefoot, buttocks

5   bare, to Egypt's disgrace. Then they will be confounded and ashamed over Ethiopia, their reliance, and Egypt,

6   their pride. And the inhabitants of this coastland at that time will say, 'Look, here are the ones we counted on for help, to save us from the Assyrian king! So what escape is there for us?' "

Isaiah 30:1-7

1   "Woe to the rebelling children!"
    Is the utterance of Yahweh,

273

"Who achieve goals, but not mine,
And form alliances alien to me,
And thus pile sin upon sin.

2 Who go down to Egypt
Without asking me,
And take refuge in the Pharaoh,
And hide in the shadow of Egypt.

3 But the refuge of the Pharaoh
Will become your disgrace,
And the protective shadow of Egypt
Will be your humiliation.

4 For though his ambassadors are in Zoan,
And his envoys as far as Hanes,

5 Everyone will be ashamed
Of a profitless ally,
Who gives no help nor benefit,
But only shame and disgrace."

6 An oracle on the animals of the Negeb:
In a land of distress and hardship,
Of lioness and roaring lion,
Of viper and flying serpent,
They carry their possessions on donkeys,
Their stores on the humps of camels,
To a people who cannot help them.

7 Egypt's aid is hollow and vain,
So I call her "Reclining Rahab."

Isaiah 31:1-3

1 Woe to those who go down to Egypt for help!
They have confidence in horses,
And put trust in many chariots,
And the great number of their horsemen.
But they do not look to the Holy One of Israel,
Nor seek the counsel of Yahweh.

2 But he too is skillful in bringing disaster,
And does not revoke his decree.

He will arise against the house of evildoers,
And the allies of those who work iniquity.
3 The Egyptians are men and not gods,
And their horses are flesh and not spirit.
Yahweh will stretch out his hand,
And the helper will stumble,
And the helped will fall,
And all will perish together.

The conclusion to which interpreters are often led by considering these materials together is that Isaiah opposed foreign alliances for Judah as substitutes for faith in God and as occasions for religious syncretism. One may hardly object to the assertion that Isaiah opposed religious syncretism of the sort practiced by Ahaz. But one may object to the conclusion that in Isaiah's eyes trust in God and trust in foreign powers were simple alternatives. To describe the conflict between Ahaz and Isaiah as one between reliance upon God and reliance upon foreign powers is to suggest that these were alternative and, to Isaiah, incompatible modes of action for the achievement of the same (or similar) ends, namely the security and well-being of Israel as a nation. But the conflict was deeper than this. It involved different, and partly incompatible, conceptions of the nature of true security and well-being, and corresponding notions of the proper function of kingship in Israel. It is clear from Isaiah's oracles that the well-being of Israel consisted, in his opinion, in the protection of the lives and rights of all her citizens, the nurture of such covenantal virtues as humility before God and loyalty to the neighbor, and the avoidance of magic and idolatry. Kingship, priesthood, and other forms of leadership were means to achieve these ends. However, these means had become corrupted by pride and self-interest so instead of serving as means of justice and guides to righteousness and faith, they had become ends in themselves, for the privileged few. Correspondingly, the Israelite cult had become a semi-magical means of self-indulgence and aggrandizement. Ahaz's introduction of Assyrian cult-objects into the temple of Jerusalem compounded the corruption, but the act itself was symptomatic of a disease that already pervaded the religious esablishment. The motives of worship were selfish, just like the king's motives of political action.

Isaiah did not offer faith in Yahweh as a better means than foreign alliances for achieving the goals to which the Davidic House, the aristocracy, and the priesthood aspired. He believed that some of these goals were about to be denied the leaders of Judah in any case, for he considered the Assyrian conquest of western Asia to be the ineluctable judgment of God. All the political machinations of Judah and her fellow nations were therefore futile. They could not resist what God had ordained and what Assyria obviously had the power to accomplish. Isaiah wanted the leaders of his people to surrender the objectives which had come to control their lives, and to which they seemed willing to sacrifice their subjects, and to put themselves at God's disposal in the pursuit of justice in Israel. He knew this decision would be an act of faith that would not reverse the political destiny of Judah among the nations. He did not say so, but it went without saying that a recommitment to justice and to a nonidolatrous cult would entail a certain risk on the part of the incumbent ruler. And yet he believed that God would prosper his servants in these pursuits and would continue to raise up leaders, even Davidic kings,[7] for such service, despite the subjugation of the nation to Assyria's overlordship and the failures of particular

---

[7] If the "branch from Jesse's trunk" (11:1) was meant literally and not merely figuratively. If this was the case, it remained for Jeremiah, Second Isaiah, and later Jewish and Christian writers to recognize the radical incompatibility of the exercise of absolute political power as a continuous, divine right with the achievement of selfless devotion to the people of God, that is to say, to recognize the necessity of distinguishing between Caesar and the Messiah.

Judean kings. After all, subjugation to a foreign power would not exempt the men of Israel from social and religious obligation.

The meaning of Isaiah's prophecy of God's deliverance of Mount Zion and his protection of the faithful in Israel (29:5-8, 17-24; 31:4-9; 32:1-20) was not that faith in God's miracles was a better military defense against Aram and Israel than reliance on Assyria, or a better defense against Assyria than reliance on Egypt. It was that Israel could count upon God's everlasting approval and support of acts performed on behalf of the poor, the oppressed, and the powerless, and upon God's everlasting opposition to tyranny and injustice. Isaiah prophesied God's eventual frustration of the proud tyranny of Assyria (10:15-19) and the passing away of Assyria's control over Palestine (14:24-27). But he never counseled the leaders of Judah to take military or political action for or against another nation on the basis of this prophecy. His disagreement with the kings of Israel over national policy was not merely a question of the proper timing of their assertion of Israel's independence and prestige, or their acceptance of her vassalage to another power. He disagreed with them over the far more fundamental question whether the House of David was justified in expending the lives and resources of the Israelite people in conflicts with other nations. I believe the evidence all points to the conclusion that he opposed the active participation of Israel in such conflicts, on the ground that it was subversive of justice and worship in Israel and was ultimately futile and self-defeating.

On the other hand, Isaiah's teaching does not necessarily imply a prohibition of self-defense against military attack from without or against criminal violence from within. I suspect that his oracles are silent on this issue because he assumed such action to be legitimate. Certainly he did not counsel faith in God as a miraculous means of self-defense.

It is possible to construe his teaching as a counsel of non-resistance, but we may not legitimately infer from this construction that he believed nonresistance more effective than resistance for preserving life and limb. It would be more consistent with the ethical principles explicitly affirmed in Isaiah's oracles to suppose that he believed all use of force to be evil, despite the perennial risk of injury involved in nonresistance. However, any inference concerning his motive for teaching nonresistance, if he taught it, would be exegetically frivolous.

The practical application of the principles of rule taught by Isaiah is exceedingly difficult in any age. It is never a simple thing to "establish justice in the gate," or to adjudicate the conflicting rights and claims of men. Nor is the achievement of justice ever permanent. The life of man is a continuous conflict of interests and needs, of privileges and responsibilities, among individuals, groups, and institutions. Freedom and order are threats to each other. Self-interest and pride corrupt the most civic-minded men. Today's victory for justice creates tomorrow's problem. And behind every social achievement looms the threat of physical disaster in the realm of nature, to complicate and frustrate the best purposes of men. But we need not dismiss Isaiah's teaching as simplistic or irrelevant merely because it fails to cover every eventuality or omits a concrete program of political order. Like all the prophets, Isaiah showed his awareness of the imperfection and impermanence of human achievements and of man's eternal liability to judgment and need for forgiveness. He acknowledged the hardness of man's heart and his ability to rationalize evil as good. Thus Isaiah had no illusions about the life of Israel or the life of men generally. His faith was in God and not man, and he proclaimed the creative sovereignty of God in the midst of man's faithlessness and folly. Therefore his hope was not utopian but realistic. His confidence in God was not diminished but tempered by the certainty of judgment and suffering. These were the cost of man's reconciliation to God and the cost of righteousness among men. The victory of faith was not a final, static solution to the conflict of good and evil nor an extrication from the field of battle to a private realm of timeless tranquility but a trust in the righteousness of God in the midst of conflict. It was a victory that had to be constantly rewon, and its preconditions were always the awareness of one's lostness before the Holy One of Israel and the acceptance of atonement as a gift (Isa. 6). The purpose of the prophetic word was to bring men to this awareness and to facilitate this acceptance. The word of the prophet was necessary to bring Israel again and again to this awareness, but it was rarely sufficient to do so. The historical judgment of God, in the form of social disaster, was also required. Without this judgment the truth of the prophet's teaching was inevitably obscured by the proud ambitions of men. But without the word of the prophet, the fall of the proud would have been a mere tragedy, one to be added to the injustices already committed by the proud, thus swelling the sum of evil. The word of the prophet kept open the possibility of creative response to the disasters of history, as well as the grateful acknowledgment of God's glory in creation, by which means the life of man might be fulfilled.

Chronological Table

Kings of Israel			Kings of Judah	
786-746	Jeroboam II	AMOS	783-742	Uzziah
746	Zechariah	(*ca.* 750)		
746	Shallum	ISAIAH		
746-738	Menahem	(*ca.* 740-700)	742-735	Jotham
738-737	Pekahiah			
737-732	Pekah		735-715	Ahaz
732-724	Hoshea		715-687	Hezekiah

738   Kingdoms of Israel (Menahem) and Aram (Rezin) pay tribute to Assyria.

735   Syro-Ephraimite (Aramean-Israelite) invasion of Judah. Judah (Ahaz) requests Assyrian aid and pays tribute.

733   Galilee and Transjordan (Israel) annexed by Assyria (Tiglath-pileser III).

732   Aramean kingdom of Damascus (Syria) annexed by Assyria.

722   Kingdom of Israel (Samaria) annexed by Assyria (Sargon II). Israelites exiled.

711   Assyria (Sargon) quells western rebel coalition. Ashdod captured.

705-

701   Assyria (Sennacherib) quells western rebellion. Jerusalem beseiged, 701. Hezekiah pays tribute.

Index of Biblical References

Translated passages in Amos and Isaiah are marked with an asterisk.

Index of Subjects and Authors